BUSINESS APPLICATIONS:
A Microcomputer Resource Book

BUSINESS APPLICATIONS:
A Microcomputer Resource Book

Frank Marvasti, Ph.D.

International Business and Marketing Department
California State Polytechnic University, Pomona

CONTENTS

Preface..xix

Chapter 1: Computer Revolution 1

< What is a Computer? 1
< Five Components of a Computer 1
< How Computers Get Input.. 2
< How Computers Store Information.. 2
< How Computers Process Information 2
< How Computers Deliver Information 3
< Some Applications of Computers 3
< The Fears People Have About Computers 3
< Advantages of Computers.. 4
< Computer Hardware 4
   — Microcomputers 4
   — System Chassis... 5
   — Types of Processors 5
   — Memory 6
   — Input Devices 6
   — Output Devices 7
      • The Monitor.. 7
      • Types of Monitors.. 7
      • Disks and Disk Drives... 8
      • Floppy Disks and Disk Drives 8
      • Hard Disks 8
      • Types of Disks... 9
      • Other Storage Devices... 9
      • Printers 10
< Computer Software 11
   — Operating System (System Software) 11
   — DOS and Windows 12
   — Functions of System Software 13
   — Bootstrap Loader 13

　　　　•　Diagnostic Routines...14
　　　　•　Service Functions..14
　　— Starting Your Computer 14
　　— Running Programs...14
　< Management Information System and Data Base Management............15
　　— Functional Support Role...15
　　— Organizing Data for Processing 16
　　　　•　Data 16
　　　　•　Information 16
　　　　•　Character...16
　　　　•　Field 16
　　　　•　Record 16
　　　　•　File 16
　　　　•　Data Base 16
　　— File Organization..17
　　　　•　Sequential File Organization 17
　　　　•　Random (Direct) File Organization 17
　　　　•　Indexed Sequential File Organization 17
　　— Management Reports...17
　　— Data Base Management System 18
　　　　•　Data Base Administrator..18
　　— Before Databases: Patchwork Files 18
　　　　•　File Processing..19
　　　　　　○　Advantages...19
　　　　　　○　Disadvantages...19
　　　　•　Databases 19
　　　　　　○　Advantages...19
　　　　　　○　Disadvantages...19
　< Exercise 1.1 Technology Acronyms Quiz..20

Chapter 2: Quantitative Analysis..21
　< What is Quantitative Analysis?..21
　　— Defining the Problem..21
　　— Developing a Model 22
　　— Acquiring Input Data..22
　　— Key Considerations in the Model-Building Process.........................22
　　— Developing a Solution...23
　　— Testing the Solution..23
　　— Analyzing the Results..23
　　— Implementing the Results 23
　　— Modifying the Model...23

— Support and Further Modification 24

< Reasons Why a Quantitative Approach Might Be Used 24

< Quantitative Analysis and Managerial Decision Making.................... 24

< The Decision-Making Process 25

< Decision Support Role 26

   — Decision Support Systems 26

     • Benefits of DSS 26

     • Applications of DSS.. 27

Chapter 3: Review of Spreadsheet (Excel) Commands & Procedures.... 28

< Formatting 28

< Cell Width and Heights 32

< Formulas 33

< Printing.. 33

< Relative and Absolute Addressing 34

   — Relative Addressing.. 34

   — Absolute Addressing 35

   — Mixed Addressing 35

< Exercise 3.1 Spreadsheet Addressing 36

< Logical Statements 37

   — Simple Logical Statements 37

   — Nested Logical Statements 38

   — Compound Logical Statements... 38

     • AND Compound Statement 39

     • OR Compound Statement... 39

< Logical Statements and Excel 39

   — Simple Logical Statements in Excel... 39

   — Nested Logical Statements in Excel... 39

   — Compound Logical Statements in Excel.. 40

< Exercise 3.2 Logical Statements 41

Chapter 4: Financial Statements 42

< Income Statement 42

< Balance Sheet 42

< Financial Statements and Excel... 43

   — Useful Tips for Creating Financial Statements Using Excel 43

< Computer Assignment 45

   — Requirements 45

   — Useful Guidelines 45

   — XYZ Company Income Statement.. 47

   — XYZ Company Balance Sheet... 48

Chapter 5: Loans and Amortization Tables..49
<   Exercise 5.1 Loans and Amortization Tables.....................................51
<   Computer Assignment 52
  — Overview...52
  — Instructions 52
  — Loan Calculation and Amortization Table Assignment 53
<   Creating an Amortization Table in Excel 54

Chapter 6: Income Tax Calculation 56
<   Introduction...56
<   Calculation of Tax on Base 56
<   Calculation of Tax Liability 57
<   Exercise 6.1 Income Tax 58
<   Computer Assignment 59
  — Purpose..59
  — Procedure 59
  — Income Tax Computer Assignment..................................60
<   Tax Calculation in Excel...61
  — Calculation of Tax on Base in Excel 61
  — Calculation of Tax Liability in Excel 61

Chapter 7: Advanced Logical Statements...63
<   Introduction...63
<   Computer Assignment 64
  — Purpose..64
  — Instructions 64
  — Student Grades Assignment 65
  — Procedure 66
    • Inputting Data..66
    • How to Create Formulas..66
      1. Quiz Average 66
      2. Exam Average 67
      3. Course Average 68
      4. Assigning Letter Grades 69
      5. Assigning Point Grades....................................70
      6. Calculating Sample Statistics for the Entire Class 71
      7. Printing the Grade Sheet and Cell Formulas 72
<   Curving the Grades...72
  — Example 7.1 72
    • Solution 72

Chapter 8: Payroll Calculation..74
  < Introduction..74
  < Computer Assignment 75
     — Purpose...75
     — Assumptions 75
     — Requirements 75
  < Solving the Payroll Problem Using Excel 76
     — Procedure 76
      • Step 1...77
      • Step 2...77
      • Step 3...77
      • Step 4...78
      • Step 5...78
      • Step 6...79
      • Step 7...80
      • Step 8...80
  < Snapshot of the Entire Payroll Worksheet................82

Chapter 9: Sales and Profit Forecasting: Pro Forma Financial
      Statements 83
  < Introduction..83
  < Computer Assignment 83
     — Purpose...84
     — Assumptions 84
     — Requirements 84
  < Procedure 85
  < Sensitivity (What-If) Analysis 88
     — Data Table Type I 89
     — Data Table Type II 92
  < Pro Forma Income Statement Assignment................94
  < Graphical Presentation of Results 95
     — Graph for Data Table I 95
     — Graph for Data Table II 98
     — Avoid Broken Lines in Line Charts 99

Chapter 10: Sales and Profit Forecasting in the International Arena.......100
  < Introduction..100
  < Computer Assignment 101
     — Purpose...101
     — Assumptions 101
     — Requirements 102

< Procedure 102
— Data Table Type I 105
— Data Table Type II 108

Chapter 11: Expense Reports and Advanced Graphing 111
< Computer Assignment 111
— Purpose 111
— Requirements 111
< Procedure 112
— Graphing the Results 113
— The Pie Chart 113
— The Bar Chart 115

Chapter 12: Business/market Analysis Using Excel's Drawing Tools 117
< Customer Service Example 119
< Using Quadrants in Market Analysis 120
— Product-market Growth Strategies 120
• Product Penetration in Existing Markets 120
• Product Development for the Existing Market 120
• Market Development Using Existing Products 121
• Diversification 121
— Product Positioning Quadrant 121
— Market Penetration: Product Depth Quadrant 122
— Market Penetration in Comparison to Consumer Spending 123
< Brand Loyalty Matrix 124
< The BCG Growth-Share Matrix 125
< The Competitive Strength Grid 127
< Advertising Scheduling 128
< Computer Assignment 130
— Purpose 130
— Instructions 130

Chapter 13: Frequency Distributions and Descriptive Summary
Measures of Data 131
< Frequency Distributions 131
— Procedure 131
< Descriptive Summary Measures of Ungrouped Data 133
— Measures of Location 133
• The Mean 133
• The Median 133
• Quartiles 133
• The Mode 134

— Measures of Dispersion...134
   • The Range...134
   • The Inter-quartile Range 135
   • The Variance and Standard Deviation 135
   • The Coefficient of Variation...135
— Measures of Shape (Skewness) 136
< Descriptive Summary Measures of Grouped Data 137
   — Approximating the Mean..137
   — Approximating the Median..137
   — Approximating the Quartiles 138
   — Approximating the Variance and the Standard Deviation............139
< Exercise 13.1 (Ungrouped Data) 140
< Exercise 13.2 (Grouped Observations) 141
< Computer Assignment 142
   — Procedure to Do the Assignment 142
   — Mean 145
   — Median...146
   — Third Quartile..146
   — Variance and Standard Deviation.................................147
< Solving the Problem Using Excel.......................................147

Chapter 14: Resource Allocation Using Linear Programming............153
< Procedure...155
< Simplex Tableau 156
< Minimization Problem 156
< Exercise 14.1 Resource Allocation Problems.....................158
< Exercise 14.2 Transportation Problem 159
< Exercise 14.3 Production Problems 160
< Computer Assignment 161
   — Solving Linear Programming Problems with Excel.....................162

Chapter 15: Simple Linear Regression and Correlation Analysis.......166
< Procedure...166
< Computer Assignment 171
   — Regression Solution Using Excel..................................172
   — Scatter and Residual Plots..175

Chapter 16: Multiple Regression Analysis...177
< Procedure...177
< Computer Assignment 181
< Solving Multiple Regression Problems Using Excel............................182
   — Residual Plots..184

Chapter 17: Time Series Analysis (Annual Data)........187
< Measuring the Trend Component 188
— Simple Regression........188
< Smoothing the Series........189
— Moving Averages........189
— Exponential Smoothing 189
< Computer Assignment 190
< Solving Annual Time Series Problems Using Excel 191
— Graphing the Results 193

Chapter 18: Time Series Analysis (Monthly Or Quarterly Data) 196
< Procedure........196
— Seasonal Analysis 197
— Cyclical Analysis 197
< Computer Assignment 198
— Solving Quarterly Or Monthly Time Series Using Excel 199
— Predicting Future Values of Sales........203
— Graphing the Results 203

Chapter 19: Chi-Square Test of Independence 206
< Procedure........206
< Exercise 19.1 Contingency Table........209
< Exercise 19.2 Contingency Problem Using Excel........210
< Computer Assignment 212

Chapter 20: Breakeven Analysis 214
< The Breakeven Formula 214
— Fixed Costs........214
— Variable Costs........214
< Example 20.1 (Determining the Breakeven Point)........214
< Derivation of Breakeven Formula........215
< Graphical Solution 216

Chapter 21: The Business & Marketing Plans 218
< Cover Page 218
< Table of Contents........218
< Executive Summary........218
< The Business 219
— Description........219
— Management........219
< The Opportunity and Marketing Plan 220

— 4Ps of Marketing 220
— The Product or Service 220
— Pricing Strategy 220
— The Market 220
— Promotion/Sales 220
— Competitive Analysis 221
— STP (Segmentation, Targeting, Positioning) 221
< Strategies for Building the Business 221
— Website 221
— E-Mail Marketing 221
— Personal Touch 221
< Production 221
— Location 222
— Facilities 222
— Materials/Supplies 222
— Personnnel 222
— Setup 222
< Financial Data 223
— Required Investment 223
— Break-Even Analysis 223
— Balance Sheet 223
— Pro Forma Income Statements 223
— Pro Forma Cash Flow 223
— Historical Financial Reports 223
< Sample Business Plan 224
— Table of Contents 225
— Executive Summary 226
— The Business Venture 226
— The Company 227
— Management 228
— The Product 229
— The Marketplace 229
— Market Size 230
— The Competition 231
— Auto-Switch's Advantage 232
— Marketing Opportunities 232
• Products and Services 233
• Research 233
o Preliminary New Product Planning and Testing 233
• Competitive Advantages 234
— Marketing Strategy 235
• Target Markets 235

— Promotion Strategy 235
   • Personal Selling 236
   • Advertising 237
   • Sales Promotion 237
     ◦ Brochure 237
   • Publicity 237
     ◦ Trade Shows 238
— Pricing Strategy 238
— Distribution Strategy 238
— Sales Plan 239
— Sales Forecast 240
— Sources of Market Information 241
— Product Development 242
— Production 242
— Product Costs 243
— Gross Profit 243
— Financial Requirements 244

Chapter 22: Creating a Web Page 246
  < Example 22.1 246
  < Tags 248
  < Example 22.2 249
  < Nested Lists 250
  < Example 22.3 251
  < Linking to Other Web Pages 252
  < Linking Between Your Own Pages 252
  < Linking Between Different Parts of the Same Web Page 253
  < Creating a Table 253
  < Example 22.4 254
  < Putting Graphics on a Web Page 255
  < Changing the Background 255
  < Preserving Spaces and Line Breaks 255
  < Changing Font Size and Colors 256
  < Marquees 256
  < Example 22.5 256
  < Forms 257
    — Text 257
    — Checkbox 257
    — Radio 257
    — Select 258
    — Textarea 258

    — Submit...258
    — Reset...258
  <   Colors 259

Appendix A
  <   Computer Acronyms..261
  <   Chronological History of Computers 261

Appendix B: Solutions to Select Exercises and Computer Assignments 262

References 301

Index...305

DEDICATION

Dedicated to my family for their patience and invaluable support.

PREFACE

QUANTITATIVE ANALYSIS IS an important tool in helping managers to make decisions, the most important function of a manager. Organizations are filled with decision-makers at various levels, as all managerial activity revolves around decision-making. Historically, most managers have used the qualitative approach to decision-making, based on judgment, intuition, and knowledge acquired through experience, rather than the scientific approach, based on systematic quantitative methods. Presently, the business environment is changing and becoming increasingly more complex. We live in a global economy where electronic information, technological advancements, and environmental factors have become major determinants of our lifestyle. Such drastic changes necessitate significant modifications in the decision-making process. Decision-makers must become more sophisticated by learning to use both quantitative and qualitative analysis.

The purpose of this book is to teach quantitative analysis to solve a variety of different business problems, using the Microsoft Excel® software program. The book is primarily written for business students and executives who want to increase their quantitative and computer skills for better decision-making. It covers both theoretical and applied material, starting with several introductory chapters on computer literacy and concluding with applied statistical problems, business plans, and designing Web pages.

The book contains 22 chapters and 2 appendices. The first three chapters are introductory chapters dealing with computer literacy. Practical business problems are covered in chapters 4 through 20. How to write a business/marketing plan is covered in chapter 21. The book concludes with a chapter on how to design and create a Web page. All chapters contain practical assignments, to be done using a computer. While some chapters contain elementary exercises, the majority are fairly advanced. Prior to using this book, users should have some familiarity with statistics, accounting, and marketing. They should also be comfortable with using computers, particularly spreadsheets, and have some knowledge of Internet.

The book can be adopted in semester or quarterly courses. All the chapters can be covered in a one semester course. However, for quarterly courses, the following chapters may be omitted without a significant loss of substantive content: Chapter 10 (Pro Forma Income Statements in the International Arena), Chapter 14 (Linear Programming), Chapter 16 (Multiple Regression Analysis), and Chapter 18 (Time Series Analysis: Monthly or Quarterly Data). It is suggested that group projects be utilized as a supplement to this book.

Most of the assignments and projects in this book have been used in courses at California State Polytechnic University, Pomona and the University of Redlands. Group projects were utilized in these courses, as a supplement to this material. One such project included writing a business plan and developing a Web page for a fictitious company.

Many people have assisted me in the preparation of this material. In particular, I would like to thank the copyeditor, Mr. Jay Winderman of Claremont, California. I also would like to express my gratitude to many of my former students who have been helpful in developing and improving the projects and problems in this book.

Frank Marvasti

CHAPTER 1

Computer Revolution

COMPUTERS AND INFORMATION technologies offer great potential for the world economy and society. Our world has become much smaller, communities more interrelated, and information technologies are starting to have a deeper impact on business organizations.

The information society is still in its youth and is constantly changing. The ongoing development of new technologies is making significant changes in our lives. We are witnessing constant creation of new products and services, new markets, new channels of communication, new ways of conducting business, and major social and cultural changes.

WHAT IS A COMPUTER?

A computer is a processing machine that manipulates information at a very high speed. The tasks that a computer can perform may be as simple as adding numbers or as complicated as forecasting sales and profits or weather conditions. A computer is basically a fast and versatile machine that can be used to solve problems, manage large amounts of data, and summarize information.

FIVE COMPONENTS OF A COMPUTER

A computer consists of five components. These components are input, processor, storage, output, and programs (software).

The first four components are physical parts that are tangible and you can touch, such as the keyboard, monitor, disk, printer, and mouse. These components are called hardware. The last component is called software. It enables the computer to manipulate and process the information you enter into it. Software is intangible and cannot be touched.

Because computers can process information, you can use them to access and change numbers, text, pictures, sound, and even movies. Using a computer, it is easy to manipulate words or to calculate the results of a complicated formula. To perform any task, though, you first have to get the information into your computer.

HOW COMPUTERS GET INPUT

Input devices are used to input information into your computer before it can be processed. You can input text with a keyboard, sound with a microphone, or pictures with a digital camera. Even a mouse that you use to navigate around the screen is an input device.

HOW COMPUTERS STORE INFORMATION

Before information can be processed, computers need to store it. Otherwise, it would be lost permanently. Computers store the information they receive as input, the commands and instructions they need, and the results they receive from the software they are using. To store all this, they use two kinds of storage: temporary and permanent.

Random Access Memory (RAM) is an example of temporary storage. Computers store temporary work in RAM memory like a scratch pad. Permanent information is stored on a variety of devices such as diskettes, hard disks, CD & DVD disks, tapes, and flash memory. The information on disks can be modified later. However, computers also need information that they use over and over again, such as the commands and instructions they need when they are turned on. These commands and instructions are stored in read only memory (ROM), a type of memory that cannot be modified.

HOW COMPUTERS PROCESS INFORMATION

A computer has a microprocessor. The microprocessor is an integrated circuit (chip) in the computer that performs the tasks we ask the computer to do. This ability is what makes the computer such a versatile machine in performing tasks such as word processing, mathematical calculations or playing a game. Instead of being designed to do one thing, microprocessors are designed to do many tasks according to the software you select.

HOW COMPUTERS DELIVER INFORMATION

A computer sends the results of its processing to an output device such as the monitor. Other kinds of output devices are speakers attached to your computer, a printer, or a disk that can save your work.

SOME APPLICATIONS OF COMPUTERS

1. Handling money (ATM)
2. Commerce (UPC), optical scanners
3. Transportation (run rapid transit systems, airline reservations)
4. Production (computerized robots in auto industry)
5. Agriculture (helping farmers)
6. Education and training
7. Health and medicine (bone scanners, diagnosis)
8. The sciences
9. Government (The federal government is the largest single user of computers.)
10. Human assistant (handicapped)
11. Art and design
12. Games
13. Internet and email

THE FEARS PEOPLE HAVE ABOUT COMPUTERS

1. When computers fail, people are happy.
2. Some people have shot their computers.
3. Computers can cause psychological problems (computer anxiety and phobia).
4. Computers can cause physical problems (eye strain, back and wrist problems, radiation, etc.).
5. Some people are nervous about the mathematical sound of the word "computer".
6. Some people are intimidated by machines.
7. Programming languages seem to be difficult to understand.
8. Software programs are not very intuitive.
9. People are afraid that they may damage something.

10. People are afraid that the computer is out to get them (also security concerns).
11. Some people do not like to type (or cannot type).
12. People are afraid of depersonalization (ID #, etc.)
13. The availability of faster, better software, and the internet may reduce the intimidation factor.

ADVANTAGES OF COMPUTERS

1. Speed—people expect fast service.
2. Computers are reliable.
3. Computers are accurate (GIGO).
4. Computers can reduce paperwork. Do we waste more paper now?
5. Computers are able to perform boring, dangerous, or highly sensitive jobs.
6. Databases—computers can hold large amount of (financial, geographical, logistical, etc.) information. Information can be accessed fast.
7. Computers increase productivity and bring costs down.

COMPUTER HARDWARE

Computers are divided into four classes, each with different ranges of size, power, and price. These classes are: super computers, mainframe computers, mini computers, and micro computers. Furthermore, there are three types of micro-computers: desktop, laptop, and dumb terminals.

Mainframe, mini, and super computers are used by governments, large organizations such as airlines or banks, and large universities to control an entire business operation. They are very powerful and expensive. By contrast, micro computers are less expensive and easier to use. In this book, the emphasis is on micro computers, particularly the IBM personal computer and compatible machines.

MICROCOMPUTERS

Microcomputers (sometimes called personal computers, desktop computers, or laptops) are the least expensive and the least powerful of all classes of computer. They are small enough to fit on a desk and have limited expansion capacity. They are used as stand-alone computers or are connected to other large or small computers in a network.

Microcomputers can be intelligent or dumb. An intelligent computer performs most of the processing locally, whereas a dumb terminal has very limited processing capabilities itself, but allows you to connect it to a more powerful computer such as a mainframe. When you process your data from the dumb terminal, the more powerful machine at the other end of the network performs most of the processing.

SYSTEM CHASSIS

The system chassis (motherboard) holds the **central processing unit** (**CPU**), the computer's memory (RAM and ROM), expansion slots, and electronic circuitry for manipulating information.

The CPU (sometimes called microprocessor) is the brain of the computer that performs the actual calculations and data manipulations. The CPU controls all of the actions of a computer. Since early 1970s, manufacturers have produced the central processing unit on a single semiconductor chip. The CPU chips used in the IBM family of personal computers are made by **Intel** and **AMD** corporations and have the classifications summarized in Table 1.1.

Table 1.1. Types of Processors	
Intel **8088**	16-bit CPU chip used in IBM PC, XT, and compatible computers
Intel **80286**	16-bit CPU chip used in IBM AT, some PS/2 models, and compatibles
Intel **80386**	32-bit CPU chip used in IBM PS/2 model 70 and 80, and all 386 compatibles
Intel **80486**	an enhanced 386 design developed in 1989
Intel **Pentium**	this chip was introduced in 1993 and can execute two instructions at once
Intel **Pentium Pro**	developed in 1995 and can execute three instructions simultaneously
Intel **Pentium II**	developed in 1997
Intel **Pentium III**	developed in 1999
Intel **Pentium IV** and AMD **Athlon**	developed in 2000 and used in high end computers

The smallest unit of information that a computer handles is called a **BIT** (**binary digit**). A BIT is either **ON** (**1**) or **OFF** (**0**). Data can be represented by combining different combinations of BITs. For example, an alphanumeric character such as "A", "9", or "&" can be represented by eight BITs, also called a **BYTE**.

MEMORY

Computers use small memory chips to store programs and data. Before a computer can execute a program, the program must reside inside memory. There are two types of memory inside the computer. The **Random Access Memory (RAM)**, also known as primary memory, can be thought of as a temporary storage device. This memory is volatile because while the power is on, the memory chips are used to temporarily hold information. You can access this memory very quickly and change its contents. The information in RAM is erased after the computer is turned off. Memory capacity, measured in bytes, can be increased by adding memory chips to the system board or by adding RAM chips to an optional memory card in an expansion slot. RAM capacity must be large enough to hold the largest application program. In general, the more RAM a machine has, the faster it can operate.

The second type of memory, called **Read Only Memory (ROM)**, contains information permanently recorded on it at the factory. This information is in the form of programs that control the computer's internal input/output operations when it is started. Application programs use ROM to access basic system devices. Information inside ROM cannot be modified by users.

Another type of memory is **Complementary Metal Oxide Semiconductor (CMOS).** It is a bank of RAM memory that stores a PC's permanent configuration information, including type of drives installed in the PC, the amount of RAM present in the system, and current date and time. The information inside CMOS is backed up by a small battery on the motherboard.

INPUT DEVICES

Input devices are used to send information to the central processing unit. The keyboard is the primary input device that people use to communicate with a computer. Most keyboards have the alphanumeric keys (alphabet letters, punctuation marks, mathematical symbols, and numbers) arranged in a typewriter (QWERTY) layout. In addition to these keys, most keyboards for the IBM PC have special keys that allow you to perform different tasks and communicate more effectively with your computer. The most widely used special keys are the Esc (escape), Alt (alternate), Ctrl (control), Shift, direction arrows, Home, End, PgUp, PgDn, Del (delete), Num Lock (number lock), PrtScr (print screen), Caps Lock (uppercase characters), Backspace, Enter (or

Return), and F1-F12 (function) keys. The function that you can perform with each key varies with the application programs.

Other important input devices are mice, joysticks, disk drives, tape drives, punch cards, paper tapes, light pens, and optical scanners.

OUTPUT DEVICES

Output devices are used to receive information from the central processing unit. The most widely used output devices are monitors, printers, disk drives, tape drives, speakers, and punch cards.

The Monitor

The monitor (or screen) displays the results of computer operations such as the execution of a program. A monitor is controlled by display controller circuitry on the motherboard or by a video controller expansion card. The two monitor types used on personal computers are monochrome (green, amber, or black-and-white), and color displays. Each type of monitor requires a different type of controller card. The most common types of color monitor/adapters for the IBM PC family of computers are CGA (color graphics adapter), EGA (extended or enhanced graphics adapter), VGA (video graphics adapter), and SVGA (super VGA).

Monitors display information as combinations of dots. Each dot is called a pixel (short for picture element). The screen resolution is measured in terms of the number of horizontal and vertical pixels. Table 1.2 summarizes the maximum resolution and screen colors for various display adapters.

Table 1.2. Types of Monitors		
Type	Resolution	Colors
Monochrome	720h x 350v	1
CGA	320h x 200v	4
EGA	640h x 350v	16
VGA	640h x 480v	256
SVGA	1024h x 768v & higher	Millions

A new class of monitors, called multi-sync monitors, was developed in late 1980s. They were fully compatible with monochrome, CGA, EGA, and

VGA display adapters. The multi-sync monitors were generally more expensive than the other monitors.

Disks and Disk Drives

The disk drive is a device that allows you to save data and programs on a disk for long term storage (output). It also functions as a device to read information from a disk (input). Disk drives are classified by the type of disk that they use: 5.25-inch floppy disk, 3.5-inch mini disk, and hard or fixed disk. Some computers may have more than one type of disk drive.

Floppy Disks and Disk Drives

There are three classes of 5.25-inch disk drives: single-head, double-head, and double-head high-density drives. Single-head drives can only use one side of a diskette whereas double-head drives can use both sides of a diskette. The 5.25-inch drives use floppy diskettes. Floppy diskettes are flexible, made of plastic with a metallic coating, and enclosed in a plastic jacket. On the right side of the jacket is a notch called the write-protect notch. If this notch is covered with a piece of tape, the diskette becomes write-protected because the disk drive can read from but not write to this diskette. In addition, write-protected diskettes cannot be formatted or erased.

The 3.5-inch disk drives are also divided into two classes: 720K, and 1.44M (high-density) drives. In general, higher-density drives can use lower-density disks, but lower-density drives cannot use higher-density disks. The 3.5-inch drives use mini diskettes. Mini diskettes are enclosed in a stronger, more rigid plastic jacket. These diskettes also have a write protect notch. The notch can be found near one corner. If a small block within the notch is pushed toward the corner of the disk so that the hole in the notch is open, the diskette becomes read only and cannot be erased or formatted.

Floppy disk drives are rapidly being replaced by faster and higher capacity storage devices.

Hard Disks

Hard disks are metallic platters enclosed in a sealed disk drive with several read/write heads and arms. Hard disk can be installed permanently inside the computer or they can be attached as an external drive. Hard disks/drives are heavier, faster, and more expensive than floppy disks/drives. Table 1.3 summarizes the most common disks and their capacities:

Table 1.3. Types of Disks	
Type	Capacity
SS/SD, 5.25 inches	80K or 81,920 bytes
SS/DD, 8 sectors, 5.25 inches	160K or 163,840 bytes
SS/DD, 9 sectors, 5.25 inches	180K or 184,320 bytes
DS/DD, 8 sectors, 5.25 inches	320K or 327,680 bytes
DS/DD, 9 sectors, 5.25 inches	360K or 368,640 bytes
DS/HD, 15 sectors, 5.25 inches	1.2M or 1,228,800 bytes
DS/DD, 9 sectors, 3.5 inches	720K or 737,280 bytes
DS/HD, 18 sectors, 3.5 inches	1.44M or 1,474,560 bytes
Hard disk	capacity varies from 1 to more than 500 gbytes

Note: SS: Single Sided; DS: Double Sided; SD: Single Density; DD: Double Density; HD: High (Quad) Density

Other Storage Devices

Tapes are primarily used for backup purposes. A tape backup unit allows you to copy the contents of a hard disk onto a tape cartridge at a relatively fast rate. Tapes are relatively inexpensive and hold a lot of information. However, information on a tape can only be accessed sequentially.

A **Zip drive** combines the convenience of a floppy diskette with the storage capacity of a hard disk. It uses removable storage disks, each having the capacity of a hard disk. In effect, it is a device with infinite storage capacity. The data access time for a Zip drive is slower than a hard disk. Zip drives are rapidly being replaced by other types of drives such as CD, DVD, and flash drives.

An **optical disk (laser disk)**, also called **CD ROM** or **CD-R**, works like an audio compact laser disk (CD). An optical disk can hold vast amounts of information (650 megabytes) for long-term storage. A newer and higher capacity optical disk is called **DVD** (Digital Versatile Disk or Digital Video Disk). The capacity of DVDs can vary from 4.7 gigabytes for normal DVDs up to 50 gigabytes on High Definition DVDs.

Flash drives are solid-state compact and easy-to-use devices that are similar in use to computer hard drives. They were originally developed to be used in portable devices such as digital cameras and Personal Digital Assistants (PDAs). However, slightly modified models, **USB flash drives**, are currently used as portable storage devices on microcomputers. You can slip USB flash drives into your pocket, or on a keychain for ultimate portable storage. Their capacity is from 8 megabytes up to 8 gigabytes.

Printers

The output of a computer on a monitor cannot be distributed to others and disappears when the power is turned off. In addition, a monitor cannot display large amounts of data at the same time. To solve these problems, most people use printers to produce a hard copy of their work. Printers fall into two general categories: impact printers and nonimpact printers. Impact printers include **dot-matrix** and **daisy-wheel** printers. They create an image on paper by striking a ribbon against the paper. Dot-matrix printer heads are made of a column (matrix) of print wires or pins. Under the control of a microprocessor inside the printer, the pins strike a ribbon against the paper to make readable characters or graphs. Dot-matrix printers are generally the least expensive of all printers and come with 9 (lower quality) or 24 (higher quality) pins. They are available in three sizes: 80 columns, 132 columns, and 256 columns.

Daisy-wheel printers are similar to daisy-wheel typewriters in that they can only use characters that are embossed on the tip of spokes of their print wheel. These printers are called daisy-wheel printers because the wheel and the spokes resemble the petals of a daisy. Daisy-wheel printers are much slower than dot-matrix printers and cannot print graphs and images. However, their letter quality output distinguishes them from dot-matrix printers. These printers have completely disappeared from the market.

Nonimpact printers include laser printers, thermal printers, ink-jet printers, and plotters. These printers are generally more expensive (with the exception of ink-jet printers) and capable of producing high quality output. Laser printers use laser beams, ink-jet printers spray ink, and thermal printers use a heat process to produce images on paper. Plotters are used to produce graphics output.

COMPUTER SOFTWARE

Computer software performs an enormously wide range of tasks. Software is divided into two categories: **system software** and **application software**.

OPERATING SYSTEM (SYSTEM SOFTWARE)

An Operating System is a program or series of programs that control the overall operations of a computer. The Operating System gives you the ability to work with a computer, use applications software and programs that you have saved on disks, and accepts commands from you and carries them out. You can communicate with a computer through its Operating System. It works as a translator between you and your computer.

This software manages the operation of the computer system, coordinates the running of the programs, allocates resources, and manages communications with the user. From the viewpoint of the user of application software, the most important piece of system software is the Operating System. The Operating System interprets your commands to run programs, manages program execution, and provides the means for you to interact with the programs while they are running. Moreover, the Operating System provides you with housekeeping programs for copying files, formatting disks, and determining the contents of diskettes and hard disks. In summary, an Operating System performs the following tasks:

- accepts and interprets user commands,
- manages the programs being run,
- makes diagnostic checks on the operation of the hardware, and
- provides application programs with access to the various components (application programs use system software to write data onto a diskette, read data from the keyboard, and to write data to the monitor).

Operating Systems may be classified into several categories:

Command-Line   In a command-line Operating System, all commands are typed on the keyboard. A mouse has limited use. Examples are: Digital Research CPM, MS-DOS, PC-DOS, VAX VMS.

GUI   A GUI (Graphical User Interface) Operating System contains graphics and icons and is commonly navigated

	by using a computer mouse. Some examples of GUI Operating Systems are: Linux, Mac OS, Windows 95, 98, 2000, XP, and CE.
Multi-User	A multi-user Operating System allows for multiple users to use the same computer at the same time and/or different times. Some examples of multi-user Operating Systems are: Linux, Mac OS, UNIX, Windows 2000, XP.
Multi-processing	An Operating System capable of supporting and utilizing more than one computer processor. Examples of multi-processing Operating Systems are: Linux, Mac OS, UNIX, Windows 2000, XP.
Multi-tasking	An Operating System that is capable of allowing multiple software processes to be run at the same time. Some examples of multi-tasking Operating Systems are: Mac OS, UNIX, Windows 2000, Windows XP.
Multi-threading	An Operating System that allows different parts of a software program to run concurrently. Operating Systems that fall into this category are: Linux, Mac OS, UNIX, Windows 2000, XP.

DOS AND WINDOWS

The Operating System that originally controlled the IBM personal computers (IBM-PC) was called PC-DOS. Most other compatible computers used a generic version of the Operating System called MS-DOS. These programs were developed by Microsoft Corporation. There were only a few minor differences between PC-DOS and MS-DOS.

As computer hardware and software improved and the need for DOS capabilities increased, Microsoft and IBM released new versions of DOS. DOS versions were upward compatible. This means that features that worked in early versions generally worked in later versions.

DOS was not a user-friendly program. In addition, it did not have a GUI interface. As a result, Microsoft developed an enhanced operating system with a GUI interface called Windows. Windows did not become a viable alternative to DOS until 1995 when Microsoft announced the Windows 95 operating system program. Table 1.4 summarizes the history of DOS and Windows since the introduction of the IBM PC in 1981.

Table 1.4. Operating Systems		
Version	**Date**	**Explanation**
DOS 1.0	1981	Original disk operating system
DOS 1.25	1982	Double-sided diskette support
DOS 2.0	1983	Hard-disk & Subdirectory support
DOS 2.01	1983	International symbols support
DOS 2.11	1983	Bugs in previous versions were fixed
DOS 2.25	1983	Support for extended character set
DOS 3.0	1984	1.2MB floppy diskette support
DOS 3.1	1984	Local Area Network support
DOS 3.2	1986	Support for 3.5 inch diskettes
DOS 3.3	1987	IBM PS/2 support
DOS 4.0	1988	Increase in user friendliness
DOS 6.0	1992	additional utilities, memory management, disk
Windows 3.1	1990	GUI interface
Windows 95	1995	Enhanced GUI interface and file manipulation
Windows 98	1998	Bug fixes and inclusion of Internet Explorer
Windows 2000	2000	Bug fixes and enhanced performance
Windows XP	2002	Security fixes and enhanced performance

FUNCTIONS OF SYSTEM SOFTWARE

Managing a computer system is a complex task requiring many different programs. Accordingly, the system software consists of many components, including the following.

Bootstrap Loader

This is the program that starts up the computer system when you turn on the power. This program is stored in ROM chip and the circuitry of the computer automatically runs this program whenever the computer is first turned on.

Diagnostic Routines

These programs are also stored in ROM chip and start up when you turn on the power. They test the operation of RAM, the CPU, and the various system components. The diagnostic routines give you some assurance that the computer is operating properly before you run any application programs.

Service Functions

These are programs stored in ROM chip and CMOS, which are used by application programs to perform "low level" hardware manipulation, such as writing characters onto a diskette, reading characters from the keyboard, and writing characters to the monitor. By using these functions, applications programs can access and use the system's hardware. The service functions are collectively called the **BIOS**—**B**asic **I**nput **O**utput **S**ystem.

STARTING YOUR COMPUTER

The process of turning your computer on and loading the Operating System into memory is called **booting or loading the system**. All IBM and compatible personal computers have a small program stored in their ROM that directs the actions of the computer when it is first turned on. This program loads the Operating System from the disk into the computer's memory (RAM) and gets the system running.

The Operating System is stored on diskettes, CD Rom or hard disk. As part of the system start-up, the bootstrap loader program reads the Operating System into RAM and turns the control of the computer to the Operating System. The bootstrap loader programs of most microcomputer systems are designed to check the first disk drive for the presence of a diskette. If one is present, the computer attempts to read the Operating System from the diskette. If no diskette is in the drive, the bootstrap loader checks for the presence of a hard disk. If one is present, the computer attempts to read the Operating System from there.

RUNNING PROGRAMS

Once the Operating System is loaded in RAM, you may request the Operating System to run a program (either an application program or an

Operating System command). In response to such a request, the following will happen.

1. The Operating System reads the program (from hard disk or diskette) into RAM.
2. The Operating System instructs the CPU to begin executing the program.
3. When program execution is done, control of the CPU is returned to the Operating System.
4. The Operating System awaits further instructions from you.

MANAGEMENT INFORMATION SYSTEM AND DATA BASE MANAGEMENT

In order to make better decisions, managers require a computer system designed to help them plan and direct business and organizational operations. A Management Information System (MIS) may be defined as a system that collects data, processes and manipulates data, and provides information to managers at all levels who use it for decision making, planning, program implementation, and control. An information system usually includes hardware, software, people, communication systems, and the data itself.

FUNCTIONAL SUPPORT ROLE

A Management Information System supports the operations of a business by

- recording and storing sales data, purchase data, investment data, payroll data and other managerial records;
- processing these records into financial statements such as income statement, balance sheet, statement of cash flow, and other pertinent financial information;
- recording and storing inventory data, work in process data, marketing data, equipment repair and maintenance data, supply chain data, and other production/operations records;
- processing the operations records into production schedules, production controllers, inventory systems, and production monitoring systems;
- recording and storing personnel data, salary data, employment histories, and other human resources records;

- processing the human resources records into employee expense reports, and performance based reports;
- recording and storing market data, customer profiles, customer purchase histories, marketing research data, advertising data, and other marketing records;
- processing the marketing records into advertising effectiveness reports, marketing plans, and sales activity reports;
- recording and storing business intelligence data, competitor analysis data, industry data, corporate objectives, and other strategic management records;
- processing the strategic management records into industry trends reports, market share reports, mission statements, and portfolio models; and
- use of all the above to implement, control, and monitor plans, strategies, tactics, new products, new business models or new business ventures.

ORGANIZING DATA FOR PROCESSING

Some of the activities involved in constructing a management information system are inputting of data, processing of data into information, storage of data and information, and the production of outputs such as management reports. Some of the most common terms in the construction of a data base management are summarized.

Data: Data are the raw material to be processed by a computer.
Information: Processed data becomes information—data that is organized, meaningful, and useful.

To be processed by the computer, raw data must be organized into characters, fields, records, files, and data bases.

Character: A character is a letter, number, or special character (such as $).
Field: A field contains an item of data. One or more characters comprise a field.
Record: A record is a collection of related fields.
File: A file is a collection of related records.
Data Base: A data base is a collection of interrelated data stored together with minimum redundancy.

FILE ORGANIZATION

Sequential File Organization
Sequential file organization simply means records are organized in sequential order.

Random (Direct) File Organization
Random file organization means records are organized randomly.

Indexed Sequential File Organization
Indexed file organization is a combination of the above two: Records are organized sequentially, but, in addition, indexes are built into the file so that a record can be accessed either sequentially or directly (randomly).

MANAGEMENT REPORTS

A computer system can produce four kinds of reports:

1. Detail Reports.
2. Summary Reports.
3. Exception Reports.
4. On-Demand Reports.

Managers at different levels have different needs and do not need all four reports. In general, managerial levels and their needs can be described as:

- **Low-Level Managers** need detail reports for day-to-day operations of the business.
- **Middle-Level Managers** need summary and exception reports for organizing functions and tactical planning.
- **Top-Level Managers** need on-demand reports for strategic planning, historic information, analysis of data trends, and general decision-making.

It should be clear that an MIS must be capable of delivering information not only of the predictable, detailed sort but also of the unpredictable, general sort.

DATA BASE MANAGEMENT SYSTEM

A database is an organized collection of records stored in a computer in a way that a computer program can access it to answer questions. Typically, for a given database, there is a structure which describes the way facts are held in that database. The structure describes the objects that are represented in the database, and the relationships among them. There are a number of different ways of organizing databases. The most common method in use today is the relational model, which represents all information in the form of multiple related tables each consisting of rows and columns.

The computer program used to manage and query a database is known as a database management system (DBMS). DBMS's are found at the heart of database applications. Typical examples of DBMS applications are accounting, human resources, and customer support systems. Originally databases were used only in large organizations with the computer hardware needed to support large data sets. However, DBMSs have nowadays become a standard part of any company.

Data Base Administrator

A Data Base Administer (DBA) is the person or group of persons who are responsible for monitoring and coordinating all activities related to the data base. The DBA has four major functions:

1. To coordinate users.
2. To monitor data base system performance.
3. To plan recovery procedures.
4. To monitor the security system.

BEFORE DATABASES: PATCHWORK FILES

In the early days of electronic computing most DBMSs were custom programs written that were tightly linked to multiple database files in order to gain speed at the expense of flexibility. In addition, each department within the organization had its own set of custom files (patchwork files) that were not linked to other files within the organization. As computers grew in capability, a number of general-purpose database systems emerged that allowed organizations to adopt one system to manage its database needs.

File Processing

Advantages:
1. Simple.
2. Inexpensive.

Disadvantages:
1. Redundancy (data duplication).
2. Data integrity.
3. Data dependence (the program logic was designed to fit the data).
4. Poor response to user requests.

Databases

Advantages:
1. Reduced redundancy.
2. Data integrity.
3. Data independence.
4. Shared data.
5. Fast response to user requests.
6. Centralized security.

Disadvantages:
1. Complexity.
2. Expense.
3. Vulnerability.

EXERCISE 1.1

Table 1.5. Technology Acronyms Quiz	
AI	LAN
ANSI	MIPS
ASCII	MIS
ATM	MPEG
CAD	OCR
CCD	OEM
CMOS	PC
CPU	PCI
CRT	PIN
DLP	PLU
DOS	PnP
DSP	POS
ECR	RAM
EFT	ROM
ESL	SKU
FAT	UNIX
I/O	UPC

CHAPTER 2

Quantitative Analysis

Q UANTITATIVE ANALYSIS HAS different meanings in different cases and applications. In most cases it is an alternative approach that is known as qualitative analysis.

WHAT IS QUANTITATIVE ANALYSIS?

Quantitative analysis is the scientific (using numerical and mathematical techniques) approach to managerial decision making. It usually involves collecting raw and unprocessed data. These data are then manipulated, processed, and summarized into meaningful information. Information is used by managers to make decisions. This process of converting raw data into useful information is the essence of quantitative analysis.

The steps required in quantitative analysis approach are: defining a problem, developing a model, acquiring input data, developing a solution, testing the solution, analyzing the results, implementing the results, modifying the model, and support.

Defining the Problem

The first step in the quantitative analysis approach is to develop a clear, accurate, and meaningful definition of the problem. Problem definition is the most important step in quantitative analysis as it gives direction and meaning to the manager.

Developing a Model

After we have a full understanding of the problem, the next step is to develop a model. A model is a mathematical representation of a problem and may require certain assumptions (see Table 2.1 and Turban, E. and Meredith, Ref. 52).

Acquiring Input Data

Solving any managerial problem requires data. It is important that we obtain good and reliable input data. Improper or inaccurate data will result in unreliable solutions and improper decisions. This is the reason why people use the expression **G**arbage **I**n, **G**arbage **O**ut (GIGO).

We can use different sources to obtain the required data. A primary source is usually company reports, financial statements, and other unpublished documents. Another major and important source of data is interviews with employees or other managers of the firm.

Table 2.1. Key Considerations in the Model-building Process		
Key Consideration	**Model-Building Approach**	
Resources Required	**Complex Model**	**Simple Model**
Cost	High	Low
Time	High	Low
Labor	High	Low
Organizational Acceptance		
Involving people	Low	High
Understanding the effort	Low	High
Implementation of the result	Low	High
Result		
Solution to the real problem	Good (Accurate)	Approximate

Developing a Solution

In order to arrive at the best or optimal solution, we need to manipulate the model. In some problems, there may be several solutions. Our task in such cases is to determine the best possible solution.

Testing the Solution

The next step in quantitative analysis is to test the accuracy of the solution and robustness of the model. Generally, we need some input data to test the validity and accuracy of the solution. In addition, we need to test the accuracy and validity of the input data.

Analyzing the Results

Before a solution can be implemented, it needs to be analyzed. The first step is to investigate the implications of implementing the new solution. In most cases, a new solution to a managerial problem may have a significant effect on the way an organization is structured or managed.

The second step in analyzing the results is to perform sensitivity analysis. Sensitivity analysis is the process by which we investigate the sensitivity of the solution to changes in the model and input data.

Implementing the Results

The final step is to incorporate the solution into the company. This may not be an easy task and may require several months. It is not unusual for members of an organization to resist change, even if the new solution is a significant improvement over the existing system. In addition, there are usually additional costs involved in implementing a new solution.

Modifying the Model

Once a model has been implemented, additional modifications may be required to better meet the needs of the decision makers.

Support and Further Modification

Long term support and further modifications are generally required for two reasons: to provide help and training for new users, and to make further modifications due to changes in needs and environmental factors such as technology.

REASONS WHY A QUANTITATIVE APPROACH MIGHT BE USED

The problem is sophisticated and complex. It is not possible for the manager to develop a reasonable solution without using quantitative analysis.

1. The problem is of strategic importance or a great deal of money is involved, and the manager is under pressure to use all available analysis before making a decision.
2. The problem is relatively new (e.g., due to technological changes), and the manager cannot rely on qualitative analysis as he/she has no prior experience to draw upon.
3. The problem occurs often and is repetitive. The manager can save time, money, and effort by using quantitative procedures to make decisions.

QUANTITATIVE ANALYSIS AND MANAGERIAL DECISION MAKING

In general, managers use resources (human, capital, energy, materials, technology, time) in order to achieve certain goals. These resources are called inputs of the process, and the results are viewed as the output of the process. The success or failure of a manager is in terms of the ratio of outputs to inputs. This ratio is commonly referred to as productivity.

Productivity = outputs (products, services) / inputs (resources)

Most organizations are concerned about productivity as it is considered to be a measure of the efficiency and well-being of the organization. Productivity is also of concern to politicians at the national level as it determines the well-being (e.g., employment level, inflation, economic growth) and standard of living of a country.

Traditionally, management and decision-making have been considered to be an art, a talent you are born with (such as creativity, intuition, and judgement) or you have attained through years of experience. However, the environment in which we make decisions have changed. We live in the global economy where technological advancements, environmental factors, and electronic information have become a significant part of our lives.

Business and its environment are more complex today for three reasons:

1. The number of available alternatives is much larger and more complex today because of technological changes.
2. The long-term consequences of our decisions are more difficult to predict because of increased uncertainty.
3. The cost of making incorrect decisions has increased because of the increase in complexity and significantly larger and more global markets.

Because of these major changes and advancements, decision-making is therefore has become more sophisticated—it is considered to be a combination of both art and science (see Figure 2.1 and Turban, E. and Meredith, Ref. 52).

Figure 2.1 The Managerial Decision-Making Process

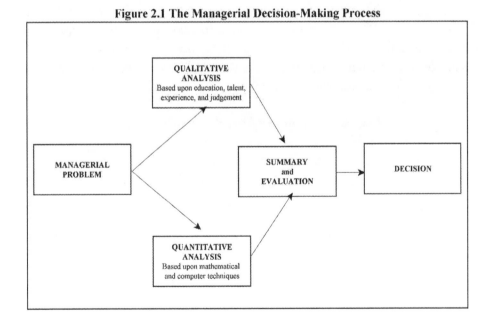

Although the quantitative approach to problem solving can be achieved without the use of computers, it would be impractical, unreliable, or totally impossible to apply quantitative analysis without computers.

DECISION SUPPORT ROLE

An integral part of a good information system is its decision-making support role. It allows managers to perform sensitivity analysis and ask what-if questions such as

- What if we reduce prices by 10%?
- What if inflation rises by 6%?
- What if we have serious labor problems in the future?

DECISION SUPPORT SYSTEMS

A decision support system (DSS) supports rather than replace managerial decision making. Ordinarily, decision support systems are used in poorly defined problems and unstructured situations. An effectively designed DSS must be flexible, interactive, and allow managers to enter different input data and try out different decisions.

Although there is no common or acceptable definition for DSS, it is generally defined as a computer-based information system consisting of hardware, software, documentation, and the human resources, designed to help decision makers with poorly defined and unstructured problems. In summary, DSS must have the following characteristics:

- DSS is designed to support rather than replace decision makers.
- DSS should help decision makers at all levels.
- DSS emphasizes poorly defined, semi-structured, and unstructured tasks.
- DSS requires hardware.
- DSS requires software.
- DSS requires human resources (designers, programmers, and users).

BENEFITS OF DSS

1. Increase in the number of alternatives examined
2. Better understanding of the business
3. Fast response to unexpected situations
4. Ability to carry out ad hoc (formed or done for a particular purpose only) analysis

5. New insights and learning
6. Improved communication
7. Improved control
8. Cost savings
9. Better decisions
10. More effective teamwork
11. Time savings
12. Making better use of data resources

APPLICATIONS OF DSS

Some of the most recent applications of DSS are:

1. What-if analysis. If, for example, labor costs increase by 5%, what will happen to the cost of a product?
2. Goal-seeking. As an example, how much you should charge for a particular unit in order to generate $500,000 profit or how much should you advertise in order to generate $20,000,000 in total sales.
3. Sensitivity analysis. For example, what is the maximum price that you should pay for energy resources and still make a profit, or how much overtime can you pay and still be cost-effective.
4. Exception reporting analysis. For example, reporting on the region that generated the highest total sales, managers that performed better than average, or the factory that spent more than the allocated budget.

CHAPTER 3

Review of Spreadsheet (Excel) Commands & Procedures

THE MOST BASIC and most versatile business decision making tool is the spreadsheet. Although there are other more-sophisticated programs available, spreadsheets can perform graphics, database management, and also incorporate statistical decision making tools like regression, forecasting, and sensitivity analysis.

Microsoft Excel is an example of a spreadsheet software program that can be highly useful in decision-makers' daily business activities. It enables them to shorten the time they would spend in creating a professional looking worksheet. The following are some of the most common and helpful commands to know when using Excel.

FORMATTING

Numbers that are entered into cells can be formatted according to many different styles (see Figure 3.1). While formatting, it is important to stay with one style throughout the worksheet so that all the numbers line up and look consistent.

Figure 3.1. Excel's Format Cells Menu

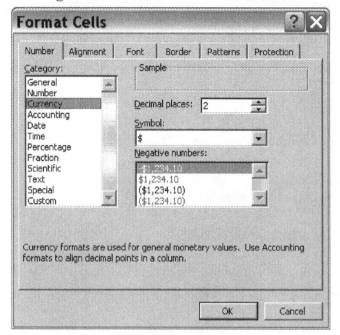

Note: Cells that are to be formatted must first be highlighted. They do not need be adjacent to each other.

To Highlight Cells in Different Parts of the Worksheet
Press and hold the Ctrl key and then highlight all the desired cells by clicking the mouse in them.

To Format a Number According to Accounting Format
Highlight the number(s) and then click on Format, Cells, Number, and Accounting. Specify the number of decimals and whether you want a $ sign or no $ sign and press Ok.

To Format a Number According to Currency Format
Highlight the number(s) and then click on Format, Cells, Number, and Currency. Specify the number of decimals and whether you want a $ sign or no $ sign and press Ok.

Note: The accounting format has the advantage of ensuring that all numbers will have the same width. However, it leaves a gap between the numbers and the $ sign. The currency format does not leave a gap between the numbers and the $ sign. However, the numbers will not have equal widths. The following examples demonstrate the difference between these two formats.

Accounting Format	Currency Format
$ 123,45.67	$123,45.67
$ 89.10	$89.10

To Format a Number According to Date Format

Type in a date (e.g., February 8, 2006) in a cell. Highlight the cell and then click on Format, Cells, Number, and Date. Specify how you want the date to be displayed and press Ok.

To Underline a Formatted Number

Highlight the number(s) and then click on Format, Cells, and Font. Specify single or double underlining and press Ok. For single underlining, you can also click on the "U" icon (see Figures 3.2 and 3.3).

To Center the Contents of a Cell

Highlight the cell(s) and then click on Format, Cells, and Alignment. Specify vertical or horizontal, click on center, and press Ok. For horizontal centering, you can also click on the centering icon (see Figures 3.2 and 3.3).

Figure 3.2. Excel's Formatting Bar

To Center a Title Across a Block of Cells (e.g., A2 Through F2)

Type the title in cell A2 and then highlight cells A2 to F2 and click on ▦ (Merge and Center) icon on the toolbar (see Figure 3.2).

Figure 3.3. Excel's Underlining Menu

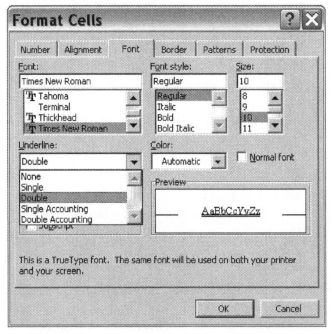

To Edit the Contents of a Cell
Click with your mouse on that cell or press the F2 key.

Renaming Cells
Use the Insert, Name, and Define command to replace cell references with easy-to-remember names in a problem.

To Add Line Breaks in One Cell
Press the Alt and Enter keys.

To Copy the Content of a Cell with the Fill Handle
Highlight the cell. Go to the right bottom corner of the cell and drag it down or to the right.

To Enter a Series of Numbers
- Enter the first number in a cell.
- Enter the second number in an adjacent cell (to the right or below it).
- Highlight both cells.
- Get the fill handle and drag it down or to the right.

To Enter a Series of Dates
- Type a date in a cell (e.g., March 21, 2007).
- Highlight the cell and drag the fill handle down or to the right.
- Excel will create a series of consecutive dates (i.e., March 22, 2007, March 23, 2007, etc.).
- Now, type two dates in two adjacent cells (e.g., March 10 and March 15).
- Highlight both cells and pull the fill handle down or to the right.
- Excel will create a new series of dates corresponding to the difference between the first two dates (i.e., March 20, March 25, etc.).

To Freeze Columns and Rows

Freezing columns and rows allows you to select data that remains visible when scrolling in a sheet. For example, keeping row and column labels visible as you scroll.

- To freeze a column, go to the adjacent column to the right of it and click on a cell.
- To freeze a row, go to the row directly below it and click on a cell.
- Next, click on Window from the toolbar and select Freeze Panes.

CELL WIDTH AND HEIGHTS

CELL WIDTHS

Method 1

Point your cursor on the top row (column headings row, A, B, C, D, . . .), and DRAG the cell to the right to increase the column width or to the left to decrease the column width.

Method 2
- Highlight the column(s).
- Choose FORMAT from the tool bar.
- Choose COLUMN from the drop down menu.
- Choose WIDTH from the menu.
- Type in the size needed.

CELL HEIGHT

Method 1

Pointing your cursor on the first column (row headings column 1, 2, 3, 4 . . . , etc.), DRAG the cell up to increase the cell (row) height or down to decrease the cell (row) height.

Method 2
- Highlight the row(s).
- Choose FORMAT from the tool bar.
- Choose ROW from the drop down menu.
- Choose HEIGHT from the drop down menu.
- Type in the size needed.

FORMULAS

Typing Method

Go to the desired cell and type the formula. For example,

$$=A5 + B7 - G3 * H9 + (C10 - D18) / 4 - C14$$

Built-In Functions

Go to the desired cell and type one of the built-in functions. For example,

$$=SUM(B6:B10, F9:F16, AA5, 12) \text{ or } STDEV(E4, G5, H8)$$

Pointing Method

Highlight the cell where you want the answer to appear and click on, for example, the SUMMATION sign, "Σ".

PRINTING

Setting the Print Area
- Highlight the cells you want printed.
- Click File, Print Area, Set Print Area, Print, and Ok.
- If this is not the first time your are printing in Excel, clear the print area first before setting it.

Figure 3.4. Excel's Page Setup Menu for Printing

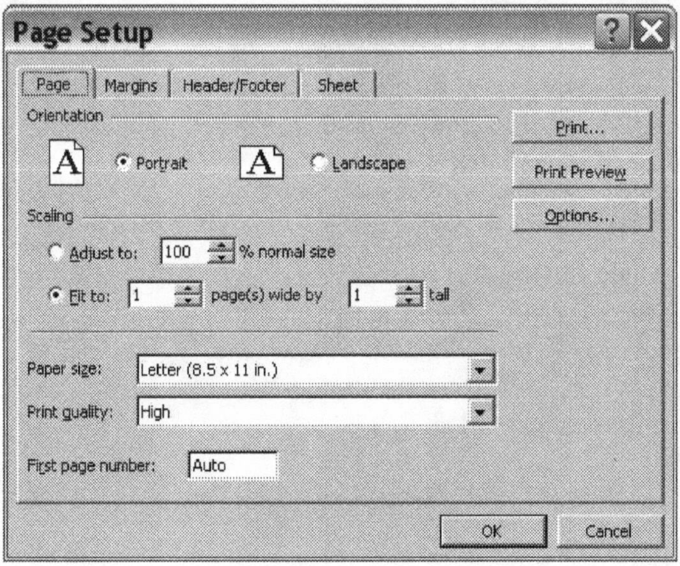

To Make Sure Your Worksheet Prints on One Page

Highlight the area you want to print and then click File, Print Preview, and Setup. Put a check mark in the Fit to One Page box (see Figure 3.4).

To Show Cell Formulas

Click on Tools, Options, and View. Put a check mark in the Formula box. To print cell formulas, follow the instructions above.

RELATIVE AND ABSOLUTE ADDRESSING

There are two methods of entering a formula into a cell:

RELATIVE ADDRESSING

Assume that you enter a formula such as =A4 + B5 + C2 into cell B8. All spreadsheets, including Excel, record this formula in cell B8, not as the sum of the values in cells A4, B5, and C2, but as the sum of values of the cells:

1 column to the left, 4 rows up + same column as B, 3 rows up + 1 column to the right, 6 rows up

This type of formula represents relative addressing, and the cell addresses in the formula are defined relative to where they are. If, for example, we enter the same formula =A4 + B5 + C2 into cell H3, the formula will find a completely new meaning:

7 columns to the left, 1 row down + 6 columns to the left, 2 rows down + 5 columns to the left, 1 row up

If the cell B8 is copied to cell K10, the formula will change to =J6 + K7 + L4 and if cell H3 is copied to K10, the formula will change to =D11 + E12 + F9.

What appears to be the same formula has two different meanings depending on its location. Relative addressing is the most common type of addressing in spreadsheets, and their use is appropriate when you want a formula to adjust when copied.

ABSOLUTE ADDRESSING

In some situations, particularly when you are referring to constants in a problem, you may want to override relative addressing. In such cases, we freeze the cell reference as it appears by putting a $ sign in front of the cell address. For example, the formula =$A$6 + $B$3 means exactly as it appears: the sum of cell A6 and B3. This type of addressing is referred to as absolute addressing and formulas using this type of addressing will not adjust when copied.

MIXED ADDRESSING

If part of a cell reference needs to be locked in and part of it requires relative reference, we use mixed addressing. For example, $E23 or G$34.

EXERCISE 3.1
SPREADSHEET ADDRESSING

1. Describe the type of addressing and the meaning of the following:

    a. =J5 + I8
    b. Cell H6 contains the formula =J5 + I8
    c. Cell K10 contains the formula =J5 + I8
    d. Cell A4 contains the formula =$J5 + I$8

2. Suppose B4, B5, B6 contain the numbers 3, 2, 4, respectively.

    a. Calculate the result in A7 if it contains the formula =STDEV(B4:
        B6)?
    b. If cell A7 is copied to cell E20, what formula will be displayed in E20?

LOGICAL STATEMENTS

A logical (if-then-else) statement is used to choose which of two alternative statements to execute, depending on the true/false value of a condition. Below we see the format for using if-then-else.

> if (condition 1), statement A
> else   if (condition2), statement B
>   else   if (condition3), statement C
>   else   statement D.

If condition A is true, statement A will be performed and program flow will jump over all other else conditions and quit. If condition 1 is false, condition 2 will be tested. If it is true, statement B will be executed. If both condition 1 and condition 2 fail, condition 3 will tested and if true, statement C will be executed. If all three conditions, 1,2, and 3 are false, then statement D will be performed.

Logical statements are among the most powerful tools in working with computers—the logic is to compare two things, for example, *if A > 2 then* to do something or *else* do something else. There are different types of logical statements: simple, nested, and compound.

SIMPLE LOGICAL STATEMENTS

Assume in a problem we have variables A and B with values 4 and 12, respectively. The value of variable C in the problem can change, depending on the result of the following simple logical statement:

> IF A > B THEN
>   Let C = 5 * A
> ELSE
>   Let C = A + B.

Since variable A is smaller than variable B, the answer for C will be 4 + 12 =16.

You can use the following operands in IF statements:

> \> greater than
> < less than

>= greater than or equal to

<= less than or equal to

< > not equal to.

NESTED LOGICAL STATEMENTS

In some problems, it may be appropriate to include an IF statement within another IF statement. These types of IF statements are referred to as **Nested IF Statements**. Here is an example:

```
IF A > B THEN
        Let C = 5 * A
ELSE
        IF A < 2 THEN
            LET C = B - 3
        ELSE
            Let = A * B.
```

In this case, the value of C will be equal to 4 * 12 = 48. The format of the nested if statement is as follows:

```
IF . . . THEN
        . . .
ELSE
        IF . . . THEN
            . . .
        ELSE
            IF . . . THEN
                . . .
            ELSE
                . . .
```

COMPOUND LOGICAL STATEMENTS

Simple and nested IF statements can be combined with one another to test multiple conditions.

AND Compound Statement

When the AND condition is used, both conditions must be satisfied. For example, the statement IF (A > B AND A > 0) THEN . . . means that not only must A be greater than B, but it must also be greater than zero (positive).

OR Compound Statement

When the OR condition is used, as long as only one of the conditions is met, we are satisfied. It is not necessary for both conditions to be true. For example, IF (B < A OR B < 0) THEN . . . means that for the statement to be satisfied, either B must be less than A or B must be negative. It is not necessary for B to be less than A and also be negative.

LOGICAL STATEMENTS AND EXCEL

The following examples demonstrate how logical statements are used in Excel.

Simple Logical Statement in Excel

An IF statement can be entered in any cell. Excel uses commas for THEN and for ELSE. You must also start an IF statement with a left parenthesis and close it with a right parenthesis. For example, you can enter the following formula in cell A6.

=IF(D20<=F15,"Error!!!",B10-B12)

If the value in D20 is less than or equal to the value in F15, the error message will display in cell A6. Otherwise, the answer to B10-B12 will appear in A6. The first comma in the IF statement represents THEN and the second comma represents ELSE. Note also that any message must be in double quotation marks.

Nested Logical Statements in Excel

Each IF statement must have its own commas and parenthesis.

=IF(. . . , . . . , IF(. . . , . . . , IF(. . . , . . . , . . .)))

Compound Logical Statements in Excel

=IF(AND(K12<30,K12>5),"INCORRECT",IF(OR(F18>100,L
16< 50), (F18-$H$7)*$A$4,$G$8+L16*$B$3))

Note that for each IF statement, there is a corresponding closed parenthesis
at the end.

EXERCISE 3.2
LOGICAL STATEMENTS

1. Assume cells B7, B8, and B9 contain numbers 76, 83, and 78.

   a. Write a formula in cell H10 to find the highest of these numbers.
   b. Write another formula in cell H11 to find the lowest of these three numbers.
   c. Write an IF statement in cell H12 to find the second highest number.

2. Suppose K is equal to 4 and L is equal to 8. Determine the values for K and L after the following commands are executed.

   a. If K < L then let K = L + 1
   b. Let L = K + 3
   c. If K < 7 then let L = L + 2
   d. Let K = L – 2

CHAPTER 4

Financial Statements

FINANCIAL STATEMENTS SERVE various purposes. Managers need them to see how effectively their enterprises are being run. Federal and state governments need them to assess taxes in a reasonable manner. Finally, investors need them to make intelligent financial decisions.

INCOME STATEMENT

The *income statement* summarizes a firm's revenues and expenses over a period of time, for example, a year. The result is either a profit or a loss for that period. Profits can be taken out of the company by the owners or re-invested back into the company as retained earnings.

In detail, the income statement shows the amount of gross sales, net sales, cost of goods sold, all expenses for the period including operating expenses and general and administrative expenses, income from operations, other income, and net income.

BALANCE SHEET

The *balance sheet* shows the firm's assets and the claims against those assets. Assets are typically shown in the order of their liquidity; claims (liabilities & stockholder's equity) are listed in the order in which they must be paid. The balance sheet can be thought of as a snapshot of the firm's financial position at a point in time, for example, the last day of the year. The balance sheet changes every day as inventory is increased or decreased, fixed assets are added or retired, cash flows in and out of a company, etc.

In detail, the balance sheet shows current assets (cash, notes receivable, inventory, etc.), long-term assets (plant and equipment), current liabilities (notes payable, accounts payable, salaries payable, and unearned revenue), long-term liabilities (mortgage payable), and finally the owners' equity. The important thing to know while doing the balance sheet is that the total assets have to equal to the total liabilities plus owners' equity.

$$\text{Assets} - \text{Liabilities} - \text{Preferred stock} = \text{Common stockholders'}$$
$$\text{equity (net worth)}$$

A major difference between the balance sheet and the income statement is that the income statement represents a 12-month period and the balance sheet represents only one day.

FINANCIAL STATEMENTS AND EXCEL

Microsoft Excel can be used for preparing financial statements as well as many other reports.

Useful Tips For Creating Financial Statements Using Excel

Centering Headings and Titles:

> Click on Al cell to make it active and type in your heading. Center the heading by highlighting the cells that the heading needs to be centered across and then pressing the "Merge and Center" icon on the toolbar. The heading should be centered after all information has been entered. Only one line can be centered at a time.

Formatting Numbers Without $ Sign:

> Highlight the number that you want to format, go to "Format" on the menu bar, click on "Cells", and then select the "Number" and pick the category of "Accounting" with "0" decimal and "None" for symbol.

Formatting Numbers With $ Sign:

> Highlight the number that you want to format, go to "Format" on the menu bar, click on "Cells", and then select the "Number" and pick the category of "Accounting" with "0" decimal and "$" for symbol.

To underline (single or double):

> Highlight the number that you want to underline, go to "Format" on the menu bar, click on "Cells", and then select "Font." On "Underline", select "Single Line" or "Double Line."

To change the width of columns:

> Highlight the cell or cells to be formatted and click "Format", "Column", "Width", and enter the width for the column or columns.

Row Height:

> In order to make the rows the same size, go to "Format" on the menu bar, click on "Row", and then click on "Height." Enter the row size that you want.

Entering dots:

> Use the period button on the keyboard and press continuously for cells with account titles.
> Use the copy and paste feature to display dots for cells between account titles and numbers.

Basic formulas when creating financial statements:

> = SUM(A1, A2) or = A1+A2 for adding two cells
> = SUM(A1:A9) for adding a range of consecutive cells
> = SUM(Al-A2) or = A1−A2 for subtracting two cells.

View Formulas:

> Highlight all the cells that you want to view the formulas for. Click on "Tools" on the menu bar, click on "Options", under "View" tab, and select "Formulas."

To print the worksheet:

> Highlight all the active cells, click on "File", "Print Area", "Set", "Print."

To make sure that all necessary data from spreadsheet fit on one page:

> Click on "File" on tool bar, then choose option "Page Setup", then click on "Page folder" to specify "Fit to: 1 page", then to "Print Preview" window to check if all necessary data is in the print page. Then to finalize, click on "Print" to print page.

To highlight cells in different parts of the worksheet:

> Press and hold the Ctrl key while highlighting all the desired cells.

Editing contents within a cell:

> Press the F2 key or click on the cell, and then change the content.

COMPUTER ASSIGNMENT

Create a detailed Income Statement (as in Table 4.1) and a detailed Balance Sheet (as in Table 4.2) for a fictitious firm using Excel.

REQUIREMENTS

1. Printout for Income Statement (one page)
2. Printout for Balance Sheet (one page)
3. Printout of cell formulas for Income Statement (one page)
4. Printout of cell formulas for Balance Sheet (one page)
5. A summary report
   - Briefly explain Financial Statements.
   - Briefly explain the Commands and Procedures used.
   - Briefly explain the formulas, formatting numbers, underlining, merging cells, printing, etc.

USEFUL GUIDELINES

Use the following steps to do this lab assignment:

- Open "Excel", right click on "Sheet 1" and rename it Income Statement, right click on 'Sheet 2' and rename it Balance Sheet.

- Go to "File", "Save" and save the workbook as LAB1.xls.
- Adjust the width of the columns. Adjust four columns (B, D, C, and E) for Income Statement and three columns (B, C, and D) for Balance Sheet to make sure all have the same size by highlighting the columns across any row and click on "Format", "Column", "Width" and type a number (e.g., 12).
- Enter all labels first so that you can identify the cells where you will enter data and formulas.
- Enter the appropriate numbers and formulas.
- To format numbers, highlight all the number and click on "Format", "Cells", "Number", "Accounting". Insert zero for decimal places. Only the first number in a column, totals, and subtotals require $ signs. The rest of the numbers in the column do not require $ signs. However, they should still be formatted to make sure that they have commas and they line up with all the other numbers.
- To print out the Income Statement and the Balance Sheet, highlight all the labels and numbers, click on "File", "Print Area", "Set" then click on "Setup", "Fit to 1 Page" and click on "OK."

Table 4.1. Income Statement

	A	B	C	D	E
1					
2		XYZ COMPANY			
3		Income Statement			
4		For the Year Ended December 31, 20 - -			
5					
6	Gross sales			$	1,500,000
7	Less: Sales returns & allowances		$	36,000	
8	Sales discounts			23,000	
9	Net sales			$	1,441,000
10	Cost of goods sold:				
11	Inventory, Jan. 1			$ 125,000	
12	Purchases	$	885,000		
13	Less: Purchase returns & allowances	$ 42,000			
14	Purchase discounts	31,000	73,000		
15	Net purchases		$ 812,000		
16	Add: Transportation-in		62,000		
17	Cost of goods purchased			874,000	
18	Cost of goods available for sale			$ 999,000	
19	Less: Inventory, Dec. 31			180,000	
20	Cost of goods sold				
21	Gross profit on sales			$	622,000
22	Operating expenses:				
23	Selling expenses:				
24	Sales salaries		$ 232,000		
25	Advertising		41,400		
26	Depreciation: building		9,000		
27	Depreciation: store equipment		10,400		
28	Depreciation: delivery equipment		8,500		
29	Insurance		4,000		
30	Miscellaneous		1,500		
31	Total selling expenses			$ 306,800	
32	Administrative expenses:				
33	Office salaries		$ 147,800		
34	Dues and subscriptions		1,080		
35	Depreciation: building		5,000		
36	Insurance		2,600		
37	Miscellaneous		700		
38	Total administrative expenses			$ 157,180	
39	Total operating expenses				
40	Income from operations			$	158,020
41	Interest earned on investments				
42	Net income			$	165,520

Table 4.2. Balance Sheet

	A	B	C	D	E
1					
2			XYZ COMPANY		
3			Balance Sheet, December 31, 20 - -		
4					
5			Assets		
6					
7	Current assets:				
8	Cash			$	253,000
9	Government bonds				110,000
10	Notes receivable				135,000
11	Accounts receivable				252,000
12	Inventory				365,000
13	Prepaid expenses				32,000
14	Total current assets			$	1,147,000
15					
16	Plant and equipment:				
17	Land		$	215,000	
18	Building	$	345,000		
19	Less: Accumulated depreciation		29,200	315,800	
20	Store equipment	$	104,000		
21	Less: Accumulated depreciation		28,800	75,200	
22	Delivery equipment	$	38,000		
23	Less: Accumulated depreciation		9,000	29,000	
24	Total plant and equipment			635,000	
25					
26	Other assets:				
27	Land (future building site)				152,000
28	Total assets			$	1,934,000
29					
30			Liabilities & Owner's Equity		
31					
32	Current liabilities:				
33	Notes payable			$	146,000
34	Accounts payable				290,000
35	Salaries payable				24,500
36	Unearned revenue				31,000
37	Total current liabilities				$
38					
39	Long-term liabilities:				
40	Mortgage payable (due in 15 years)				276,000
41	Total liabilities			$	767,500
42					
43	Owner's equity:				
44	XYZ, capital				1,166,500
45	Total liabilities & owner's equity			$	1,934,000

CHAPTER 5

Loans and Amortization Tables

A LOAN IS A sum of money lent at interest for temporary use. Amortization is the process of cost allocation that assigns the original cost of an asset over the number of periods that asset was in use. A loan amortization table shows the loan amount, interest rate, term of the loan, and payment per month. It also shows how much of the payment is interest and how much of it is principal. In the last column, it shows the ending balance after each period.

To calculate the periodic payment on a loan, we use the present value of an annuity formula

$$PV = PMT \cdot \frac{1 - 1 / (1 + k)^n}{k}$$

If we rearrange the above formula to solve for PMT, we obtain

$$PMT = PV / \{[1 - (1 / (1+k)^n)] / k\}$$

where:

PV	=	principal or present value of the loan,
PMT	=	periodic payment
k	=	interest rate per compound period
n	=	total number of compound periods

To construct the first row of an amortization table, we multiply the loan balance by the rate, k, to determine the interest due. Then, we subtract the interest amount from the payment, PMT, to calculate the principal paid out of the first payment. Next, we subtract the principal paid from the loan balance to determine the outstanding balance after the first payment. This procedure will be repeated for each loan period until the loan is fully paid up.

EXERCISE 5.1
LOANS AND AMORTIZATION TABLES

1. a) Assume $30,000 is borrowed for 3 years at 10% interest. The loan is to
    be repaid in three (3) *annual* payments. Find the annual payment.

    b) Use Table 5.1 to construct an amortization table for this loan.

Table 5.1. Amortization Table				
Period	**Payment**	**Interest**	**Principal**	**Balance**
0	—	—	—	$30,000.00
1				
2				
3				

COMPUTER ASSIGNMENT

OVERVIEW

The goal of this assignment is to create an Excel spreadsheet to calculate the periodic payment on a loan and then create an amortization table. This assignment focuses on creating more complex formulas, using absolute and relative addressing, as well as basic Excel commands.

INSTRUCTIONS

1. Follow the format in Table 5.2.
2. In cell D8 create a formula, PMT = PV / ((1 − 1/(1 + k)^n) / k), to calculate the periodic payment on a loan.
3. In cell F8 use the built-in function =PMT(k, n, PV). You should get identical answers.
4. Create an amortization table (use absolute and relative addressing where appropriate).
5. Print the worksheet.
6. Change the loan amount and the rate (everything should adjust automatically) and print it again.
7. Print the cell formulas (force to one page).
8. Write a report and explain all formulas and procedures.
9. Submit the four printouts.

Table 5.2. Loan Calculation and Amortization Table

	C	D	E	F	G
2		LOANS AND AMORTIZATION TABLES			
3					
4	Loan Amount:	$50,000.00			
5	Rate:	9.00%	Per Year	0.75%	Per Month
6	Term:	3	Years	36	Months
7					
8	PMT:	$1,589.99	Per Month	$1,589.99	
9					
10	Period	PMT	Interest	Principal	Balance
11	0	–	–	–	$50,000.00
12	1	$1,589.99	$375.00	$1,214.99	48,785.01
13	2	1,589.99	365.89	1,224.10	47,560.91
14	3	1,589.99	356.71	1,233.28	46,327.63
15	4	1,589.99	347.46	1,242.53	45,085.11
16	5	1,589.99	338.14	1,251.85	43,833.26
17	6	1,589.99	328.75	1,261.24	42,572.02
18	7	1,589.99	319.29	1,270.70	41,301.32
19	8	1,589.99	309.76	1,280.23	40,021.10
20	9	1,589.99	300.16	1,289.83	38,731.27
21	10	1,589.99	290.48	1,299.50	37,431.77
22	11	1,589.99	280.74	1,309.25	36,122.52
23	12	1,589.99	270.92	1,319.07	34,803.45
24	13	1,589.99	261.03	1,328.96	33,474.49
25	14	1,589.99	251.06	1,338.93	32,135.56
26	15	1,589.99	241.02	1,348.97	30,786.59
27	16	1,589.99	230.90	1,359.09	29,427.50
28	17	1,589.99	220.71	1,369.28	28,058.22
29	18	1,589.99	210.44	1,379.55	26,678.67
30	19	1,589.99	200.09	1,389.90	25,288.78
31	20	1,589.99	189.67	1,400.32	23,888.46
32	21	1,589.99	179.16	1,410.82	22,477.63
33	22	1,589.99	168.58	1,421.40	21,056.23
34	23	1,589.99	157.92	1,432.06	19,624.16
35	24	1,589.99	147.18	1,442.81	18,181.36
36	25	1,589.99	136.36	1,453.63	16,727.73
37	26	1,589.99	125.46	1,464.53	15,263.20
38	27	1,589.99	114.47	1,475.51	13,787.69
39	28	1,589.99	103.41	1,486.58	12,301.11
40	29	1,589.99	92.26	1,497.73	10,803.38
41	30	1,589.99	81.03	1,508.96	9,294.42
42	31	1,589.99	69.71	1,520.28	7,774.14
43	32	1,589.99	58.31	1,531.68	6,242.46
44	33	1,589.99	46.82	1,543.17	4,699.29
45	34	1,589.99	35.24	1,554.74	3,144.55
46	35	1,589.99	23.58	1,566.40	1,578.15
47	36	1,589.99	11.84	1,578.15	0.00
48	Total:	$57,239.52	$7,239.52	$50,000.00	

CREATING AN AMORTIZATION TABLE IN EXCEL

In this assignment, we learn how to produce a loan and amortization table in Excel. In order to do so, we will have to use both relative and absolute addressing. To learn about these types of cell reference, please review Chapter 3.

To create the table, use these procedures:

1. Type in the loan amount ($50,000), rate (9%), and term (3 years) in cells D4, D5, and D6.
2. To get the rate per month, refer to the cell containing the interest rate for the loan and divide it by twelve (i.e., F5: = D5/12 = 0.09/12 = .0075 or 0.75%).
3. To get the number of months for the loan, refer to the cell for the term and multiple it by twelve (i.e., F6: =D6*12 = 3 * 12 = 36).
4. For the payment per month cell, enter in the following formula in cell D8.

$$PMT = PV / ((1 - 1/(1+k)^\wedge n) / k)$$

   In Excel format, the formula = $D4/((1 - 1/(1 + F5)^\wedge F6)/F5)$ is entered in Cell D8.

   Alternatively, the built-in function = PMT(k, n, PV) can be used in cell F8.

5. Next, set up the amortization table by entering dash in the first three cells. Since Excel expects a formula after typing the minus sign, it may not allow you to enter it by itself. If that happens, make sure you format the cell according to TEXT format.
6. To number the periods from 0 to 36, type in 0 in cell C11. Then in cell C12, enter the formula =C11+1 and drag it all the way down to cell C47.
7. Enter the periodic payment, =$D$8 into cell D12. We use absolute addressing to make sure that this formula does not adjust when it is copied.
8. The interest amount is the ending balance of the previous period multiplied by rate of interest per month. In cell E12, we should use mixed addressing and type =G11*$F$5, because we want the balance to change and the interest rate to remain the same.

9. The principal is the payment amount minus the interest amount. Therefore, cell F12 will contain the formula =D12-E12. We want to use relative addressing because the payment and the interest amounts will change from period to period.

10. The outstanding balance is the balance amount from the previous period minus the principal of the current period, =G11-F12. We used relative addressing for the same reason as in step nine.

11. After completing all the formulas in row 12, copy them all the way down to rows 13 through 47.

12. For the total of each column, put the formula =SUM(D12:D47) in cell D48 and then copy it across to cells E48 and F48.

13. To format the rates in percentages, highlight the cells, then go to "format", "cells", and "percentage". You can also specify the number of decimal places.

14. To put dollar signs and two decimal places for the top row of the amortization table, highlight them, then "format", "cells", "currency", "2" for number of decimals, and "$".

15. For the rest of the numbers in the amortization table, highlight them, then "format", "cells", "currency", "2" for number of decimals, and "none" for no $ sign.

16. Finally, you can work on making your table look professional by putting boxes around the table and centering the titles.

17. Next, make cell formulas appear by highlighting the whole document, then go to "tools", "options", and check "formulas". Print out the formula sheet and change the document back to the original by going to "tools", "options", and uncheck "formulas".

18. Print worksheets by going to "file", "print area", "clear print area", "set print area", then go back to "file", "page set up", and adjust to fit to one page. Before printing, go to print preview to double check how your printout will look.

In this assignment, when we change the loan amount and the rate of interest, the numbers in all cells will adjust automatically. This is because we used formulas instead of typing in the numbers. Furthermore, we used relative and absolute addressing. By applying relative and absolute addressing, we had to create the formulas only once. When the formulas were copied to other cells, the payment, interest, principal, and balance for each period were calculated automatically.

CHAPTER 6

Income Tax Calculation

INTRODUCTION

INCOME TAX IS an assessment levied on individual or corporate incomes. Although some states do not have income tax (Nevada), all people are subject to the federal income tax. Individuals are not the only ones required to pay income tax; but corporations are too. Personal incomes below a certain level are exempt from individual income tax, the level differing for single and for married persons with or without dependents. The tax is applied to the net income after certain deductions and exemptions, and the rate becomes progressively higher for larger incomes. To determine the amount of income tax to be paid, we use a tax table. A tax table contains information about taxable income, tax rate, and the tax on base. This table helps us in figuring out what the tax amount would be on a particular amount of taxable income.

In this chapter, we learn how to calculate the income tax on any level of income by using the logical (if-then-else) statements. We assume that the income tax brackets and the income tax rates have already been provided. The calculation involves three steps. First, we need to input the information into a tax table. Second, we need to calculate the Tax on Base column to complete the tax table. Finally, we need to write IF STATEMENTS to calculate the amount of tax liability.

CALCULATION OF TAX ON BASE

For any level of income, the Tax On Base is defined as total taxes that must be paid for all levels of income below the current level. Assume Table 6.1 represents the progressive income tax table.

Table 6.1. Tax Table		
Income	Tax Rate	Tax on Base
0 - 5,000	5%	
5,000 - 15,000	10%	
15,000 - 20,000	15%	
20,000 - 28,000	20%	
28,000 - 35,000	25%	
35,000 - 50,000	30%	
>=5 0,000	35%	

To calculate the amount of tax on base, follow the formulas in Table 6.2.

Table 6.2. Tax on Base Formulas	
0 - 5,000	no previous tax bracket = $0
5,000 - 15,000	0 + (5000-0) x 0.05 = 250
15,000 - 20,000	250 + (15,000 - 5,000) x 0.10 = 1,250
20,000 - 28,000	1,250 + (20,000 - 15,000) x 0.15 = 2,000
28,000 - 35,000	2,000 + (28,000 - 20,000) x 0.20 = 3,600
35,000 - 50,000	3,600 + (35,000 - 28,000) x 0.25 = 5,350
>= 50,000	5,350 + (50,000 - 35,000) x 0.30 = 9,850

CALCULATION OF TAX LIABILITY

To calculate the tax liability, we have to use if-then-else statements. Before writing the actual statements in computer format, it is a good idea to first write them in pseudo code. Pseudo codes are not real computer codes, but rather a combination of words, symbols, and numbers. This helps in understanding the logic we will be using in the actual code.

Using pseudo code allows you to set up the parameters of the problem at hand, and it provides you a map to figure out the computer format. In pseudo code we use a less structured language that is easier to understand. It gives us an opportunity to project the necessary functions needed for solving the problem on the computer. For the example, for the problem in Table 6.1, the logical statement in pseudo code is illustrated in Table 6.3.

Table 6.3. Pseudo Code to Calculate Tax Liability
if income < 5,000 then
0 + (income - 0) * 0.05
else if income < 15,000 then
250 + (income - 5,000) * 0.10
else if income < 20,000 then
1,250 + (income - 15,000) * 0.15
else if income < 28,000 then
2,000 + (income - 20,000) * 0.20
else if income < 35,000 then
3,600 + (income - 28,000) * 0.25
else if income < 50,000 then
5,350 + (income - 35,000) * 0.30
else
9,850 + (income - 50,000) * 0.35

EXERCISE 6.1
INCOME TAX

Given the tax information in Table 6.4.

Table 6.4. Income Tax Exercise		
Income	Tax Rate	Tax on Base
$0 - $5,000	0%	
5,000 - 12,000	10%	
12,000 - 20,000	15%	
20,000 - 35,000	20%	
35,000 - 60,000	25%	
>= 60,000	30%	

a. Complete the Tax on Base column.
b. Suppose your taxable income is $42,000. Calculate the tax liability.
c. Given the level of taxable income, write an IF STATEMENT in pseudo code to calculate the amount of tax liability.

COMPUTER ASSIGNMENT

PURPOSE

1. To become familiar with tax tables and the significance of progressive taxes
2. To learn how to calculate tax on base
3. To learn how to calculate tax liability, given a certain level of taxable income
4. To learn how to use logical statements to calculate income tax
5. To learn how to use if-then-else statements in Excel

PROCEDURE

1. Input income levels and tax rates in columns B, C, D, and E (see Table 6.5).
2. Enter a formula in F10 to calculate tax on base.
3. Copy the formula in cell F10 to cells F11, F12, F13, F14, and F15.
4. Enter the taxable income of three individuals in cells D20, E20, F20.
5. Enter an if statement in cell D22 to calculate the tax liability of the first individual.
6. Copy the formula in D22 to cells E22 and F22.
7. Print the worksheet.
8. Print the cell formulas.
9. Prepare a report summarizing all steps and procedures used.

Table 6.5. Income Tax Computer Assignment

	B	C	D	E	F	
2						
3			INCOME TAX CALCULATION			
4						
5						
6	TAX TABLE:					
7						
8	Income			Tax Rate	Tax on Base	
9	0	–	$5,000	5.0%	$0	
10	$5,000	–	15,000	10.0%	250	
11	15,000	–	20,000	15.0%	1,250	
12	20,000	–	28,000	20.0%	2,000	
13	28,000	–	35,000	25.0%	3,600	
14	35,000	–	50,000	30.0%	5,350	
15		>=	50,000	35.0%	9,850	
16						
17						
18						
19			Individual 1	Individual 2	Individual 3	
20	Taxable Income:		$120,000	$35,000	$2,500	
21						
22	Tax Amount:		$34,350	$5,350	$125	
23						

If income < 5,000 then

0 + (income – 0) * 0.05

else if income < 15,000 then

250 + (income – 5000) * 0.10

else if income < 20,000 then

1,250 + (income – 15,000) * 0.15

else if income < 28,000 then

2,000 + (income – 20,000) * 0.20

else if income < 35,000 then

3,600 + (income – 28,000) * 0.25

else if income < 50,000 then

5,350 + (income – 35,000) * 0.30

else

9,850 + (income – 50,000) * 0.35

TAX CALCULATION IN EXCEL

CALCULATION OF TAX ON BASE IN EXCEL

To perform this assignment, utilize the following procedure:

1. First, open a worksheet in Microsoft Excel. Enter the income brackets in columns B, and D. In column C, enter a minus sign. To make sure the minus signs appear properly, format the cells according Text format. Next, enter the tax rates in column E.
2. Tax on Base calculations should appear in column F. Start by putting zero in cell F9 because there are no previous brackets. In cell F10, take the Tax on Base from the previous level, F9, add it to the difference of the previous income levels (D9-B9), multiply that by the tax rate of the previous tax level, E9, and copy it down for the whole tax table. To do this, highlight cell F10, press "Edit" from the top menu, click on "Copy", highlight the cells F11 to F15, and then click on "Paste". Once the cell is copied, the formulas for each cell will look like the following.

   Cell F10: =F9+(D9-B9)*E9
   Cell F11: =F10+(D10-B10)*E10
   Cell F12: =F11+(D11-B11)*E11
   Cell F13: =F12+(D12-B12)*E12
   Cell F14: =F13+(D13-B13*E13
   Cell F15: =F14+(D14-B14)*E14

3. Input taxable income of three individuals in cells D20, E20, and F20.

CALCULATION OF TAX LIABILITY IN EXCEL

1. To compute the tax liability, we need to follow the logic of the pseudo code given in the bottom of Table 6.5. However, we have to convert the if-then-else statement into Excel's syntax. This is demonstrated in Table 6.6.

Table 6.6. Cell Formula to Calculate Tax Liability

	D

22	=IF(D20 < $D$9, $F$9 + (D20 - $B$9)*$E$9,
	IF(D20 < $D$10, $F$10 + (D20 - $B$10) * $E$10,
	IF(D20 < $D$11, $F$11 + (D20 - $B$11) * $E$11,
	IF(D20 < $D$12, $F$12 + (D20 - $B$12) * $E$12,
	IF(D20 < $D$13, $F$13 + (D20 - $B$13) * $E$13,
	IF(D20 < $D$14, $F$14 + (D20 - $B$14) * $E$14,
	$F$15 + (D20 - $D$15) * $E$15))))))

2. The above IF STATEMENT for $120,000 of taxable income, for example,
    is translated to

    = if(120,000 < 5,000 then 0 + (120,000 – 0) * 0.05 else if 120,000
    < 15,000 then 250 + (120,000 – 5000) * 0.10 else if 120,000 <
    20,000 then 1,250 + (120,000 – 15000) * 0.15 else if 120,000 <
    28,000 then 2,000 +(120,000 – 20,000) * 0.20 else if 120,000 <
    35,000 then 3,600 + (120,000 – 28,000) * 0.25 else if 120,000
    < 50,000 then 5,350 + (120,000 – 35,000) *0.30 else 9,850 +
    (120,000 – 50,000) * 0.35))))))

3. Copy the formula in D22 to cells E22 and F22.
4. In this formula, relative addressing was used when referring to the cell
    containing the individual's income and absolute addressing was used
    when referring to tax rates and tax on base. When the formula in D22
    is copied to E22 and F22, the taxable income will adjust automatically,
    leaving the rest of the formula the same.

CHAPTER 7

Advanced Logical Statements

INTRODUCTION

IN CHAPTER 6, WE used tax tables to learn about logical statements. We noticed that once you insert the correct formula to calculate the income tax for one person, we can simply copy that formula for as many people as are required without the tedious task of redoing the formula. This has the added advantage of reducing errors in our worksheet. In this chapter we learn about more advanced logical statements. For this purpose, we will use an example of grading in a course by an instructor.

Microsoft Excel serves as an excellent tool for tracking grades in a course. But its power is not limited to its ability to organize information in rows and columns. Using formulas and functions in Excel, we can simplify the grading process. With Excel we can sort students by GPA, grades, or whatever characteristics we choose. We can also set up a grade scale or percentages in advance and have Excel automatically assign letter grades to each of the students. When we change the scale, percentages, or test scores, the letter grades will change automatically.

A table like this could be very useful because it takes away all the unnecessary tedious calculations we once did by hand. By entering one formula for a student, we can copy and paste it to all other students. Not only does it save a great deal of time, it also prevents any mistakes that could be detrimental to an individual's grade.

COMPUTER ASSIGNMENT

PURPOSE

1. Learn and make use of more advanced "logical statements"
2. Introduce "Compound IF-Statements"
3. Introduce formulas that calculate the maximum, minimum, and second highest numbers by using more sophisticated formulas
4. Understand how to break a long formula into several cells
5. Learn and analyze how to use grade scales in assigning letter grades and point grades
6. Get additional practice with "Absolute" and "Relative" addressing

INSTRUCTIONS

1. In this assignment, you are asked to construct a grade table for a class of 15 to 20 students (see Table 7.1). The table consists of grades for four quizzes, three exams, and one final exam. Formulas should be used to find the average of the three highest quiz grades, the average of the highest two exam scores, the course average, the letter grade, the point grade, the total class average, the class standard deviation, and the highest and lowest grades in the class.
2. Quiz Average = Average of the three highest quizzes; note that not all the quiz grades are from a scale of 0 to100.
3. Find the highest exam grade in cell AA5, the lowest in cell AB5, and the second highest in cell AC5. Use the following formulas:

   AA5: =Max(G5:I5);
   AB5: =Min(G5:I5);
   AC5: use IF statements to find the second highest exam.

4. Exam Average = Average of the highest and second highest exam, J5:

   =AVERAGE(AA5,AC5).

5. The course average in cell L5 is the weighted average of quizzes, exams, and final.
6. For columns M and N, use **IF Statements** to assign letter and point grades. If the formulas get too long, you may have to split them and put them into two different cells.

7. Go to cells X5 and Y5 and use the

   =VLOOKUP(lookup_value,table_array,col_index_num)
   function to assign letter grade and point grade. Your answers should
   be identical to the values in cells M5 and N5.

8. Copy all the formulas from row 5 for the rest of the students.
9. Print the grade sheet.
10. Write a report explaining your work. Put the long formulas in your report,
    using COPY and PASTE.

	A	B	C	D	E	F	G	H	I	J	K	L	M	N	O	P	Q	R
	Table 7.1. Student Grades Assignment																	
1	Course Name					30%				35%	35%							
2	Instructor	45	30	85	60		100	100	100		100							
3						Ave				Ave		C.	Let	Pt				
4	Name	Q1	Q2	Q3	Q4	Q	E1	E2	E3	E	Fin	Ave	Gr	Gr				
5	Student1															Grade Scale		
6	Student2															0	F	0.0
7	Student3					F				F		F	F	F		55	D-	0.7
8	Student4					O				O		O	O	O		59	D	1.0
9	Student5					R				R		R	R	R		63	D+	1.3
10	Student6					M				M		M	M	M		67	C-	1.7
11	Student7					U				U		U	U	U		70	C	2.0
12	Student8					L				L		L	L	L		76	C+	2.3
13	Student9					A				A		A	A	A		79	B-	2.7
14	Student10															82	B	3.0
15	Student11															86	B+	3.3
16	Student12															89	A-	3.7
17	Student13															93	A	4.0
18	Student14																	
19	Student15																	
20	Student16																	
21																		
22	Average:				F	O	R	M	U	L	A							
23	Std. Dev.:				F	O	R	M	U	L	A							
24	Highest:				F	O	R	M	U	L	A							
25	Lowest:				F	O	R	M	U	L	A							

PROCEDURE

Inputting Data

Following is the instruction of how to do the assignment:

- Design the borders and titles for the grading table. Type students' names in the cells in Column A (see Table 7.1).
- Randomly input student quiz scores in columns B, C, D, and E for each student. The quizzes' maximum points are 45 for the first quiz, 30 for the second quiz, 85 for the third quiz, and 60 for the fourth quiz. The lowest quiz grade will be dropped. Also note that the average of the three highest quizzes will be worth 30% (typed in cell Fl) of the total grade.
- Input the three exam scores, each with maximum of 100 points, in columns G, H, and I. Note that the average of the two highest exam grades will be counted as 35% (typed in cell J1) of the total grade.
- Input the final exam score, with a maximum of 100 points, in column K. Note that this final exam will be counted as 35% (typed in cell K1) of the total grade.
- The final step in inputting data is to create a grade scale table. This can be done in cells P6 through R17.

How to Create Formulas

Once the numerical grades are established for all the students, the averages and the letter grades can be calculated with the help of basic mathematical functions and IF statements. This is a multi-step process and is summarized below:

Step 1. Quiz Average

The average of the 3 highest quizzes can be found by using the following formula:

(Sum of All Four Quiz Scores − Minimum of All Four Quiz Scores) / 3

The lowest quiz grade was dropped and that is why the numerator is divided by 3. The formula in Excel format (inserted in cell F5) is given in Table 7.2.

Table 7.2. Calculation of Quiz Average
F
5 =(SUM(B5/$B$2,C5/$C$2,D5/$D$2,E5/$E$2) - MIN(B5/$B$2,C5/$C$2,D5/$D$2,E5/$E$2))/3 * 100

Note that not all the scores are from 100. This is why each raw score had to be standardized by dividing it by the maximum score for that quiz given in cells B2, C2, D2, and E2. For example, we can take the sum of (43/45, 28/30, 80/85, 55/60) and subtract the lowest score of all 4 quizzes and then divide it by 3. Because the maximum scores are the same for all students, we must use absolute addressing when we refer to these cells. The reason that this formula is multiplied by 100 is to convert the final number to a percentage.

Step 2. Exam Average

According to the instructions, we have to find the highest, lowest, and second highest exam marks. This is not part of the table itself, so we place the formulas outside of the table. We can find the highest exam score in cell AA5, the lowest in cell AB5, and the second highest in cell AC5.

- The formula for the highest exam mark will be: =MAX(G5:I5).
- The formula for the lowest exam mark will be: =MIN(G5:I5).
- The instructions state that we should use IF STATEMENTS to find the second highest exam score. Therefore, we need to write a pseudo code (see Table 7.3) to understand the logic behind the formula. By definition, when two scores are equal, we call one the second highest.

Table 7.3. Pseudo Code for Determining the Second Highest Exam
IF (MIN< Exam 1 <MAX) THEN
Exam 1
ELSE IF (MIN< Exam 2<MAX) THEN
Exam 2
ELSE IF (MIN< Exam 3<MAX) THEN
Exam 3
ELSE IF Exam 1=Exam 2 THEN
Exam 1 (*or Exam 2*)
ELSE IF Exam 1=Exam 3 THEN
Exam 1 (*or Exam 3*)
ELSE
Exam 2 (*this implies that Exam 2 and Exam 3 are equal*)

The formula in Excel format (entered in cell AC5) is given in Table 7.4.

Table 7.4. Formula to determine the Second Highest Exam	
	AC

5	=IF(AND(G5>AB5,G5<AA5),G5,
	IF(AND(H5>AB5,H5<AA5),H5,
	IF(AND(I5>AB5,I5<AA5),I5,
	IF(G5=H5,G5,IF(G5=I5,G5,H5)))))

NOTE: The word "AND" was used because the "IF STATEMENT" is a compound statement and it compares the MAX and MIN at the same time. This formula means that if the number in G5 is greater than the number in AB5 and if G5 is less than AA5 then the second highest number is G5. This follows the logic of the pseudo code.

- Exam Average = Average of the highest and second highest exam. So we can use the following formula in cell J5: =AVERAGE(AA5,AC5).

Step 3. Course Average

The course average is determined in cell L5. This is a weighted average formula, and the pseudo code is

Course Average = Quiz Average * .30 + Exam Average * .35 + Final Exam * .35.

This formula computes the course average of the quizzes, exams, and final exam. This formula takes the average quiz cell multiplies it by the weighted percentage for the quizzes and adds that to the average exam cell multiplied by the weighted percentage for the exams and adds that to the final score and multiplies that by the exam percentage weight.

The formula in Excel format is = F5*$ F$1+J5*$J$1+K5*$K$1.

Note that since the weights of the quizzes and exams must be the same for all the students, ABSOLUTE ADDRESSING must be used when the formula refers to percentage weights in cells F1, J1, and K1.

Step 4. Assigning Letter Grades

A Grade Scale is provided on the right hand side of the grade sheet. The formulas used for determining the letter grades must refer to the cells in this grade scale. As instructed, we have to use IF STATEMENTS to assign letter grades. First, we need to write the logic of the formula in pseudo code. This is done in Table 7.5.

Table 7.5. Pseudo Code for Determining Letter Grades
IF C. AVERAGE >= 93 THEN "A" ELSE
IF C. AVERAGE >= 89 THEN "A-" ELSE
IF C. AVERAGE >= 86 THEN "B+" ELSE
IF C. AVERAGE >= 82 THEN "B" ELSE
IF C. AVERAGE >= 79 THEN "B-" ELSE
IF C. AVERAGE >= 76 THEN "C+" ELSE
IF C. AVERAGE >= 70 THEN "C" ELSE
IF C. AVERAGE >= 67 THEN "C-" ELSE
IF C. AVERAGE >= 63 THEN "D+" ELSE
IF C. AVERAGE >= 59 THEN "D" ELSE
IF C. AVERAGE >= 55 THEN "D-" ELSE "F"

The formula in Excel format to assign the letter grade for the course will be typed in cell M5. This formula becomes too long and needs to be broken up into two cells. Half of the formula will be inserted into cell M5 (Table 7.6) and the other half into cell U5 (Table 7.7). It is a good idea to write the second half of the formula in the same row (row 5 in our example). After the formulas in M5 and U5 are completed, we need to copy them down for the rest of the students.

Table 7.6. The First Part of the Formula to Calculate Letter Grades
M

=IF(L5>=$P$17,$Q$17,IF(L5>=$P$16,$Q$16,
IF(L5>=$P$15,$Q$15,IF(L5>=$P$14,$Q$14,
IF(L5>=$P$13,$Q$13,IF(L5>=$P$12,$Q$12,
IF(L5>=$P$11,$Q$11,U5)))))))

Using U5 at the end of the formula lets the current cell know that we will be continuing the formula in U5.

	U
Table 7.7. The Second Part of the Formula to Determine Letter Grades	
5	=IF(L5>=$P$10,$Q$10,IF(L5>=$P$9,$Q$9, IF(L5>=$P$8,$Q$8,IF(L5>=$P$7,$Q$7, $Q$6))))

This formula works by taking the number in cell L5 and applying it to the IF statement. The basic theme of this statement is that if L5 is greater than the number in P17 then the letter grade is the grade displayed in cell Q17. If it is not greater than P17 then go to the next part of the statement and apply the same logic there. At the end of the IF statement, if L5 is not greater than P7 then by default the grade the student will receive will be that of cell Q6.

NOTE: The built-in function VLOOKUP(L5,$P$6:$R$17,2) can also be used to assign letter grades.

Step 5. Assigning Point Grades

For point grades we use similar formulas. As part of the Grade Scale that has been provided on the right hand side of the grading sheet, the point grades can also be found. The formulas used must also refer to the cells in this grade scale. The logic of the formula is exactly the same as used to obtain the letter grades, as explained in Table 7.8.

Table 7.8. Pseudo Code for Determining Point Grades

```
IF C. AVERAGE >= 93 THEN "4.0"  ELSE
IF C. AVERAGE >= 89 THEN "3.7"  ELSE
IF C. AVERAGE >= 86 THEN "3.3"  ELSE
IF C. AVERAGE >= 82 THEN "3.0"  ELSE
IF C. AVERAGE >= 79 THEN "2.7"  ELSE
IF C. AVERAGE >= 76 THEN "2.3"  ELSE
IF C. AVERAGE >= 70 THEN "2.0"  ELSE
IF C. AVERAGE >= 67 THEN "1.7"  ELSE
IF C. AVERAGE >= 63 THEN "1.3"  ELSE
IF C. AVERAGE >= 59 THEN "1.0"  ELSE
IF C. AVERAGE >= 55 THEN "0.7"  ELSE  "0.0"
```

As before, the formula in Excel format will not fit within one cell, so it has to be divided into two parts. The first part of the formula will be written in cell N5 (Table 7.9) and the second part in cell V5 (Table 7.10). The formula in N5 refers to cell V5.

Table 7.9. The First Part of the Formula to Calculate Point
N
5 =IF(L5>=$P$17,$R$17,IF(L5>=$P$16,$R$16, IF(L5>=$P$15,$R$15,IF(L5>=$P$14,$R$14, IF(L5>=$P$13,$R$13,IF(L5>=$P$12,$R$12, IF(L5>=$P$11,$R$11,V5)))))))

The formula continues in cell V5 as in Table 7.10.

Table 7.10. The Second Part of the Formula to Determine Point Grades
V
5 =IF(L5>=$P$10,$R$10,IF(L5>=$P$9,$R$9, IF(L5>=$P$8,$R$8,IF(L5>=$P$7,$R$7, $R$6))))

After completion of the formulas in row 5, all the formulas will be copied down for the rest of the students below row 5. All the grades should adjust automatically.

NOTE: The built-in function VLOOKUP(L5,$P$6:$R$17,3) can also be used to assign point grades.

Step 6. Calculating Sample Statistics for the Entire Class

Once all the student letter grades and point grades are calculated, we need to calculate the average, the standard deviation, the highest, and the lowest of all the quizzes and exams for the entire class. First, we calculate these sample statistics for quiz 1 in column B.

- In cell B22, we type =AVERAGE(B5:B20).
- In cell B23, we type =STDEV(B5:B20).
- In cell B24, we type =MAX(B5:B20).

- In cell B25, we type =MIN(B5:B20).
- For the other quizzes and exams, we simply copy the formulas in cells B22 to B25 to all the cells in C22 through N25.

Step 7. Printing the Grade Sheet and Cell Formulas

To print the worksheet and cell formulas we follow the same procedure as is explained in chapter 3.

CURVING THE GRADES

A common request by students is that the exam results should be curved. Although there is no best method to curve the grades, the following formula is a reasonable technique that can be used.

Adjusted Grade = (Raw Grade – Raw Average) * (Forced STD / Raw STD) + Forced Average

Of course, there is some subjectivity in this technique as the instructor arbitrarily chooses a forced average and a forced standard deviation for the class. The following example demonstrates the use of this formula.

EXAMPLE 7.1. Assume the grades on an exam for 20 students are given in Table 7.11. Use the above formula to curve the grades.

Solution

In this example, the raw grades are given in column B. The average for the class is 68.7 with a standard deviation of 14.7. Let us assume that the instructor decides to increase the average to 75.0 (forced average) with a standard deviation of 15.0 (forced standard deviation). After applying the above formula to column B, we get the results in column C. The cell formulas are displayed in Table 7.12.

Table 7.11. Grades for Example 7.1		
	A	**B**	**C**
2		Raw Grades	Adj. Grades
3		47.0	53.0
4		85.0	91.6
5		88.0	94.7
6		79.0	85.5
7		87.0	93.7
8		76.0	82.5
9		83.0	89.6
10		74.0	80.4
11		66.0	72.3
12		66.0	72.3
13		64.0	70.3
14		77.0	83.5
15		57.0	63.1
16		70.0	76.4
17		40.0	45.8
18		63.0	69.3
19		60.0	66.2
20		51.0	57.0
21		50.0	56.0
22		90.0	96.7
23	Average:	68.7	75.0
24	STD:	14.7	15.0
25	Highest:	90.0	96.7
26	Lowest:	40.0	45.8

Table 7.12. Cell Formulas for Example 7.1	
B	**C**
Raw Grades	Adjusted Grades
47.0	=(B3-$B$23)*($C$24/$B$24)+$C$23
85.0	=(B4-$B$23)*($C$24/$B$24)+$C$23
88.0	=(B5-$B$23)*($C$24/$B$24)+$C$23
79.0	=(B6-$B$23)*($C$24/$B$24)+$C$23
87.0	=(B7-$B$23)*($C$24/$B$24)+$C$23
76.0	=(B8-$B$23)*($C$24/$B$24)+$C$23
83.0	=(B9-$B$23)*($C$24/$B$24)+$C$23
74.0	=(B10-$B$23)*($C$24/$B$24)+$C$23
66.0	=(B11-$B$23)*($C$24/$B$24)+$C$23
66.0	=(B12-$B$23)*($C$24/$B$24)+$C$23
64.0	=(B13-$B$23)*($C$24/$B$24)+$C$23
77.0	=(B14-$B$23)*($C$24/$B$24)+$C$23
57.0	=(B15-$B$23)*($C$24/$B$24)+$C$23
70.0	=(B16-$B$23)*($C$24/$B$24)+$C$23
40.0	=(B17-$B$23)*($C$24/$B$24)+$C$23
63.0	=(B18-$B$23)*($C$24/$B$24)+$C$23
60.0	=(B19-$B$23)*($C$24/$B$24)+$C$23
51.0	=(B20-$B$23)*($C$24/$B$24)+$C$23
50.0	=(B21-$B$23)*($C$24/$B$24)+$C$23
90.0	=(B22-$B$23)*($C$24/$B$24)+$C$23
=Average(B3:B22)	75
=Stdev(B3:B22)	15
=Max(B3:B22)	=Max(C3:C22)
=Min(B3:B22)	=Min(C3:C22)

Note that we used absolute addressing when we referred to class average and class standard deviation. This is because we created the formula for the first student in cell C3 and then copied it down for all the other students. We did not want the cells that referred to average and standard deviation to adjust. Also remember that the results depend on your choice of forced average and forced standard deviation.

CHAPTER 8

Payroll Calculation

INTRODUCTION

PAYROLL IS THE process of paying employees for services performed, after accounting for the various withholdings for taxes, social security, health insurance, retirement benefits, and other deductions. It usually involves the calculation of amounts, such as hourly wages, overtime, commissions, and other benefits. All of these monies are referred to as gross pay. From the gross pay, various items such as income tax, other taxes such as social security and Medicare (in the United States) are deducted. The amount left after all deductions from gross pay is referred to as net pay or take-home amount.

Payroll is a business function that has little margin for error. Payroll processing mistakes can have many adverse effects on the business. Due to severe tax penalties for improper or inadequate collection of payroll taxes, almost all employers either use a payroll software program or a payroll service company. As a result, in recent years, we have seen significant increases in the use of PCs for payroll accounting and other business applications. In the short term, these PC-based packages are often economical, and many small businesses find them sufficiently functional.

As time goes by, most companies grow in size and their payroll systems become more complex. Processing payroll takes precious time and energy away from the real business of managing the enterprise. There is no cost-effective way to do payroll in-house, which is why payroll has become the most significant outsourcing industry. Outsourcing payroll frees resources for other purposes and it costs much less than hiring a full-time payroll professional. Many employers find that payroll services are well worth the cost.

COMPUTER ASSIGNMENT

PURPOSE

1. To learn how payroll calculations are made
2. To learn about formatting time and how to manipulate time in Excel
3. To learn about the VLOOKUP command in searching a table

ASSUMPTIONS

A small business with five employees and a weekly payroll system has following requirements:

1. Social Security Tax is 7.5% of gross pay.
2. Medicare Tax is 1.45% of gross pay.
3. Income tax must be deducted from the employees' weekly pay based on a tax table.
4. The company pays overtime at the rate of 1.5 times the regular hourly rate.
5. Overtime is defined as the hours in excess of 40 hours per week.
6. Each employee gets a one hour lunch break per day. There is no pay for this hour.

REQUIREMENTS

Using your computer and Microsoft Excel, do the following

1. Complete the Tax on Base column in Table 8.2.
2. Calculate the number of hours worked by each employee for each day of the week.
3. Use the information in step 2 to calculate the total number of regular hours and overtime hours for each employee.
4. Calculate total gross pay (sum of regular and overtimes pay).
5. Calculate social security, Medicare, and federal income tax amounts.
6. Calculate the net pay during the week.
7. Print the results.
8. Write a report and explain how you performed each step. Make sure you include all the formulas used for your calculations.

SOLVING THE PAYROLL PROBLEM USING EXCEL

Assume the hourly wage rates of the 5 employees are given in Table 8.1 and that the income taxes are calculated on the basis of the rates in Table 8.2. Furthermore, assume that time cards specifying the hours that each employee worked during the week are also given.

Table 8.1. Hourly Wage Rates		
Employee #	Name	Salary/Hr
1120	A	$28.75
1135	B	35.63
1255	C	7.66
1276	D	16.34
1360	E	9.38

Table 8.2. Tax Table				
Income Brackets			Tax Rate	Tax on Base
$0	up to	$5,000	0.0%	
5,000	up to	12,000	10.0%	
12,000	up to	20,000	15.0%	
20,000	up to	35,000	20.0%	
35,000	up to	45,000	25.0%	
45,000	up to	60,000	30.0%	
60,000	above 60,000		35.0%	

PROCEDURE

There are multiple steps in solving this problem, and they are summarized below.

Step 1. The first step is to enter the information given above into a worksheet. This is done in Table 8.3.

	Table 8.3. Initial Data for Payroll Problem										
C	**D**	**E**	**F**	**G**	**H**	**I**	**J**	**K**	**L**	**M**	
3											
4	Each employee gets one hour of lunch time (not paid)					Tax Table					
5	Overtime:	more than	40	Hours		Income Brackets			Tax Rate	Tax on Base	
6	Social Security Tax:	7.50%				$0	up to	$5,000	0.0%	$0	
7	Medicare Tax:	1.45%				5,000	up to	12,000	10.0%	0	
8	Overtime Pay:	1.5	Regular Pay			12,000	up to	20,000	15.0%	700	
9						20,000	up to	35,000	20.0%	1,900	
10	Employee #	Name	Salary/Hr			35,000	up to	45,000	25.0%	4,900	
11	1120	A	$28.75			45,000	up to	60,000	30.0%	7,400	
12	1135	B	35.63			60,000	above 60,000		35.0%	11,900	
13	1255	C	7.66								
14	1276	D	16.34								
15	1360	E	9.38								

Step 2. Next, we will enter the information on the time cards into an Excel table. However, before we do that, we need to format the cells according to time format so that Excel represents the actual times when the employees checked in and when they checked out. To do this, we highlight the cells and click on "Format", "Cells", "Number", "Time", "1:30 PM", and then press "OK". The advantage of this type of formatting is that the times will actually be represented as real times with "AM" and "PM" after them instead of just numbers. This is demonstrated in Table 8.4.

	Table 8.4. Employee Time Cards During the Week										
C	**D**	**E**	**F**	**G**	**H**	**I**	**J**	**K**	**L**	**M**	**N**
16											
17	Employee #	Monday		Tuesday		Wednesday		Thursday		Friday	
18		IN	OUT	IN	OUT	IN	OUT	IN	OUT	IN	OUT
19	1120	8:00 AM	4:30 PM	8:15 AM	5:23 PM	8:05 AM	5:35 PM	8:00 AM	5:00 PM	8:20 AM	6:55 PM
20	1135	8:25 AM	5:15 PM	7:45 AM	4:10 PM	9:45 AM	5:34 PM	9:00 AM	6:00 PM	9:00 AM	6:08 PM
21	1255	9:15 AM	7:55 PM	10:00 AM	6:26 PM	8:15 AM	5:00 PM	8:10 AM	5:35 PM	8:12 AM	5:45 PM
22	1276	10:10 AM	4:18 PM	8:05 AM	5:10 PM	9:00 AM	5:24 PM	9:00 AM	8:30 PM	7:55 AM	6:10 PM
23	1360	8:45 AM	6:25 PM	8:25 AM	4:27 PM	8:30 AM	6:30 PM	8:30 AM	7:05 PM	8:00 AM	4:20 PM

Step 3. Use the procedure learned in Chapter 6 (Income Tax) to calculate the Tax-On-Base column. This is displayed in Table 8.5.

Table 8.5. Calculation of Tax on Base	
M	
6	0	= $0
7	=M6+(K6-I6)*L6	= 0
8	=M7+(K7-I7)*L7	= 700
9	=M8+(K8-I8)*L8 1,900	= 1,900
10	=M9+(K9-I9)*L9 4,900	= 4,900
11	=M10+(K10-I10)*L10	= 7,400
12	=M11+(K11-I11)*L11	= 11,900

Step 4.   For every day of the week, we calculate the number of hours worked by each employee. This is done by subtracting the time "IN" from the time "OUT". You should remember that Excel keeps the time as a fraction of the 24 hour clock; therefore, we need to multiply the above result by 24 to get the actual number of hours worked. Since the formulas are identical for all employees, we enter the formula for the first employee in row 27 and then copy it down to rows 28 through 31. This is displayed in Table 8.6.

Table 8.6. Calculation of the Number of Hours Worked				
E	**F**	**G**	**H**	**I**
25 Monday	Tuesday	Wednesday	Thursday	Friday
26 # Hours Worked	# Hours Worked	# Hours Worked	# Hours Worked	Hours
27 =(F19-E19)*24	=(H19-G19)*24	=(J19-I19)*24	=(L19-K19)*24	=(N19-M19)*24
28 =(F20-E20)*24	=(H20-G20)*24	=(J20-I20)*24	=(L20-K20)*24	=(N20-M20)*24
29 =(F21-E21)*24	=(H21-G21)*24	=(J21-I21)*24	=(L21-K21)*24	=(N21-M21)*24
30 =(F22-E22)*24	=(H22-G22)*24	=(J22-I22)*24	=(L22-K22)*24	=(N22-M22)*24
31 =(F23-E23)*24	=(H23-G23)*24	=(J23-I23)*24	=(L23-K23)*24	=(N23-M23)*24

Step 5.   Table 8.7 shows how the total number of regular hours and overtime hours are calculated. Note the use of IF Statements. This is done to make sure that we do not get negative numbers for overtime hours. Again, we complete row 27 and copy the formulas down for all the other employees.

	J	K	L	M
	Table 8.7. Calculation of Regular and Overtime Hours			
	J	**K**	**L**	**M**
25	Total	Total	Total	Total
26	**Hours Worked**	**Minus Lunch Hr**	**Overtime Hours**	**Regular Hours**
27	=SUM(E27:I27)	=J27-5	=IF((K27-$F$5)<0,0,K27-$F$5)	=K27-L27
28	=SUM(E28:I28)	=J28-5	=IF((K28-$F$5)<0,0,K28-$F$5)	=K28-L28
29	=SUM(E29:I29)	=J29-5	=IF((K29-$F$5)<0,0,K29-$F$5)	=K29-L29
30	=SUM(E30:I30)	=J30-5	=IF((K30-$F$5)<0,0,K30-$F$5)	=K30-L30
31	=SUM(E31:I31)	=J31-5	=IF((K31-$F$5)<0,0,K31-$F$5)	=K31-L31

Step 6.   To calculate the gross pay, we need to use the VLOOKUP function to look up the hourly wage rate of all employees by their ID numbers. The format of this function is as follows:

=VLOOKUP(lookup_value, table_array, col_index_num)

In this case the lookup_value is the employee ID # (e.g., D27 for the first employee), the table_array is the table of hourly wage rates ($D$11:$F$15), and col_index_num is column 3 as the wage rate is in the third column. Since we create this formula for the first employee and plan to copy it down for all other employees, we use absolute addressing for table_array. Also note that for overtime pay, we multiply the result of the lookup formula by $F$8. This cell contains the number 1.5 and it accounts for the higher pay rate for overtime hours. Table 8.8 displays the completed formulas for all employees.

	N	O	P
	Table 8.8. Calculation of Regular and Overtime Pay		
	N	**O**	**P**
25	Total	Total	Total
26	**Regular Pay**	**Overtime Pay**	**Gross pay**
27	=M27*VLOOKUP(D27,$D$11:$F$15,3)	=L27*VLOOKUP(D27,$D$11:$F$15,3)*$F$8	=N27+O27
28	=M28*VLOOKUP(D28,$D$11:$F$15,3)	=L28*VLOOKUP(D28,$D$11:$F$15,3)*$F$8	=N28+O28
29	=M29*VLOOKUP(D29,$D$11:$F$15,3)	=L29*VLOOKUP(D29,$D$11:$F$15,3)*$F$8	=N29+O29
30	=M30*VLOOKUP(D30,$D$11:$F$15,3)	=L30*VLOOKUP(D30,$D$11:$F$15,3)*$F$8	=N30-O30
31	=M31*VLOOKUP(D31,$D$11:$F$15,3)	=L31*VLOOKUP(D31,$D$11:$F$15,3)*$F$8	=N31+O31

Step 7.   Calculation of social security and Medicare taxes are quite simple. We only have to multiply the gross wages by the tax percentage rates. This is exhibited in Table 8.9.

Table 8.9. Calculation of Social Security & Medicare Taxes	
Q	R
25 Tax	Tax
26 Social Security	Medicare
27 =P27*$F$6	=P27*$F$7
28 =P28*$F$6	=P28*$F$7
29 =P29*$F$6	=P29*$F$7
30 =P30*$F$6	=P30*$F$7
31 =P31*$F$6	=P31*$F$7

Step 8.   The final step is to calculate the federal income tax. We need to use the procedure we learned in Chapter 6. However, in this problem, we will use the VLOOKUP function instead of IF statements. Also, the tax table has information for annual income levels, so that we need to multiply the weekly wages by 52 (the number of weeks in a year) to estimate the annual income and then divide the result (the annual tax amount) by 52 to estimate the weekly tax amount. This is displayed in Table 8.10.

Table 8.10. Calculation of Federal Income Tax & Net Pay	
S	T
26 Federal Income Tax	Net Pay
27 =(VLOOKUP(P27*52,$I$6:$M$12,5)+(P27*52-VLOOKUP(P27*52,$I$6:$M$12,1))*VLOOKUP(P27*52,$I$6:$M$12,4))/52	=P27-SUM(Q27:S27)
28 =(VLOOKUP(P28*52,$I$6:$M$12,5)+(P28*52-VLOOKUP(P28*52,$I$6:$M$12,1))*VLOOKUP(P28*52,$I$6:$M$12,4))/52	=P28-SUM(Q28:S28)
29 =(VLOOKUP(P29*52,$I$6:$M$12,5)+(P29*52-VLOOKUP(P29*52,$I$6:$M$12,1))*VLOOKUP(P29*52,$I$6:$M$12,4))/52	=P29-SUM(Q29:S29)
30 =(VLOOKUP(P30*52,$I$6:$M$12,5)+(P30*52-VLOOKUP(P30*52,$I$6:$M$12,1))*VLOOKUP(P30*52,$I$6:$M$12,4))/52	=P30-SUM(Q30:S30)
31 =(VLOOKUP(P31*52,$I$6:$M$12,5)+(P31*52-VLOOKUP(P31*52,$I$6:$M$12,1))*VLOOKUP(P31*52,$I$6:$M$12,4))/52	=P31-SUM(Q31:S31)

After all the steps mentioned above are completed, the net pay of the employees will appear in cells T27 through T31, as displayed in Table 8.11. At this time our entire worksheet should look like Table 8.12.

Table 8.11 Calculation of Weekly Wages																	
C	D	E	F	G	H	I	J	K	L	M	N	O	P	Q	R	S	T
Employee #	Monday	Tuesday	Wednesday	Thursday	Friday	Total	Total	Total	Total	Total	Total	Total	Total	Tax	Tax	Tax	Total
	# Hours Worked	# Hours Worked	# Hours Worked	# Hours Worked	# Hours Worked	Hours Worked	Minus Lunch Hr	Overtime Hours	Regular Hours	Regular Pay	Overtime Pay	Gross Pay	Social Security	Medicare	Federal		Net Pay
1120	8.50	9.13	9.50	9.00	10.58	46.72	41.72	1.72	40.00	$1,150.00	$74.03	$1,224.03	$91.80	$17.75	$253.41		$861.07
1135	8.83	8.42	7.82	9.00	9.13	43.20	38.20	0.00	38.20	1,361.07	0.00	1,361.07	102.08	19.74	301.37		937.88
1255	10.67	8.45	8.75	9.42	9.35	46.82	41.82	1.82	40.00	306.40	20.87	327.27	24.55	4.75	27.94		270.05
1276	6.13	9.08	8.40	11.50	10.25	45.37	40.37	0.37	40.00	653.60	8.90	662.99	49.69	9.61	92.13		511.15
1360	9.67	8.03	10.00	10.58	8.33	46.62	41.62	1.62	40.00	375.20	22.75	397.95	29.83	5.77	39.20		323.13

Table 8.12. Snapshot of the Entire Payroll Worksheet

Each employee gets one hour of lunch time (not paid)

Overtime:	more than	40 Hours
Social Security Tax:	7.50%	
Medicare Tax:	1.45%	
Overtime Pay:	1.5	Regular Pay

Employee #	Name	Salary/Hr
1120	A	$28.75
1135	B	35.63
1255	C	7.66
1276	D	16.34
1360	E	9.38

Tax Table

Income Brackets			Tax Rate	Tax on Base
$0	up to	$5,000	0.0%	$0
5,000	up to	12,000	10.0%	0
12,000	up to	20,000	15.0%	700
20,000	up to	35,000	20.0%	1,900
35,000	up to	45,000	25.0%	4,900
45,000	up to	60,000	30.0%	7,400
60,000	above	60,000	35.0%	11,900

Payroll Worksheet — Daily Times and Hours

Employee #	Mon IN	Mon OUT	Mon # Hrs	Tue IN	Tue OUT	Tue # Hrs	Wed IN	Wed OUT	Wed # Hrs	Thu IN	Thu OUT	Thu # Hrs	Fri IN	Fri OUT	Fri # Hrs
1120	8:00 AM	4:30 PM	8.50	8:15 AM	5:23 PM	9.13	8:05 AM	5:35 PM	9.50	8:00 AM	5:00 PM	9.00	8:20 AM	6:55 PM	10.58
1135	8:25 AM	5:15 PM	8.83	7:45 AM	4:10 PM	8.42	9:45 AM	5:34 PM	7.82	9:00 AM	6:00 PM	9.00	9:00 AM	6:08 PM	9.13
1255	9:15 AM	7:55 PM	10.67	10:00 AM	6:26 PM	8.43	8:15 AM	5:00 PM	8.75	8:10 AM	5:35 PM	9.42	8:12 AM	5:45 PM	9.55
1276	10:10 AM	4:18 PM	6.13	8:05 AM	5:10 PM	9.08	9:00 AM	5:24 PM	8.40	9:00 AM	8:30 PM	11.50	7:55 AM	6:10 PM	10.25
1360	8:45 AM	6:25 PM	9.67	8:25 AM	4:27 PM	8.03	8:30 AM	6:30 PM	10.00	8:30 AM	7:05 PM	10.58	8:00 AM	4:20 PM	8.33

Payroll Worksheet — Totals

Employee #	Hours Worked	Minus Lunch Hr	Overtime Hours	Regular Hours	Regular Pay	Overtime Pay	Gross Pay	Social Security Tax	Medicare Tax	Federal Tax	Net Pay
1120	46.72	41.72	1.72	40.00	$1,150.00	$74.03	$1,224.03	$91.80	$17.75	$253.41	$861.07
1135	43.20	38.20	0.00	38.20	1,361.07	0.00	1,361.07	102.08	19.74	301.37	937.88
1255	46.82	41.82	1.82	40.00	306.40	20.87	327.27	24.55	4.75	27.94	270.05
1276	45.37	40.37	0.37	40.00	653.60	8.99	662.59	49.69	9.61	92.13	511.15
1360	46.62	41.62	1.62	40.00	375.20	22.75	397.95	29.85	5.77	39.20	323.13

CHAPTER 9

Sales and Profit Forecasting: Pro Forma Financial Statements

INTRODUCTION

FORECASTING IS A useful and powerful technique used in many industries to predict future values of their financial statements. For example, a company may want to find the predicted sales figures for the next 3 years, or it may want to know the predicted profits on their products for the next 4 years. Although forecasting is advantageous, forecasting too far into the future is problematic. This is because macro-environmental factors can vary quite a bit and affect a company's products and its profitability. For example, if you make sales forecasts for the next 4 consecutive years, your estimates may not be accurate due to major political, economic, or technological changes.

To determine future sales and profits, many businesses construct **Pro Forma** financial statements. A pro forma financial statement is a provisional financial statement of an enterprise. Pro forma financial information can serve useful purposes. Public companies may quite appropriately wish to focus investors' attention on critical components of quarterly or annual financial results in order to provide a meaningful comparison to results for the same period of prior years or to emphasize the results of core operations.

In this chapter we learn about sales and profit forecasting. There are different types of forecasting, such as trend analysis and regression analysis. In trend analysis, past history is used to predict the future; if there is no history, then the history of competitors can be used. Regression analysis looks at the relationship between two variables (X and Y) and provides a "best fit" mathematical equation for the coefficients of the two variables. The purpose of this analysis is to predict or estimate what variable "Y" will be for a given value of variable "X."

When looking at growth, a forecast can begin by making an initial assumption of a certain percentage growth, for example 5%, and make forecasts of the future based on this assumption. Once the forecast has been made, we need to apply sensitivity analysis. Sensitivity ("what if") analysis looks at the various scenarios that may take place if the initial assumptions do not hold. For instance, if we start out with an initial assumption of 5% growth in sales, we also want to see what the numbers will be if growth declines to 1% (worst scenario) or if it increases to 10% (best scenario) and of course, all the possibilities within this range. In this chapter, we will again use Excel program to prepare a pro forma income statement. We then link the information to graphs that show the effect on net profit of growth rate of sales and cost of goods sold.

COMPUTER ASSIGNMENT

PURPOSE

1. To learn about basic sales and profit forecasting using pro forma financial statements
2. To learn how to perform sensitivity (what-if) analysis
3. To learn about pivot tables (data tables) in Excel
4. To learn how to produce graphs in Excel

ASSUMPTIONS

1. Assume that sales for last year (base year or Year 0) were $8,100.
2. Assume that the growth rate of sales for the next few years is 5% a year.
3. Assume that the commission rate paid to sales staff is 2% of gross sales.
4. Assume that cost of goods sold (COGS) as a percentage of sales is 65% and stays constant for the next few years.
5. Assume that the tax rate is set at 40% of gross profit.

REQUIREMENTS

1. Based on assumptions #3 through #5 above, reconstruct the income statement for the base year (Year 0).

2. With the added assumption in #2 above, construct a set of Pro Forma Income Statements for the next 4 years (Year 1-Year 4).
3. What happens if the assumption #2 (5% growth rate) is violated? Perform sensitivity analysis (Data Table Type I) on the pro forma financial statements.
4. What if assumptions #2 (5% sales growth rate) and #4 (60% COGS) change at the same time? Perform sensitivity analysis (Data Table Type II) on the pro forma financial statements.
5. Produce line graphs for the results of the Data Tables.
6. Print the Pro Forma statements, Data Tables, and your graphs.
7. Write a report summarizing all the procedures used to complete this assignment.

PROCEDURE

The Pro Forma Income Statements presented in this assignment are designed to calculate the estimated sales and profits of a company for Years 1 through Year 4, given the figures for Year 0 (base year). The estimated sales and profits are affected by such variables as commission rate, annual growth of sales, cost of goods sold, and tax rate. When one or more of these factors change, the estimated values will also change.

This assignment starts us by asking us to reconstruct the income statement for the base year (Year 0). Following certain assumptions, we are to predict net profits for the years 1, 2, 3 and 4. The figures that are given to us are gross sales for Year 0, commission rate, tax rate, annual growth rate of sales, and cost of goods sold (as % of net sales). Given this information, we can figure out the dollar value of commissions, net sales, COGS, gross profit, tax amount, and net profit by using simple financial formulas (illustrated in Table 9.1).

Table 9.1. Financial Formulas	
Commissions:	= Gross Sales * Commission Rate
Net Sales:	= Gross Sales - Commissions
COGS:	= Net Sales * COGS Rate
Gross Profit:	= Net sales - COGS
Tax Amount:	= Gross Profit * Tax Rate
Net Profit:	= Gross Profit - Tax Amount

Table 9.2 demonstrates the initial information that is given to construct the pro forma Income Statements.

Table 9.2. Assumptions		
B	**C**	**D**
3 Gross Sales for 2005 (Given		$8,100
4 Commission Rate:		2%
5 Tax Rate:		40%
6 Annual Growth Rate of Sales:		5%
7 COGS (as % of Net Sales):		65%

Based on the information given above we can use Excel to reconstruct the Income Statement for the Year 0 (the base year) in column C (see Table 9.3).

Cell	Table 9.3. Formulas in Excel Cells		
C11	= $D$3	$8,100	Gross Sales
C12	= C11 * $D$4	8,100 x 2% = $162	Commissions = Gross Sales . Commission Rate
C13	= C11 – C12	8,100 – 162 = $7938	Net Sales = Gross Sales – Commissions
C14	= C13 * $D$7	7,938 x 65% = $5160	COGS = Net Sales . COGS Rate
C15	= C13 – C14	7,938 – 5,160 = $2778	Gross Profit = Net Sales – COGS
C16	= C15 * $D$5	2778 x 40% = $1,111	Tax Amount = Gross Profit . Tax Rate
C18	= C15 – C16	2,778 – 1,111 = $1,667	Net Profit = Gross Profit – Tax Amount

Cell C11 refers to the gross sales amount in Year 0, which was given in cell D3. Therefore, cell C11 contains the cell reference to $D$3. A relative cell reference would work as well because this cell will not be copied.

Cell C12 contain the formula =C11*$D$4. This formula multiplies the gross sales by the commission rate. It uses relative addressing for cell C11 and absolute addressing for cell D4. This allows the formula to be copied to cells D12, E12, F12, and G12 in order to calculate projected commissions for subsequent years. The commission rate stays the same for all subsequent years.

Cell 13 contains the formula =C11 – C12. This formula calculates the net sales by subtracting commissions from gross sales. It uses relative addressing for both cells C11 and C12. This allows the formula to be copied to cells D13, E13, F13, and G13 in order to calculate projected net sales for subsequent years.

Cell C14 contains the formula =C13*$D$7. This formula calculates the cost of good sold by multiplying the net sales by the given percentage. It uses relative addressing for cell C13 and absolute addressing for cell D7. This allows the formula to be copied to cells D14, E14, F14, and G14 in order to calculate projected cost of goods sold for subsequent years. The COGS rate stays the same for all years.

Cell C15 contains the formula =C13-C14. This formula calculates gross profit by subtracting the cost of goods sold from net sales. It uses relative addressing for cell C13 and cell C14. This allows the formula to be copied to cells D15, E15, F15, and G15 in order to calculate projected gross profits for subsequent years.

Cell C16 contains the formula =C15*$D$5. This formula calculates the tax amount by multiplying the gross profit by the tax rate. It uses relative addressing for cell C15 and absolute addressing for cell D5. This allows the formula to be copied to cells D16, E16, F16, and G16 in order to calculate projected tax amounts for subsequent years. The tax rate stays the same for all years.

Cell C18 contains the formula =C15-C16. This formula calculates net profit by subtracting the tax from gross profit. It uses relative addressing for both cell C15 and cell C16. This allows the formula to be copied to cells D18, E18, F18, and G18 in order to calculate projected net profits for subsequent years.

Once the income statement for the base year (Year 0) is completed, we can use it to construct projected income statements for the next 4 years by following these steps:

- Start by inserting the formula =C11*(1+$D$6) into cell D11. Cell D11 contains the forecasted gross sales for Year 1 based on a 5% growth in the Year 0 gross sales (cell C11). This formula increases the previous year's gross sales by the projected rate of growth. It uses relative addressing for cell C11 and absolute addressing for cell D6. This allows the formula to be copied to cells E11, F11, and G11 in order to calculate projected gross sales for years 0 through 4 based on the same 5% annual growth in gross sales.
- Highlight cell D11 and copy it to cells E11, F11, and G11.
- Next highlight cells C12 through C18 and copy them across to cells D12 through G18.

After copying the cells, all the formulas will adjust as in Table 9.4.

	B	C	D	E	F	G
		Table 9.4. Cell Formulas for Pro Forma Income Statements				
10		Year 0	Year 1	Year 2	Year 3	Year 4
11	Gross Sales:	= $D$3	= C11*(1+$D$6)	= D11*(1+$D$6)	= E11*(1+$D$6)	= F11*(1+$D$6)
12	Commissions:	= C11 * $D$4	= D11 * $D$4	= E11 * $D$4	= F11 * $D$4	= G11 * $D$4
13	Net Sales:	= C11 – C12	= D11 – D12	= E11 – E12	= F11 – F12	= G11 – G12
14	COGS:	= C13 * $D$7	= D13 * $D$7	= E13 * $D$7	= F13 * $D$7	= G13 * $D$7
15	Gross Profit:	= C13 – C14	= D13 – D14	= E13 – E14	= F13 – F14	= G13 - G14
16	Tax Amount:	= C15 * $D$5	= D15 * $D$5	= E15 * $D$5	= F15 * $D$5	= G15 * $D$5
17						
18	Net Profit	= C15 – C16	= D15 – D16	= E15 – E16	= F15 – F16	= G15 – G16

Once the formulas are completed, the results will appear as in Table 9.5.

	B	C	D	E	F	G
		Table 9.5. Completed Pro Forma Income Statements				
10		Year 0	Year 1	Year 2	Year 3	Year 4
11	Gross Sales:	$8,100	$8,505	$8,930	$9,377	$9,846
12	Commissions:	162	170	179	188	197
13	Net Sales:	7,938	8,355	8,752	9,189	9,649
14	COGS:	5,160	5,418	5,689	5,973	6,272
15	Gross Profit:	2,778	2,917	3,063	3,216	3,377
16	Tax Amount:	1,111	1,167	1,225	1,286	1,351
17						
18	Net Profit	$1,667	$1,750	$1,838	$1,930	$2,026

This completes the table for net profit projections through Year 4 based on the assumption of a 5% annual sales growth rate.

SENSITIVITY (WHAT-IF) ANALYSIS

Once the pro forma income statements are completed, we need to perform sensitivity analysis. For example, what will happen to net profits of the next four years if sales do not grow by 5% a year? How about COGS? How will changes in COGS rate affect net profits? We can do this in Excel with the help of Data Table commands. There are two types of Data Tables. In Type I, changes in one factor is investigated and in Data Table Type II, two factors are changed simultaneously and their effect on another factor is studied.

DATA TABLE TYPE I

To perform sensitivity analysis with one variable, we need to pick a range of possible values for that variable. Let us assume the variable of interest is the Annual Growth Rate of Sales. The pro forma income statements in the previous tables assumed that this rate is 5% and stays the same over the next four years. What if this rate changes anywhere from 1% (worst possible scenario) to 10% (best possible scenario) in increments of 1/2%. In Excel we can type these rates in cells C23 through C41, for example. The best way to do this is to enter 1% in cell C23 and enter a formula =C23+0.005 in the cell below it, C24, and then copy it down all the way to cell C41. Since we are interested in finding the effect of changes in the annual growth rate of sales on the estimated net profits of the next four years (Year 1, Year 2, Year 3, and Year 4), we need to identify the cells that contain the net profits information. Therefore, we enter:

- =D18 in cell D22 (cell D18 contains the estimated net profit of Year 1)
- =E18 in cell E22 (cell E18 contains the estimated net profit of Year 2)
- =F18 in cell F22 (cell F18 contains the estimated net profit of Year 3)
- =G18 in cell G22 (cell G18 contains the estimated net profit of Year 4)

After the completion of these steps, your worksheet should look like Table 9.6.

Table 9.6. Cell Formulas for Data Table Type I				
	C	D	E	F	G
22		=D18	=E18	=F18	=G18
23	0.01				
24	=C23+0.005				
25	=C24+0.005				
26	=C25+0.005				
27	=C26+0.005				
28	=C27+0.005				
29	=C28+0.005				
30	=C29+0.005				
31	=C30+0.005				
32	=C31+0.005				
33	=C32+0.005				
34	=C33+0.005				
35	=C34+0.005				
36	=C35+0.005				
37	=C36+0.005				
38	=C37+0.005				
39	=C38+0.005				
40	=C39+0.005				
41	=C40+0.005				

Note that cell C22 is left **blank**. Also remember that there is nothing special about cells C22 through C41 or cell D22 through G22. You can do this in any part of your worksheet as long as the cell in the upper left corner of your work area is left blank.

You can complete the process by following these steps:

- Place the cursor in cell C22 (the blank cell) and highlight the whole table from cell C22 through cell G41.
- Next click on "Data" on the menu bar.

- Press "TABLE" and the dialogue box in Figure 9.1 will appear:

Figure 9.1. Data Table I Dialogue Box

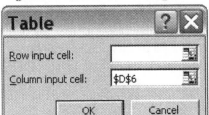

Enter D6 (the cell that holds the annual growth rates of sales in the pro forma income statements) in the "COLUMN INPUT CELL" box and press "OK".

The computer will then enter all the numbers in the first column (1.0% through 10.0%) into cell D6 and recalculate cells D18, E18, F18, and G18. All the numbers in our pro forma income statements depend on the value in cell D6. Therefore, as the value of D6 changes, all the numbers will adjust and we will get new forecasts of estimated net profits for the next four years. However, when the value of D6 becomes 5.0%, the estimated profit becomes equal to the original values in the pro forma income statement. This is demonstrated in Table 9.7.

Table 9.7. Data Table Type I				
C	**D**	**E**	**F**	**G**
20		DATA TABLE TYPE I		
21		Year 1	Year 2	Year 3	Year 4
22		=D18	=E18	=F18	=G18
23	1.0%	$1,684	$1,700	$1,717	$1,735
24	1.5%	1,692	1,717	1,743	1,769
25	2.0%	1,700	1,734	1,769	1,804
26	2.5%	1,709	1,751	1,795	1,840
27	3.0%	1,717	1,768	1,822	1,876
28	3.5%	1,725	1,786	1,848	1,913
29	4.0%	1,734	1,803	1,875	1,950
30	4.5%	1,742	1,820	1,902	1,988
31	5.0%	$1,750	$1,838	$1,930	$2,026
32	5.5%	1,759	1,855	1,957	2,065
33	6.0%	1,767	1,873	1,985	2,105
34	6.5%	1,775	1,891	2,014	2,145
35	7.0%	1,784	1,909	2,042	2,185
36	7.5%	1,792	1,926	2,071	2,226
37	8.0%	1,800	1,944	2,100	2,268
38	8.5%	1,809	1,962	2,129	2,310
39	9.0%	1,817	1,981	2,159	2,353
40	9.5%	1,825	1,999	2,189	2,397
41	10.0%	1,834	2,017	2,219	2,441

DATA TABLE TYPE II

Data Table Type II expands on the features introduced in Data Table Type I by allowing us to change two variables at the same time. Since two factors are changed at the same time, we can only investigate the effect of changes in these two factors on estimated profits of **one year only**. In our analysis, we will investigate the effect of growth rate of sales and COGS rate on the estimated profit of Year 4, as displayed in cell G18 of the pro forma income statement.

- Go to an empty area of the worksheet (for example, C45) and type a formula that refers to the cell address that holds the net profit figure for Year 4, =G18 in this case.
- Type the various COGS rates (for example, 60%, 65%, 70%, and 75%) that need to be calculated in the next four cells to the right of the cell where =G18 was typed. Instead of typing all four numbers, it is advantageous to use formulas, as demonstrated in the table 9.8.
- Enter growth rates in column C (starting in cell C46) using the same formulas described in Data Table Type I.

After completing all the steps, your table should look like Table 9.8.

Table 9.8. Cell Formulas for Data Table Type II				
C	**D**	**E**	**F**	**G**
44		COGS AS % OF NET SALES		
45	=G18	60%	=D45+.05	=E45+.05%	=F45+.05
46	0.01				
47	=C46+0.005				
48	=C47+0.005				
49	=C48+0.005				
50	=C49+0.005				
51	=C50+0.005				
52	=C51+0.005				
53	=C52+0.005				
54	=C53+0.005				
55	=C54+0.005				
56	=C55+0.005				
57	=C56+0.005				
58	=C57+0.005				
59	=C58+0.005				
60	=C59+0.005				
61	=C60+0.005				
62	=C61+0.005				
63	=C62+0.005				
64	=C63+0.005				

You are now ready to perform sensitivity analysis again.

- Highlight the whole table, from cell C45 through cell G64.
- Click on "DATA" on the menu bar.
- Press "TABLE", and the same dialogue box will appear (Figure 9.2).
- For the Row Input Cell, enter D7, the cell that holds the COGS rate in the pro forma income statements.
- For the Column Input Cell, enter D6, the cell that holds the annual growth rate of sales in the pro forma income statements.
- Click on OK.

Figure 9.2. Data Table II Dialogue Box

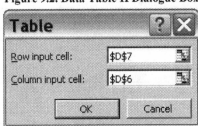

The program will insert all the values of growth rate of sales into D6 and all the values of COGS rates into D7, and recalculate the estimated net profit for Year 4 in cell G18. Note that at 5% growth rate and 65% COGS, the table gives the original value for estimated net profit (highlighted in Table 9.9).

	C	D	E	F	G
	Table 9.9. Data Table Type II				
43	**DATA TABLE TYPE II (Year 4)**				
44	**COGS as a Percentage of Net Sales**				
45	=G18	60%	65%	70%	75%
46	1.0%	$1,982	$1,735	$1,487	$1,239
47	1.5%	2,022	1,769	1,517	1,264
48	2.0%	2,062	1,804	1,547	1,289
49	2.5%	2,103	1,840	1,577	1,314
50	3.0%	2,144	1,876	1,608	1,340
51	3.5%	2,186	1,913	1,640	1,366
52	4.0%	2,229	1,950	1,672	1,393
53	4.5%	2,272	1,988	1,704	1,420
54	5.0%	2,316	$2,026	1,737	1,447
55	5.5%	2,360	2,065	1,770	1,475
56	6.0%	2,405	2,105	1,804	1,503
57	6.5%	2,451	2,145	1,838	1,532
58	7.0%	2,497	2,185	1,873	1,561
59	7.5%	2,544	2,226	1,908	1,590
60	8.0%	2,592	2,268	1,944	1,620
61	8.5%	2,640	2,310	1,980	1,650
62	9.0%	2,689	2,353	2,017	1,681
63	9.5%	2,739	2,397	2,054	1,712
64	10.0%	2,789	2,441	2,092	1,743

At this time the entire worksheet should look like Table 9.10.

Table 9.10. Pro Forma Income Statement					
B	**C**	**D**	**E**	**F**	**G**
PRO FORMA INCOME STATEMENTS					
Gross Sales for Year 0 (Given Year):	$8,100				
Commission Rate:	2%				
Tax Rate:	40%				
Annual Growth Rate of Sales:	5%				
COGS (% of Net Sales):	65%				
	Year 0	Year 1	Year 2	Year 3	Year 4
Gross Sales:	$8,100	$8,505	$8,930	$9,377	$9,846
Commissions:	162	170	179	188	197
Net Sales:	7,938	8,335	8,752	9,189	9,649
COGS:	5,160	5,418	5,689	5,973	6,272
Gross Profit:	2,778	2,917	3,063	3,216	3,377
Tax Amount:	1,111	1,167	1,225	1,286	1,351
Net Profit:	$1,667	$1,750	$1,838	$1,930	$2,026
		DATA TABLE Type I			
	Growth Rate	Year 1	Year 2	Year 3	Year 4
		=D18	=E18	=F18	=G18
	1.0%	$1,684	$1,700	$1,717	$1,735
	1.5%	1,692	1,717	1,743	1,769
	2.0%	1,700	1,734	1,769	1,804
	2.5%	1,709	1,751	1,795	1,840
	3.0%	1,717	1,768	1,822	1,876
	3.5%	1,725	1,786	1,848	1,913
	4.0%	1,734	1,803	1,875	1,950
	4.5%	1,742	1,820	1,902	1,988
	5.0%	$1,750	$1,838	$1,930	$2,026
	5.5%	1,759	1,855	1,957	2,065
	6.0%	1,767	1,873	1,985	2,105
	6.5%	1,775	1,891	2,014	2,145
	7.0%	1,784	1,909	2,042	2,185
	7.5%	1,792	1,926	2,071	2,226
	8.0%	1,800	1,944	2,100	2,268
	8.5%	1,809	1,962	2,129	2,310
	9.0%	1,817	1,981	2,159	2,353
	9.5%	1,825	1,999	2,189	2,397
	10.0%	1,834	2,017	2,219	2,441
		DATA TABLE Type II (Year 4)			
		Growth Rate of Sales & COGS			
	=G18	60%	65%	70%	75%
	1.0%	$1,982	$1,735	$1,487	$1,239
	1.5%	2,022	1,769	1,517	1,264
	2.0%	2,062	1,804	1,547	1,289
	2.5%	2,103	1,840	1,577	1,314
	3.0%	2,144	1,876	1,608	1,340
	3.5%	2,186	1,913	1,640	1,366
	4.0%	2,229	1,950	1,672	1,393
	4.5%	2,272	1,988	1,704	1,420
	5.0%	2,316	$2,026	1,737	1,447
	5.5%	2,360	2,065	1,770	1,475
	6.0%	2,405	2,105	1,804	1,503
	6.5%	2,451	2,145	1,838	1,532
	7.0%	2,497	2,185	1,873	1,561
	7.5%	2,544	2,226	1,908	1,590
	8.0%	2,592	2,268	1,944	1,620
	8.5%	2,640	2,310	1,980	1,650
	9.0%	2,689	2,353	2,017	1,681
	9.5%	2,739	2,397	2,054	1,712
	10.0%	2,789	2,441	2,092	1,743

GRAPHICAL PRESENTATION OF RESULTS

After finishing the two Data Tables, the information can be displayed in graphs so as to provide a visual interpretation of the data. These graphs can be used to complement our analysis. In addition, a graph helps to eliminate pages upon pages of endless data that might seem uninteresting to a reader. It is therefore important to include graphs whenever possible.

There are many different types of graphing techniques that can be used in Excel. In this exercise, we create a set of line graphs for each of the above data tables. Below are the instructions of how the line graphs are created.

GRAPH FOR DATA TABLE TYPE I

The line graph for this table illustrates the effect of growth rate of sales on net profits for the years1 through 4.

- Highlight the row indicating the 1 % growth rate from Table 9.7 (cells D23:G23).
- Click on the "CHART" icon from the toolbar. A "CHART TYPE" screen appears (Figure 9.3).

Figure 9.3. Chart Wizard

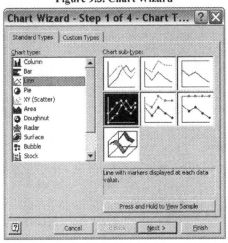

- On the "STANDARD TYPE" tab, click on "LINE" graph then click on the "FINISH" button.
- An empty graph appears with handles. The graph should be dragged to a blank area of the worksheet and its size should be adjusted using the handles.

- The line will be named by Excel as series 1 line. To name this line the 1% line, right-click on the white (blank) portion of the graph and choose "SOURCE DATA" from the menu.
- The "SOURCE DATA" dialogue box (Figure 9.4) appears. There are two tab buttons to choose: "DATA RANGE" and "SERIES".

Figure 9.4. Source Data Option of Chart Wizard

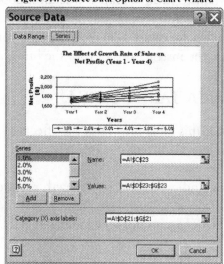

- Click on the "SERIES" tab, and click on "NAME."
- The name of the Series 1 is entered by clicking on the small red square icon in the right corner of the "NAME" field.
- The large dialogue box will be replaced by the small "SOURCE DATA – NAME:" dialogue box.
- You want to click on the value that this line represents. In this case, the value is 1%, so click on cell C23.
- When C23 appears in the minimized box, the same small square icon is clicked. This takes you back to the "SERIES" window again.
- The values for Series 1 were already entered because they were highlighted prior to starting the graph.
- For this graph the X axis represents the years 1 through 4. Therefore, click on the small red square icon in the right corner of the "CATEGORY (X) AXIS LABELS:" field and highlight cells D21:G21.
- In order to add additional lines to the same graph, right-click on the white (blank) portion of the graph and choose SOURCE DATA from the menu.
- The "SOURCE DATA" dialogue box appears. Click on the "SERIES" tab, and click on the "ADD" button.

- To identify the values that the second line represents, click on the "VALUES" icon and highlight the second series corresponding to 2% growth rate, cells D25:G25.
- You can name this graph 2% by clicking on "NAMES" icon and then clicking on cell C25.
- The remaining series are added using the same procedure. Repeat this procedure for all of the required lines up to 6%.
- The next step is to give the graph a chart title and also label the X and Y axes.
- Right click in the white (blank) area of the graph and click on "CHART OPTIONS" from the menu.
- Choose "TITLES" from the menu (Figure 9.5).
- This is where the "CHART TITLE:", "CATEGORY (X) AXIS:", and "VALUE (Y) AXIS:" are entered.
- For the "CATEGORY (X) AXIS:", enter "Years."
- For the "CHART TITLE:", enter "The Effect of Growth Rate of Sales on Net Profits (Year 1-Year 4)."
- For the "VALUE (Y) AXIS:", enter "Net Profit ($)."
- Click on the "OK" button.

Figure 9.5. Chart Options for Entering Titles

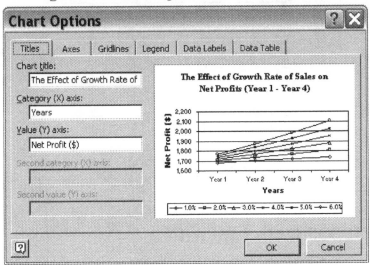

- For this problem we may need to adjust the scale of the Y-axis.
- Right click on the Y-axis and then click "FORMAT AXIS."
- Click on "SCALE."

- We can adjust the minimum and maximum values of the Y-axis.
- In this case, a value of 1600 for minimum and 2200 for maximum are appropriate.
- The font and the font size of the axes labels can also be adjusted by right-clicking on the axis and choosing the "FORMAT AXIS" and "FONT" option.
- You can also change the shape of the line markers and the color of the graph lines by right-clicking on the lines and choosing "FORMAT DATA SERIES."
- You can also change the foreground to black, and background to white.

The completed graph is displayed in Figure 9.6.

Figure 9.6. Graph for Data Table Type I

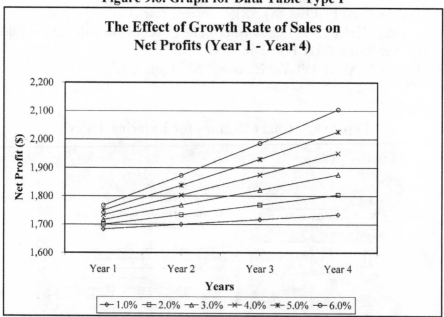

GRAPH FOR DATA TABLE II

The second graph can be created using the same procedure as the first graph. However, we need to use the information in Data Table Type II (Table 9.9). The completed graph is shown in Figure 9.7. The graph demonstrates how profits drop as the cost of goods sold increases.

Figure 9.7. Graph for Data Table Type II

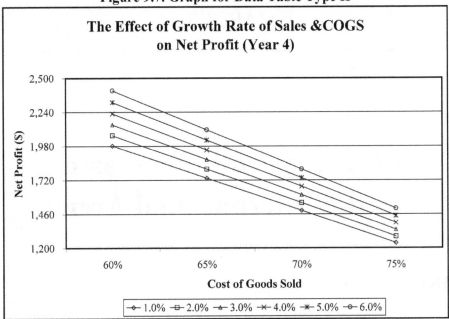

Before you print the graphs, it is a good idea to put them above one another, preferably with the same size, so that both graphs print on the same page.

AVOID BROKEN LINES IN LINE CHARTS

Excel creates a broken line chart if data are missing form one or more cells. If a cell is blank, the line will have a gap. If the cell has non-numeric data, Excel treats it as zero. You can solve the problem by inserting the formula =NA(). Since NA() is treated as "Not Available", Excel will ignore the non-numeric data and create a continuous line.

CHAPTER 10

Sales and Profit Forecasting in the International Arena

INTRODUCTION

IN CHAPTER 9 WE learned about Pro Forma Income Statements and sensitivity analysis and how they can be used to predict future sales and profits. In this chapter we can extend financial forecasting to firms that have subsidiaries in other countries and investigate how exchange rates can affect profitability of these firms, even if all the other factors remain the same.

Exchange rate volatility (risk) is a potential problem for anyone engaged in international trade. This includes importers and exporters, multinational companies, banks, investment companies, or even individuals planning to travel abroad.

Each day, billions of dollars worth of foreign exchange changes hands around the world. The value of foreign trade exchange transactions exceed the daily value of world trade. More than three quarter of these transactions involve U. S. dollars, but they do not all involve U.S. citizens or take place in the U.S.

Relatively small changes in exchange rates can have immediate and significant effects on the economy, ranging from corporate profits to overseas traveling. Large changes in exchange rates can destabilize governments, as was demonstrated in the 1990s in Mexico and Southeast Asia. Despite their importance, most people find the behavior of exchange rates confusing. A summary of some of the key ideas about exchange rate are:

- There is a widespread perception that foreign exchanges are too volatile.
- If investors interpret volatility as risk, their investment decisions may be adversely affected.

- Managing risk is of primary importance to firms engaged in international trade.
- Sometimes exchange rates are fairly stable for long periods; other times they are fairly volatile for long periods.
- Exchange rates can become volatile in a relatively short time.

COMPUTER ASSIGNMENT

PURPOSE

1. To investigate the effect of exchange rate volatility on financial statements.
2. To demonstrate how Technology (microcomputers and software) can assist decision makers in International Business.
3. To build a model to forecast sales and profits (pro forma income statements).
4. To perform sensitivity (what-if) analysis:

   - Investigate the effect of changes in the growth rate of sales of a subsidiary in another country on profitability.
   - Investigate the effect of changes in exchange rate on profitability.

5. To learn about some of the advanced features of Excel, namely Data Table and Graphical Analysis.

ASSUMPTIONS

In order to use pro forma income statements to investigate the effect of exchange rates, we need to make some assumptions:

1. A U.S.-based firm has a subsidiary in Japan. Its gross sales in Year 0 were ¥20,000.
2. The subsidiary sells all its products in Japan and is growing at a rate of 5% per year.
3. The firm relies on Japanese resources such as raw material and sales force, and pays for them in Yen. Currently, they pay a 10% commission and their COGS is 65% of net sales.
4. Since the firm is a U.S.-based company, it must pay income taxes in the U.S.; the tax rate is 40%.

5. The current exchange rate is 110 yen to the U.S. dollars, and the firm is subject to exchange rate volatility.

REQUIREMENTS

1. Use the technique learned in Chapter 9 to build four pro forma income statements for the subsidiary in Japan.
2. Convert the numbers from foreign currency (Japanese yen) to U.S. dollars.
3. Construct pro forma income statements for the firm in U.S.
4. Perform sensitivity analysis to investigate the effect of growth rate of sales and exchange rate on estimated net profits.
5. Graph your results.
6. Print your results.
7. Write a report summarizing all the steps and procedures used in this assignment.

PROCEDURE

We start by entering the above assumptions into the cells as in Table 10.1.

Table 10.1. Initial Assumptions			
	A	B	C	D
2	Pro Forma Income Statements			
3	Sales and Profit Forecasting in the International Arena			
4	(For an American Firm Selling Products in Japan)			
5				
6	Total Sales for Year 0 (in Japan):		¥20,000,000	Yen
7	Exchange Rate ($ vs. Yen):		110	
8	Commission Rate:		10%	
9	Tax Rate:		40%	
10	Annual Growth Rate of Sales in Japan:		5%	
11	COGS (% of Net Sales):		65%	

We can use the same technique learned in Chapter 9 to build pro forma statements for the firm in Japan and in the United States and also perform sensitivity analysis to investigate the effect of exchange rate volatility on profit.

To construct the growth of sales in Japan under the above assumptions, we need to insert the appropriate formulas as in Table 10.2.

Table 10.2. Cell Formulas for Growth Rate of Sales in Japan					
A	B	C	D	E	F
13	Growth of Sales in Japan (in Yen)				
14		Year 0	Year 1	Year 2	Year 3	Year 4
15 Gross Sales:	=$C$6	=B16*(1+$C$10)	=C16*(1+$C$10)	=D16*(1+$C$10)	=E16*(1+$C$10)
16 Commissions Paid in Japan:	=B16*$C$8	=C16*$C$8	=D16*$C$8	=E16*$C$8	=F16*$C$8
17 Net Sales:	=B16-B17	=C16-C17	=D16-D17	=E16-E17	=F16-F17

After completing the formulas the actual numbers appear as in Table 10.3.

Table 10.3. Growth Rate of Sales in Japan					
A	B	C	D	E	F
13	Growth of Sales in Japan (in Yen)				
14		Year 0	Year 1	Year 2	Year 3	Year 4
15 Gross Sales:	¥20,000,000	¥21,000,000	¥22,050,000	¥23,152,500	¥24,310,125
16 Commissions Paid in Japan:	2,000,000	2,100,000	2,205,000	2,315,250	2,431,013
17 Net Sales:	¥18,000,000	¥18,900,000	¥19,845,000	¥20,837,250	¥21,879,113

Now, we need to use the exchange rate to see the results in U.S. dollars (see Table 10.4).

Table 10.4. Cell Formulas for Growth of Sales in Dollars					
	A	**B**	**C**	**D**	**E**	**F**
21	Growth of Sales in Dollars					
22		Year 0	Year 1	Year 2	Year 3	Year 4
23						
24	Gross Sales:	=B16/$C$7	=C16/$C$7	=D16/$C$7	=E16/$C$7	=F16/$C$7
25	- Commissions:	=B17/$C$7	=C17/$C$7	=D17/$C$7	=E17/$C$7	=F17/$C$7
26						
27	= Net Sales:	=B24-B25	=C24-C25	=D24-D25	=E24-E25	=F24-F25
28	- COGS:	=B27*$C$11	=C27*$C$11	=D27*$C$11	=E27*$C$11	=F27*$C$11
29						
30	= Gross Profit:	=B27-B28	=C27-C28	=D27-D28	=E27-E28	=F27-F28
31	- Tax:	=B30*$C$9	=C30*$C$9	=D30*$C$9	=E30*$C$9	=F30*$C$9
32						
33	= Net Profit:	=B30-B31	=C30-C31	=D30-D31	=E30-E31	=F30-F31

After all the formulas are completed, Table 10.5 will be displayed. This table actually represents the pro forma income statements of the firm in U.S. dollars for the next 4 years.

Table 10.5. Growth of Sales in Dollars					
	A	**B**	**C**	**D**	**E**	**F**
21	Growth of Sales in Dollars					
22		Year 0	Year 1	Year 2	Year 3	Year 4
23						
24	Gross Sales:	$181,818	$190,909	$200,455	$210,477	$221,001
25	- Commissions:	18,182	19,091	20,045	21,048	22,100
26						
27	= Net Sales:	$163,636	$171,818	$180,409	$189,430	$198,901
28	- COGS:	106,364	111,682	117,266	123,129	129,286
29						
30	= Gross Profit:	$57,273	$60,136	$63,143	$66,300	$69,615
31	- Tax:	22,909	24,055	25,257	26,520	27,846
32						
33	= Net Profit:	$34,364	$36,082	$37,886	$39,780	$41,769

At this point, your entire worksheet should like Table 10.6.

Table 10.6. Pro Forma Income Statements						
	A	B	C	D	E	F
1						
2		Pro Forma Income Statements					
3		Sales and Profit Forecasting in the International Arena					
4		(For an American Firm Selling Products in Japan)					
5						
6	Total Sales for Year 0 (in Japan):		¥ 20,000,000			
7	Exchange Rate ($ vs. Yen):		110			
8	Commission Rate:		10%			
9	Tax Rate:		40%			
10	Annual Growth Rate of Sales in Japan:		5%			
11	COGS (% of Net Sales):		65%			
12						
13			Growth of Sales in Japan (in Yen)				
14		Year 0	Year 1	Year 2	Year 3	Year 4
15	Gross Sales:	¥ 20,000,000	¥ 21,000,000	¥ 22,050,000	¥ 23,152,500	¥ 24,310,125
16	Commissions in Japan:	2,000,000	2,100,000	2,205,000	2,315,250	2,431,013
17	Net Sales:	¥ 18,000,000	¥ 18,900,000	¥ 19,845,000	¥ 20,837,250	¥ 21,879,113
18	COGS:	11,700,000	12,285,000	12,899,250	13,544,213	14,221,423
19	Gross Profit:	¥ 6,300,000	¥ 6,615,000	¥ 6,945,750	¥ 7,293,038	¥ 7,657,689
20						
21			Growth of Sales in U.S. Dollars				
22		Year 0	Year 1	Year 2	Year 3	Year 4
23						
24	Gross Sales:	$ 181,818	$ 190,909	$ 200,455	$ 210,477	$ 221,001
25	Commissions:	18,182	19,091	20,045	21,048	22,100
26						
27	Net Sales:	$ 163,636	$ 171,818	$ 180,409	$ 189,430	$ 198,901
28	COGS:	106,364	111,682	117,266	123,129	129,286
29						
30	Gross Profit:	$ 57,273	$ 60,136	$ 63,143	$ 66,300	$ 69,615
31	Tax:	22,909	24,055	25,257	26,520	27,846
32						
33	Net Profit:	$ 34,364	$ 36,082	$ 37,886	$ 39,780	$ 41,769

DATA TABLE TYPE I

In row 33 we have the estimated net profits for years 1, 2, 3, and 4. If any one of the assumptions of this problem (for example, exchange rate) changes, it can drastically affect the estimated profits. This type of what-if analysis can be performed with the help of data tables type I and type II. The procedure for setting up data table was explained in Chapter 9. We can use similar procedure for this problem. First, set up the data table as in Table 10.7. Make sure cell I10 is blank. In cells J10, K10, L10, and M10 type the formulas where the original estimated net profits were calculated. In this case, they were =C33, =D33, =E33, and =F33.

Table 10.7. Cell Formulas for Data Table Type I				
I	**J**	**K**	**L**	**M**
4	What if exchange rate changes? Assume the range is between 100 to 120.			
5	Sensitivity Analysis: (What-if Analysis)			
6	DATA TABLE TYPE I			
7	The effect of exchange rate volatility on estimated net profit in U.S. $			
8					
9		Year 1	Year 2	Year 3	Year 4
10		=C33	=D33	=E33	=F33
11	100				
12	101				
13	102				
14	103				
15	104				
16	105				
17	106				
18	107				
19	108				
20	109				
21	110				
22	111				
23	112				
24	113				
25	114				
26	115				
27	116				
28	117				
29	118				
30	119				
31	120				

Now highlight the table starting from cell I10 through cell M31. From the task bar, click on "DATA", and "TABLE". A dialogue box will appear (see Figure 10.1). Enter C7 for column input cell on and press "OK."

Figure 10.1. Data Table I Dialogue Box

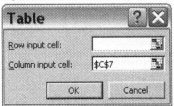

Table 10.8 will be displayed. The table represents all values of estimated net profits of years 1 through 4 at varying rates of exchange.

	I	J	K	L	M
	Table 10. 8. Data Table Type I				
4	What if exchange rate changes? Assume the range is between 100 to 120.				
5	Sensitivity Analysis: (What-if Analysis)				
6	DATA TABLE TYPE I				
7	The effect of exchange rate volatility on estimated net profit in U.S. $				
8					
9		Year 1	Year 2	Year 3	Year 4
10		=C33	=D33	=E33	=F33
11	100	$39,690	$41,675	$43,758	$45,946
12	101	39,297	41,262	43,325	45,491
13	102	38,912	40,857	42,900	45,045
14	103	38,534	40,461	42,484	44,608
15	104	38,163	40,072	42,075	44,179
16	105	37,800	39,690	41,675	43,758
17	106	37,443	39,316	41,281	43,345
18	107	37,093	38,948	40,896	42,940
19	108	36,750	38,588	40,517	42,543
20	109	36,413	38,233	40,145	42,152
21	110	$36,082	$37,886	$39,780	$41,769
22	111	35,757	37,545	39,422	41,393
23	112	35,438	37,209	39,070	41,023
24	113	35,124	36,880	38,724	40,660
25	114	34,816	36,557	38,384	40,304
26	115	34,513	36,239	38,051	39,953
27	116	34,216	35,926	37,723	39,609
28	117	33,923	35,619	37,400	39,270
29	118	33,636	35,317	37,083	38,937
30	119	33,353	35,021	36,772	38,610
31	120	33,075	34,729	36,465	38,288

DATA TABLE TYPE II

Similarly, Data Table Type II can be set up for two factors, exchange rate and annual growth rate of sales. This will show the effect of these factors on estimated net profit of Year 4 (as calculated in cell F33). The first step is to set up the table as in Table 10.9.

	H	I	J	K	L	M	N	O	P	Q	R
	Table 10. 9. Cell Formulas for Data Table Type II										
34	What if exchange rate and growth rate of sales change?										
35	Assume the exchange rate changes between 100 to 120 & sales grow between 1 and 10%.										
36	Sensitivity Analysis: (What-if Analysis)										
37	DATA TABLE TYPE II (Year 4)										
38	The effect of exchange rate & sales volatility on estimated net profit in U.S. dollars.										
39											
40	=F33	1%	2%	3%	4%	5%	6%	7%	8%	9%	10%
41	100										
42	101										
43	102										
44	103										
45	104										
46	105										
47	106										
48	107										
49	108										
50	109										
51	110										
52	111										
53	112										
54	113										
55	114										
56	115										
57	116										
58	117										
59	118										
60	119										
61	120										

After the table is set up, highlight cells H40 through R61 and from the task bar, click on "DATA", "TABLE". The dialogue box in Figure 10.2 will appear.

Figure 10.2. Data Table II Dialogue Box

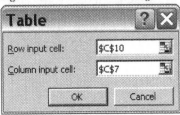

On the dialogue box, enter C10 for row input cell and C7 for column input cell and press "OK." The completed data table, displayed in Table 10.10, will appear.

	Table 10.10. Data Table Type II										
	H	I	J	K	L	M	N	O	P	Q	R
34	What if exchange rate and growth rate of sales change?										
35	Assume the exchange rate changes between 100 to 120 & sales grow between 1 and 10%.										
36	Sensitivity Analysis: (What-if Analysis)										
37	DATA TABLE TYPE II (Year 4)										
38	The effect of exchange rate & sales volatility on estimated net profit in U.S. dollars.										
39											
40	=F33	1%	2%	3%	4%	5%	6%	7%	8%	9%	10%
41	100	$39,335	$40,916	$42,544	$44,221	$45,946	$47,722	$49,548	$51,426	$53,358	$55,343
42	101	38,945	40,511	42,123	43,783	45,491	47,249	49,058	50,917	52,829	54,795
43	102	38,564	40,114	41,710	43,354	45,045	46,786	48,577	50,418	52,312	54,258
44	103	38,189	39,724	41,305	42,933	44,608	46,332	48,105	49,929	51,804	53,731
45	104	37,822	39,342	40,908	42,520	44,179	45,886	47,642	49,449	51,306	53,214
46	105	37,462	38,968	40,518	42,115	43,758	45,449	47,189	48,978	50,817	52,708
47	106	37,108	38,600	40,136	41,718	43,345	45,020	46,743	48,516	50,338	52,210
48	107	36,762	38,239	39,761	41,328	42,940	44,600	46,307	48,062	49,867	51,722
49	108	36,421	37,885	39,393	40,945	42,543	44,187	45,878	47,617	49,405	51,244
50	109	36,087	37,538	39,031	40,569	42,152	43,781	45,457	47,180	48,952	50,773
51	110	35,759	37,196	38,677	40,201	$41,769	43,383	45,044	46,751	48,507	50,312
52	111	35,437	36,861	38,328	39,838	41,393	42,992	44,638	46,330	48,070	49,859
53	112	35,120	36,532	37,986	39,483	41,023	42,609	44,239	45,917	47,641	49,413
54	113	34,810	36,209	37,650	39,133	40,660	42,232	43,848	45,510	47,219	48,976
55	114	34,504	35,891	37,320	38,790	40,304	41,861	43,463	45,111	46,805	48,546
56	115	34,204	35,579	36,995	38,453	39,953	41,497	43,085	44,719	46,398	48,124
57	116	33,909	35,272	36,676	38,121	39,609	41,139	42,714	44,333	45,998	47,709
58	117	33,620	34,971	36,363	37,795	39,270	40,788	42,349	43,954	45,605	47,302
59	118	33,335	34,675	36,054	37,475	38,937	40,442	41,990	43,582	45,218	46,901
60	119	33,054	34,383	35,751	37,160	38,610	40,102	41,637	43,216	44,838	46,507
61	120	32,779	34,097	35,454	36,851	38,288	39,768	41,290	42,855	44,465	46,119

The last step is to graph the results. We can create one set of line graphs from Data Table Type I and one set from Data Table Type II. The procedure is explained in Chapter 9. The results are displayed in Figures 10.3 and 10.4.

Figure 10.3. Exchange Rate Volatility

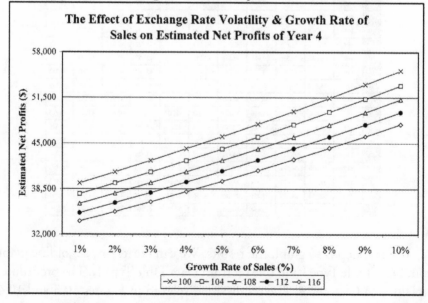

The Effect of Exchange Rate Volatility on
Estimated Net Profits (Year 0 - Year 4)

Estimated Net Profits ($)

Exchange Rates

→ Year 1 —□— Year 2 —△— Year 3 —✕— Year 4

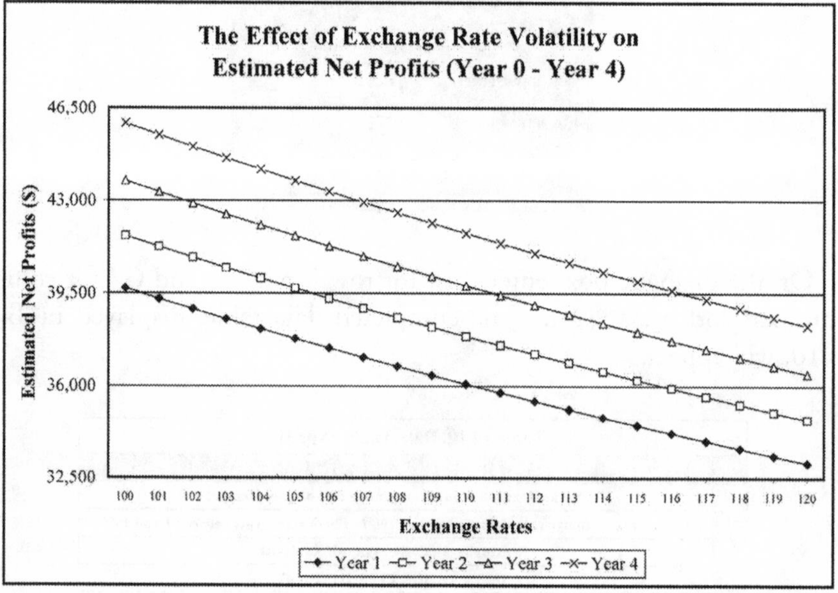

Figure 10.4. Exchange Rate Volatility & Growth Rate of Sales

The Effect of Exchange Rate Volatility & Growth Rate of
Sales on Estimated Net Profits of Year 4

Estimated Net Profits ($)

Growth Rate of Sales (%)

—✕— 100 —□— 104 —△— 108 —●— 112 —◇— 116

CHAPTER 11

Expense Reports and Advanced Graphing

P REPARING A MONTHLY sales and expense report is highly useful for small as well as large firms. It is of particular use to people in sales and consulting that travel often.

COMPUTER ASSIGNMENT

PURPOSE

1. To learn about monthly expenses reports
2. To learn how to calculate Year-To-Date expenses and profits
3. To learn more advanced graphs beyond line graphs

REQUIREMENTS

1. Prepare a monthly sales and expense report for a traveling salesperson.
2. Enter the appropriate formulas to calculate the monthly and year-to-date totals.
3. Create a Pie Chart and a Stacked Bar graph of the results.
4. Print your results.
5. Prepare a report and explain all the steps and procedures that were used.

PROCEDURE

Table 11.1 demonstrates how the Excel program can be used to create monthly expense statements. This table shows the company's monthly profits from January through May.

Table 11.1. Monthly Expense Report						
A	**B**	**C**	**D**	**E**	**F**	**G**
2	CONSULTING SERVICE					
3		JAN	FEB	MAR	APR	MAY	Y.T.D.
4 **Sales:**	$1,600	$1,600	$1,600	$1,800	$1,700	$8,300
5 **Expenses:**						
6 Rent	400	400	400	400	400	$2,000
7 Supplies	300	270	340	295	210	$1,415
8 Utilities	130	130	120	85	75	$540
9 Travel	120	90	160	100	120	$590
10 **Total Expenses:**	$950	$890	$1,020	$880	$805	$4,545
11 **Monthly Profits:**	$650	$710	$580	$920	$895	$3,755
12						
13 **Y.T.D. Profits:**	$650	$1,360	$1,940	$2,860	$3,755	

The formulas used to create the monthly expense report are given in Table 11.2.

Table 11.2. Cell Formulas for Monthly Expense Report						
A	B	C	D	E	F	G
2	CONSULTING SERVICE					
3		JAN	FEB	MAR	APR	MAY	Y.T.D.
4 Sales:	$1,600	$1,600	$1,600	$1,800	$1,700	=SUM(B4:F4)
5 Expenses:						
6 Rent	400	400	400	400	400	=SUM(B6:F6)
7 Supplies	300	270	340	295	210	=SUM(B7:F7)
8 Utilities	130	130	120	85	75	=SUM(B8:F8)
9 Travel	120	90	160	100	120	=SUM(B9:F9)
10 Total Expenses:	=SUM(B6:B9)	=SUM(C6:C9)	=SUM(D6:D9)	=SUM(E6:E9)	=SUM(F6:F9)	=SUM(G6:G9)
11 Monthly Profits:	=B4-B10	=C4-C10	=D4-D10	=E4-E10	=F4-F10	=G4-G10
12						
13 Y.T.D. Profits:	=B11	=B13+C11	=C13+D11	=D13+E11	=E13+F11	

GRAPHING THE RESULTS

In addition to line graphs, there are other graphing options available in Excel, such as pie charts and bar charts. These graphs can also be plotted in three dimensions and pie charts can also be blown up or portions moved away from the pie for emphasis. In this exercise we will create both of these charts from the monthly sales and expense report tables.

THE PIE CHART

This chart illustrates the relative monthly profits from January through May. A section of the pie chart is separated (exploded) from the whole pie itself. This is usually performed to emphasize that segment in relation to the whole pie. For example, why was the profit for the month of April greater than for the other months.

To create a Pie Chart we need to do the following.

8. In Table 11.1, highlight monthly profits from January through May (cells B11:F11).
9. Click on the **Chart Wizard** icon on the toolbar.
10. From the window, choose the pie chart and the 3-D view, and click on the finish button.
11. Once the pie chart appears, drag it into an area that suits your report.
12. The right hand button on the mouse is then clicked anywhere in the clear (blank) area of the pie chart's box. A drop down menu appears.
13. Choose the "SOURCE DATA" option.
14. A window appears with the "DATA RANGE" and "SERIES" tabs. Only the Data Range is needed for the pie chart. The Data Range is already entered because it was highlighted prior to chart wizard. Click "OK."
15. The right hand button on the mouse is again clicked anywhere in the pie chart's box, but this time the "CHART OPTIONS" is chosen from the pull down menu. This option allows us to enter the title of the chart and change the legend, if needed.
16. Choose "DATA LABELS" from the available tabs, and check the boxes "CATEGORY NAME", "PERCENTAGE", and "SHOW LEADER LINES." This will automatically set the format of your pie and label its sections.
17. Choose the "TITLES" tab. This allows you to enter in the title of your pie chart, such as "Monthly Profits (Jan-May)."

18. Next choose the "LEGEND" tab. This allows you to change the legend position, or in this case hide the legend by un-checking the "SHOW LEGEND" from the list. Click "OK" and all is completed.

19. We can slice a segment of the pie to emphasize it. In this case the month of April is emphasized.

20. Click on the section you want to separate, and once there are handles on that one piece, carefully drag it away.

21. If you want your pie to look slightly tilted, you can do so by clicking on the right-hand button of the mouse in any part of the chart's box, this will access the pull down menu bar. Chose the "3-D" view from the given menu.

22. This will give you a window that allows you to elevate your pie, thicken the base of your pie, or rotate the pie. There are two arrows in the window to elevate the pie: ↓ and ↑, or you can manually type in a number. As you click on the arrows, an outline of a pie will show you what the final view will look like.

23. Once you are finished, click "OK."

24. To enlarge the whole pie, highlight it by placing the cursor on the outer rim. Once handles appear around the pie, drag the pie outward until it suits your taste.

25. The data labels section can also be changed or corrected. Right click on the data labels and handles will appear. Choose the font tab, and change the font size or color. Click "OK" when finished. Your pie chart will look like Figure 11.1.

Figure 11.1. Pie Chart

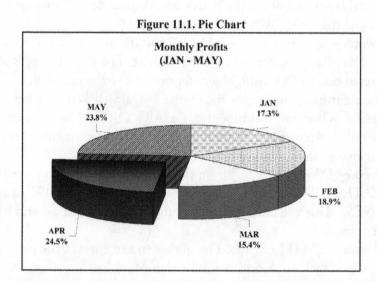

THE BAR CHART

This graph illustrates the monthly expenses for the consulting company. The monthly expenses shown are from January through May. The legend to the right of the graph identifies each bar, so it provides easy reference to the chart.

Below are the steps required to create a bar graph.

- In table 11.1, highlight rent expenses from January through May (cells B6:F6).
- Click on the "CHART WIZARD" icon on the toolbar.
- Choose the specific bar chart that you need from the window and click the finish button.
- Once the bar chart appears, drag it into an area that suits your report.
- Click the right hand button of the mouse in the clear (blank) part of the bar chart's box.
- A drop down menu appears.
- Choose "SOURCE DATA" from the menu.
- A window appears with the "DATA RANGE" and "SERIES" tabs. The Series tab is needed for the bar chart.
- Excel will automatically name this bar Series 1. To change the name, click on the small red square icon in the bottom right corner of the "NAME" field. Once the Series window disappears you can highlight the cell that states the name of your Series 1. In this case, the name is "Rent", cell A6.
- When it appears in the minimized box, the same small square icon is clicked again. This takes you back to the main "SERIES" window again.
- Each new series is added via the "ADD" button and then by highlighting the name and the values. They are entered using the procedure that we used in Chapter 9.
- Values for Series 2 are entered by clicking on the small red square icon at the bottom right-hand corner of the "VALUES" box.
- The row of values stating the supplies expense are highlighted (cells B7: F7), and the small square icon is clicked again to return to the "SERIES" window.
- The remaining series are added using the same procedure. A series is added every time by clicking on the "ADD" button until there are no more series to add.

- To enter the values of the X axis, the red square icon located at the bottom right-hand corner of the "CATEGORY (X) AXIS LABELS" box is clicked.
- The information for the X axis is highlighted. For this graph, the X axis is the months January through May, cells B3:F3.
- When finished, the small square icon on the given box is clicked.
- Next the chart title and the X and Y axes have to be labeled.
- Right click the mouse within the clear (blank) area of the graph.
- Choose "CHART OPTIONS" from the pull-down menu.
- From the tabs, "TITLES" is chosen. The titles are entered as:

> Chart title: Monthly Expenses (Jan-May)
> Category (X) axis: Months
> Value (Y) axis: Expenses ($)

- The Y scale can be changed to match our needs.
- To do this, right click on the Y axis.
- The "AXIS FORMAT" option is chosen from the drop down menu.
- The "SCALE" tab is chosen.
- You can change the scale by setting the "MINIMUM" and/or the "MAXIMUM", and not having Excel automatically arrange it for us.
- Once the scale is adjusted, click on the "OK" button.
- The graph is now complete (Figure 11.2). Minor adjustments can be made to adjust its size.

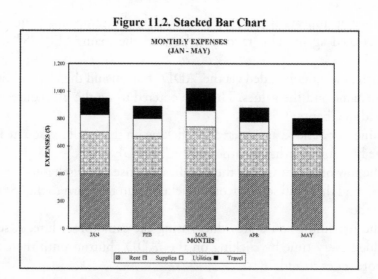

Figure 11.2. Stacked Bar Chart

Business/Market Analysis Using Excel's Drawing Tools

E XCEL'S DRAWING TOOLBAR enables you to add lines, shapes, boxes, text boxes, text art, and clip art to your document, and change their size, location, and colors. The drawing toolbar is also available in Word and PowerPoint and offers the same set of tools in each application. To make the toolbar appear on the screen in Excel, click on VIEW, TOOLBARS, and DRAWING. The toolbar will appear on the left hand side or bottom of the screen. Figure 12.1 demonstrates how to access Excel's toolbar by clicking on one of the options in the lower-left part of the screen.

Figure 12.1. Excel's Drawing Toolbar

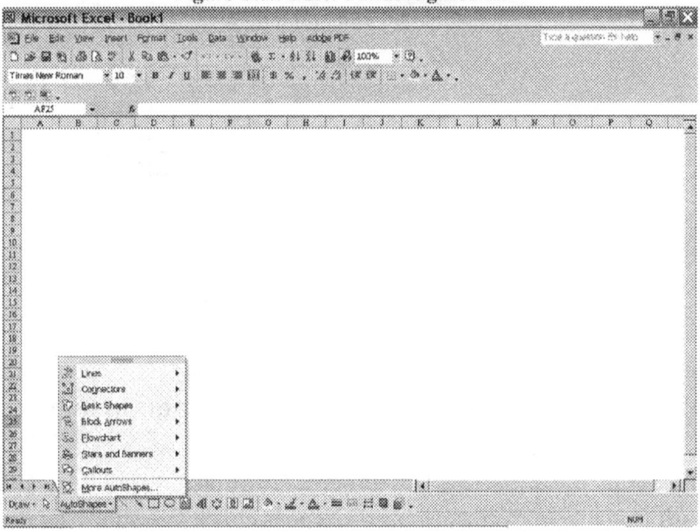

Figure 12.2 exhibits the Block Arrows toolbar and Figure12.3 exhibits the Flowchart toolbar. Both of these options are accessed by clicking on Autoshapes toolbar.

Figure 12.2. Excel's Block Arrows Toolbar

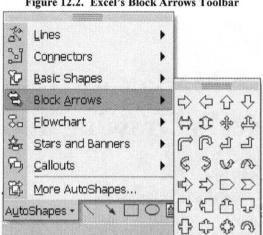

Figure 12.3 Excel's Flowchart Toolbar

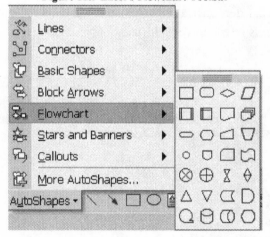

When using the toolbars, keep the following points in mind:

- The tools (Line, Arrow, Rectangle, Oval, and all of the Autoshapes) work by clicking on them and then drawing the shape or line.

- Each time you click on a drawing tool and use it, the tool turns off as soon as the object is created. To use the same tool again, you must click on the tool again.

In the following sections, there are several common and important business applications where the drawing tools are used to add borders, directions, text boxes, and messages.

CUSTOMER SERVICE EXAMPLE

An important factor in developing a positive image in the minds of your customers is to create a good and effective customer service. One area of major concern to most consumers, particularly in the area of technology, is customer service calls. Monitoring customers' telephone calls on a regular basis helps to alleviate any concerns that your customers might have, and is an effective step in building a positive relationship with your customers. Figure 12.4 exhibits such an example. It also demonstrates an application where Excel's drawing tools, lines, and two types of callouts can make your analysis more productive (see Blattner et. al., 1999, pp. 188-189).

Figure 12.4. Customer Service Calls

	B	C	D	E	F	G	H	I
1	Customer Service Calls							
2		Monday	Tuesday	Wednesday	Thursday	Friday		
3	Number of Calls	250	100	150	260	300		
4	Average Minutes on Hold	15.4	9.5	8.3	12.0	14.3		
5	Average Length of Call	12.6	11.1	6.4	11.3	13..5		
6	Average No. of Dropped Calls	6	7	10	8	9		
7								
8								
9								
10		Average duration was the highest on Monday and Friday						
11								
12		For some unexplained reason Wednesday had						
13		the highest number of dropped calls.						
14								

Highest number of calls received on Friday

USING QUADRANTS IN MARKET ANALYSIS

You can use quadrants to understand your product strategy in the market place and compare it to that of your competitors. You can also use quadrants to measure your market share and penetration in each section. A third way to use quadrants is comparative analysis for two market factors, such as market share and penetration against consumer spending. The quadrant examples in the following sections fully utilize Excel's drawing tools to demonstrate effective business strategies.

PRODUCT-MARKET GROWTH STRATEGIES

Product-market strategies involve selecting specific markets and reaching them through marketing mix strategies. In the product-market matrix, shown in Figure 12.5, four growth options are shown. The first is to increase the penetration of existing products in existing markets. The second involves creating new product offerings for existing markets. The third is to market the existing products in new markets. The fourth growth option is to diversify and develop new products for new markets. A summary of alternative strategies in each segment is given below (see Stauble, 2000, pp. 308-309).

Product Penetration in Existing Markets
$ Increase market share.
$ Increase product usage.
$ Provide reminder communications.
$ Position the product for regular or frequent Use
$ Make the use easier.
$ Provide incentives
$ Reduce undesirable consequences of frequent use.
$ Revitalize the Brand
$ New applications for existing product users.

Product Development for the Existing Market
$ Add to product features.
$ Develop product extensions.
$ Develop new-generation products.
$ Develop new products for existing markets

Market Development Using Existing Products
$ Expand geographically.
$ Expand into new market segments.

Figure 12.5. Product-Market Strategies

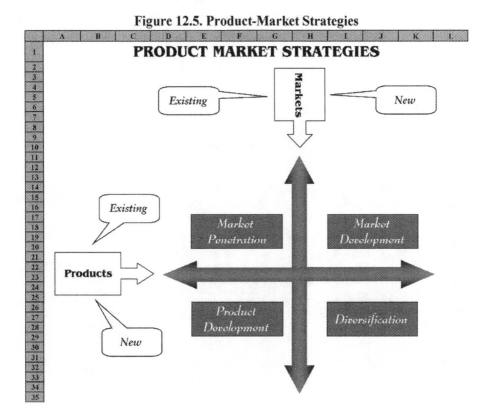

Diversification
$ Develop new products.
$ Arrange for mergers (horizontal, vertical, conglomerate).
$ Form joint ventures.
$ Export to other countries.

PRODUCT POSITIONING QUADRANT

A product positioning quadrant helps you to understand your market coverage for all your products (see Figure 12.6). Note that the products are situated in different locations in the quadrant. This means that each product has a different coverage. For example, Product C's location in the upper-left quadrant indicates that this product is at the middle of the versatile level and the edge of the easy market (see Blattner et. al., 1999, pp. 683-685).

To create the quadrant in Figure 12.6, use one of the block arrows from Excel's drawing toolbar. Then click on the Draw button from the toolbar and use the Rotate and Flip option to place arrows facing in the opposite direction.

Figure 12.6. Product Positioning Quadrant

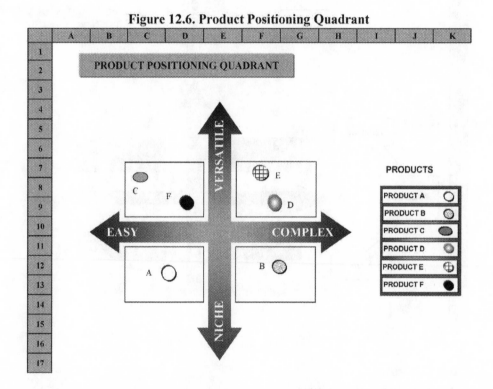

MARKET PENETRATION: PRODUCT DEPTH QUADRANT

Quadrants can be used to demonstrate product or positioning focus in a particular market, or the entire market as a whole. This is done in Figure 12.7. Use the Freeform tool from the Lines toolbar to draw the market penetration into each quadrant, and then fill the inner spaces with a fill color. Use text to enter the percentages in each quadrant.

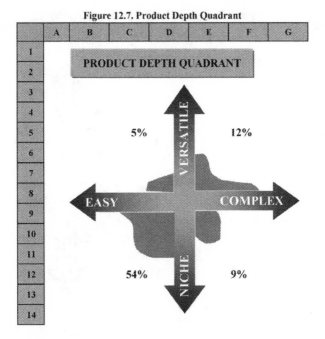

Figure 12.7. Product Depth Quadrant

MARKET PENETRATION IN COMPARISON TO CONSUMER SPENDING

Figure 12.8 demonstrates a company's market penetration relative to the amount of consumer spending. By using this technique, the managers can understand where the market opportunities lie and where their focus should be in current and future markets.

Use the Freeform tool from the Lines toolbar to draw consumer spending in each quadrant and then fill the inner spaces with a fill color. Use Connectors from the Autoshapes toolbar and text to show the dollar amounts in each quadrant.

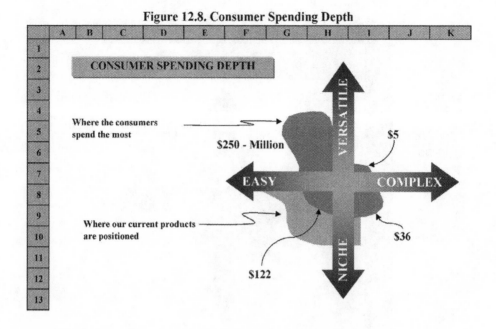

Figure 12.8. Consumer Spending Depth

BRAND LOYALTY MATRIX

Market segmentation is an effective technique in developing a sustainable competitive advantage. Segmentation is the art/science of identifying customer groups that respond differently than other groups to a firm's competitive strategies. In general, it is costly to develop a different strategy for each segment. The effectiveness of a segmentation strategy is measured by whether it will pay for the added cost of the investment required.

An important consideration in segmentation strategy is brand loyalty. It can be analyzed using a loyalty matrix, as shown in Figure 12.9. This matrix can help us identify the customers in each group, estimate the size of each of group, and design strategic programs that will influence their brand choice and loyalty level. By analyzing the loyalty matrix, we learn that the brand fence-sitters, both customers and non-customers, should have high priority. It is highly desirable to convert the fence-sitters into loyal customers (see Aaker, 2001, pp.45-46).

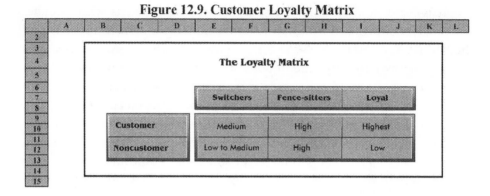

Figure 12.9. Customer Loyalty Matrix

THE BCG GROWTH-SHARE MATRIX

The Growth-Share Matrix is a model that is used to evaluate a company's overall strategic position and to help its managers to allocate resources across products and markets. This model was developed by Boston Consulting Group (BCG) and uses a two-dimensional matrix, shown in Figure 12.10. The matrix can easily be produced with Excel's Drawing Tool and clip art.

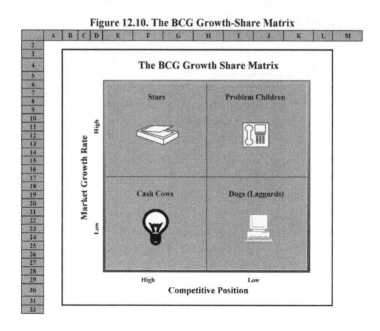

Figure 12.10. The BCG Growth-Share Matrix

It is reasonable to allocate resources to those products with a higher potential for growth and withdraw resources from those that are less attractive. In the matrix, the stars (high-share, high-growth quadrant) are market leaders in a high-growth industry and important to the current businesses, and they should receive the most resources. Problem children (low-share, high-growth quadrant) are in a growing market but not in a leading market position, and are assumed to need substantial outlays before they become stars and eventually cash cows. Cash cows (high-share, low-growth quadrant) have a high share in a slow-growth market and should be the source of significant cash flows that can be diverted to other products. Dogs (low-share, low-growth quadrant) are products with lower share in a slow-growth market and are potential cash traps (see Aaker, 2001, pp. 125-126 and Stauble, 2000, pp.310-311).

The BCG growth-share matrix is an important way of matching the company's core competencies with different market opportunities. When both company and market opportunities are positive, the company should attempt to invest and grow. When both company and market opportunities are negative, then it would be best to either harvest the business and take some cash out or to liquidate the business. It is important to understand that strategies must be flexible because company and market opportunities are not static and can change, especially if the current strategy is applied. Some of the relevant strategies that can be applied in each quadrant are summarized in the following:

Stars
- Invest more for future growth.
- Invest to penetrate.

Cash Cows
- Invest to hold.
- Use profits to finance growth in stars and problem children.

Problem Children
- Invest to rebuild (modify strategy).
- Invest selectively.

Dogs
- Harvest (low investment, take cash out).
- Divest (liquidate and accept the loss).

THE COMPETITIVE STRENGTH GRID

Market analysis is further concerned with how a company competes with firms in the same industry. The first step in competitor analysis is to identify current and potential competitors and prepare a SWOT (strengths, weaknesses, opportunities, threats) statement. The statement should contain any strategic outcomes that may be created by competitor (new or potential) actions.

After the relevant strength and competencies are identified, the next step is to prepare a competitive grid statement and measure a company against its major competitors. Figure 12.11 exhibits such a grid for three U.S. firms competing against three Japanese and three German firms (see Aaker, 2001, pp.71-73).

Figure 12.11. Competitive Strength Grid

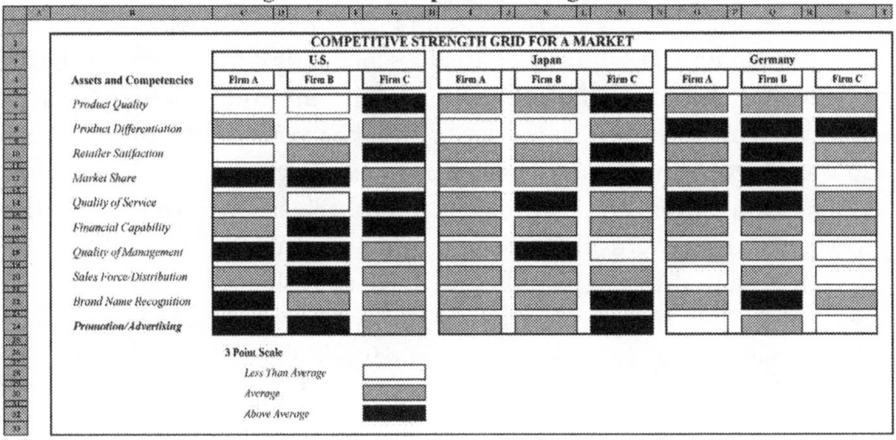

ADVERTISING SCHEDULING

An important decision in developing a promotion strategy is the choice of appropriate media to carry the company's message to its target customers. The media selected must be capable of carrying through the objectives of the promotion strategy—informing, persuading, and reminding the target audience of the product, service, or message being promoted (see Boone & Kurtz, 2001, pp. 506-508).

Once the media that best match the objectives of the firm and its promotional budget are selected, attention should be directed to media scheduling. For example, in an advertising campaign, setting the timing and sequence for a series of advertisements is important because a variety of factors such as sales patterns, repurchase cycles, and competitors' reactions influence this decision.

In many industries such as sporting goods, summer wear, and heating products, seasonal sales patterns are quite common. Repurchase cycles also affect the timing and sequence of media scheduling. Products with shorter repurchase cycles, such as batteries, soaps, and most durables, will require more frequent media schedules throughout the year. Competitors' actions also affect media schedules. A small firm, for example, may more likely follow its larger competitors or may decide to completely avoid advertising during periods of heavy advertising by its larger competitors.

Figure 12.12 depicts a hypothetical media schedule for introduction of a new product. It is assumed that the product is introduced in November with a direct-mail campaign, informing potential customers about this product, followed by outdoor advertising to support the direct-mail campaign. The firm increases its spending during holiday specials in December.

Figure 12.12. Media Advertising Schelue

Hypothetical Media Schedule for a New Product Introduction

Medium	Jan	Feb	Mar	Apr	May	June	July	Aug	Sept	Oct	Nov	Dec
Direct Mail											$150	
Outdoor Advertisig										$60	$40	$30
Newspaper	$30	$35	$40	$46	$60	$60	$45	$45	$68	$68	$75	$65
Television	$30	$35	$40	$99	$55	$65	$30	$35	$45	$50	$70	$60
Holiday Special												$129
Selected Shows	$1,120	$209	$259	$250	$160	$320	$200	$250	$200	$340	$300	$150
Football	$450									$800	$400	$700
Baseball	$550		$150	$205	$150	$150	$150	$206	$166	$400	$150	
Magazine				$170	$175	$235	$368	$300				
Magazine 1	$13	$28	$36	$34	$35	$45	$50	$45	$35	$45	$38	$35
Magazine 2	$15	$45	$15	$17	$15	$15	$15	$15	$35	$30	$40	$60
Magazine3	$10	$10	$10	$10	$10	$10	$10	$10	$10	$10	$10	$10
Semi-Monthly Ad. Budget:	$650	$295	$591	$478	$554	$668	$733	$555	$408	$1,395	$1,237	$1,480
Monthly Ad. Budget:	$1,410	$624	$1,069	$960	$1,159	$1,323	$1,433	$1,130	$888	$3,018	$2,392	$2,760
Total Yearly Ad. Budget:						$18,166						

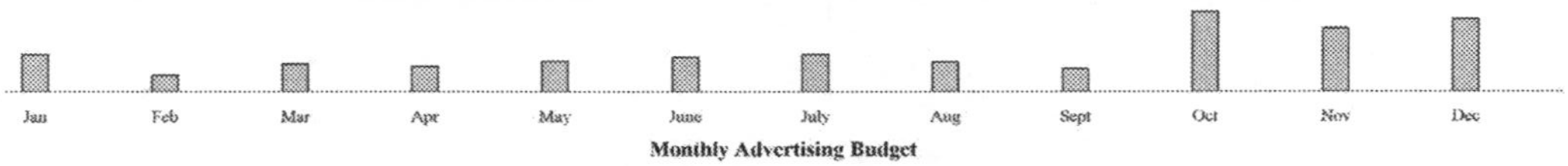

Monthly Advertising Budget

	Jan	Feb	Mar	Apr	May	June	July	Aug	Sept	Oct	Nov	Dec

COMPUTER ASSIGNMENT

PURPOSE

The purpose of this assignment is two-fold:

1. To learn/review some of Business/Marketing Analysis techniques
2. To use some of the features of Excel's Drawing Toolbar

INSTRUCTIONS

1. Use Excel's Drawing Toolbar to prepare a Product/Market Growth Strategies quadrant as in Figure 12.5.
2. Use Excel's Drawing Toolbar to prepare a BCG Growth Share Matrix as in Figure 12.10.
3. Prepare a Media Advertising Schedule as in Figure 12.12.
4. Print your results.
5. Prepare a report and explain all the steps and procedures that were used.

CHAPTER 13

Frequency Distributions and Descriptive Summary Measures of Data

FREQUENCY DISTRIBUTIONS

A SERIES OF OBSERVATIONS collected by an investigator is referred to as raw or ungrouped data. In order to make the task of interpreting raw data easier, a frequency distribution is constructed. A frequency distribution is a table that groups data into a series of classes and shows the number of observations from the data set that fall into each of the classes. The number of observations in a given class is called the frequency of that class.

In order to summarize data into a frequency distribution, we need to establish the number of classes and class widths. The class width is the difference between the upper and lower class limits. The center of a class, called class midpoint, can be found by summing the lower and upper class limits and dividing the result by two. It is usually best if all the classes have the same width.

Procedure

To construct a frequency distribution table, the following steps must be taken.

1. Decide on how many classes you want to use. The number of classes should be small enough to make the task of interpreting the data

effective, yet large enough to avoid losing important information. As a rule of thumb, the number of classes should be between 5 and 20.

2. Sort the data in ascending (from the smallest to the largest) order. An ordered sequence of data is called an ordered array.
3. Determine the range by finding the difference between the largest value and the smallest value:

$$Range = Highest\ Value - Lowest\ Value$$

4. Determine the width of class intervals by dividing the number of classes into range:

$$Class\ Width = \frac{Range}{Number\ of\ Classes}$$

The following formula, developed by Sturges, gives an alternative suggested class width:

$$Suggested\ Class\ Width = \frac{Range}{1 + 3.322\log_{10}(Total\ Freq.)} = \frac{Range}{1 + 1.443\ \mathrm{1n}_e(Total\ Freq.)}$$

5. The answer in step 4 should be rounded. Using the class width determined in step 4, determine the class limits by starting with the smallest value in the data set.
6. Count the number of observations that fall into each class. This number is the frequency of that class.
7. Divide the frequency in each class by the total number of observations to obtain the relative frequency of that class.
8. Construct the frequency and relative frequency distribution table by listing the class intervals in one column and their respective frequencies in another column.

DESCRIPTIVE SUMMARY MEASURES OF UNGROUPED DATA

MEASURES OF LOCATION

The Mean

The mean is found by summing all the observations and dividing the total by the number of observations. Therefore, the mean can be expressed as:

$$\bar{X} = \frac{\sum X_i}{n} = \frac{X_1 + X_2 + \ldots + X_n}{n}$$

where:

$\bar{X}$ = *sample arithmetic mean*
X_i = *individual observations*
n = *sample size*

The Median

The median is the observation in the middle of an ordered data set. If $X_1, X_2, \ldots, X_n$ represent a random sample of size n, then the median is computed as follows:

$$M_d = X_{(n + 1)/2} \qquad \textit{if n is odd}$$

and

$$M_d = \frac{X_{n/2} + X_{n/2 + 1}}{2} \qquad \textit{if n is even}$$

Quartiles

The quartiles divide the ordered data array into four quarters. The first quartile, Q_1, is the value where 1/4 of the observations are smaller and 3/4 of the observations are larger than it.

$$Q_1 = value\ corresponding\ to\ the\ \frac{n+1}{4}\ ordered\ observation$$

The second quartile, Q_2, is the value in the middle of the ordered array—1/2 of the observations are smaller and 1/2 of the observations are larger. The second quartile is also called the median.

$$Q_2 = value\ corresponding\ to\ the\ \frac{2(n+1)}{4}\ ordered\ observation$$

The third quartile, Q_3, is the score such that 3/4 of the observations are below it and 1/4 of the observations are above it.

$$Q_3 = value\ corresponding\ to\ the\ \frac{3(n+1)}{4}\ ordered\ observation$$

The Mode

The mode is defined as the most commonly observed value in the sample. It is the observation with the highest frequency of occurrence. Some populations may have more than one mode, and they are called multi-modal distributions. The mode can easily be found from an ordered array.

MEASURES OF DISPERSION

The Range

The range is the difference between the largest and smallest observations in a set of data, and can easily be obtained from an ordered array:

$$Range = Maximum - Minimum$$

The range is affected by extreme observations and is generally not considered to be a very good measure of dispersion.

The Inter-quartile Range

The inter-quartile range is another measure of dispersion in the data set, and is computed by the following formula:

$$\textit{Inter-quartile Range} = \textit{Third Quartile} - \textit{First Quartile} = Q_3 - Q_1$$

The inter-quartile range is not affected by extreme observations in the data set.

The Variance and Standard Deviation

The variance measures the average of the squared differences between each observation and the mean. The formula for sample variance is

$$S^2 = \frac{\sum_{i=1}^{n}(X_i - \bar{X})^2}{n-1} = \frac{\sum_{i=1}^{n}X_i^2 - \dfrac{\left(\sum_{i=1}^{n}X_i\right)^2}{n}}{n-1}$$

and the formula for standard deviation is

$$S = \sqrt{\frac{\sum_{i=1}^{n}(X_i - \bar{X})^2}{n-1}}$$

where:

$$\begin{aligned}
\bar{X} &= \textit{sample mean} \\
S^2 &= \textit{sample variance} \\
S &= \textit{sample standard deviation} \\
X_i &= \textit{individual observations}
\end{aligned}$$

The Coefficient of Variation

The coefficient of variation is defined as the ratio of the standard deviation to the arithmetic mean of the sample of observations, and is expressed by

$$CV = \frac{S}{\overline{X}} \times 100\%$$

where:

$\overline{X}$ = *sample mean*
CV = *coefficient of variation*
S = *sample standard deviation*

The coefficient of variation is a relative measure, and is expressed as a percentage rather than the units of the particular data.

MEASURES OF SHAPE (SKEWNESS)

Another important characteristic of a set of observations is its shape. A frequency distribution that is symmetrical has no skewness. If the distribution is not symmetrical, it is said to be skewed. Skewness refers to the lack of symmetry in a frequency distribution. A formula was developed by Karl Pearson to measure the amount and direction of skewness:

$$S_k = \frac{3\,(\overline{X} - M_d)}{S}$$

where:

$\overline{X}$ = *sample mean*
S_k = *coefficient of skewness*
M_d = *sample median*
S = *sample standard deviation*

This coefficient generally falls between -3 and $+3$. The sign and magnitude of the coefficient determine the degree and direction of skewness:

If $S_k > 0$,   the distribution is positively skewed or skewed to the right
If $S_k = 0$,   the distribution is symmetrical or has zero skewness
If $S_k < 0$,   the distribution is negatively skewed or skewed to the left

DESCRIPTIVE SUMMARY MEASURES OF GROUPED DATA

If original (raw) data are not available and it is necessary to obtain descriptive summary measures from grouped data, only approximations of these measures can be obtained. The following sections describe the approximation methods for the mean, the median, the variance, and the standard deviation of grouped data.

Approximating the Mean

The mean of grouped data can be approximated by the following formula:

$$\bar{X} \approx \frac{\sum_{i=1}^{c} f_i \cdot m_i}{n}$$

where:

$$
\begin{aligned}
\bar{X} &= \text{sample mean} \\
S^2 &= \text{sample variance} \\
c &= \text{number of classes} \\
f_i &= \text{frequency of the } i^{th} \text{ class} \\
m_i &= \text{midpoint of the } i^{th} \text{ class} \\
n &= \text{sample size}
\end{aligned}
$$

Approximating the Median

For grouped data, the median can be approximated by

$$M_d = L + \frac{\frac{n}{2} - F}{f} \cdot W$$

where:

M_d = *median*
L = *lower limit of the median class*
n = *total number of observations*
F = *cumulative frequency before the median class*
f = *frequency of the median class*
W = *class width*

Approximating the Quartiles

The formulas for the first and third quartiles of grouped data are similar to the formula for the median:

$$Q_1 \approx L_1 + \frac{\frac{n}{4} - F_1}{f_1} \cdot W$$

where:

Q_1 = *the first quartile*
L_1 = *lower limit of the first quartile class*
n = *sample size*
F_1 = *cumulative frequency before the first quartile class*
f_1 = *frequency f the first quartile class*
W = *class width*

and

$$Q_3 \approx L_3 + \frac{\frac{3n}{4} - F_3}{f_3} \cdot W$$

where:

Q_3 = *the third quartile*
L_3 = *lower limit of the third quartile class*
n = *sample size*

F_3 = *cumulative frequency before the third quartile class*
f_3 = *frequency of the third quartile class*
W = *class width*

Approximating the Variance and the Standard Deviation

To obtain an approximation for the variance and standard deviation of grouped data, the following formulae can be used:

$$S^2 \approx \frac{\sum_{i=1}^{c}(m_i - \bar{X})^2 \cdot f_i}{n - 1}$$

and

$$S \approx \sqrt{\frac{\sum_{i=1}^{c}(m_i - \bar{X})^2 \cdot f_i}{n - 1}}$$

where:

$\bar{X}$ = *sample mean*
S^2 = *sample variance*
S = *sample standard deviation*
c = *number of classes*
m_i = *midpoint of the ith class*
f_i = *frequency of the ith class*
n = *total number of observations*

EXERCISE 13.1
(Ungrouped Data)

1. For the following observations:

    97 93 92 89 87 85 85 84 82 79
    78 78 76 76 76 76 75 72 70 69
    67 67 67 67 67 66 66 66 66 65
    64 63 63 63 63 62 61 60 60 60
    57 57 56 55 53 50 47 45 43 35

    a. Calculate the median.
    b. Calculate the mode.
    c. Calculate the first, second, and third quartiles.

2. Calculate the standard deviation of the following numbers:

    5

    8

    12

    15

    20

EXERCISE 13.2
(Grouped Observations)

Given the following table:

Age	Freq.
20-30	10
30-40	20
40-50	22
50-60	8

a. Calculate the mean.
b. Calculate the standard deviation.
c. Calculate the median.
d. Calculate the third quartile.
e. Calculate the 20th percentile.
f. Calculate the 90th percentile.

COMPUTER ASSIGNMENT

- Collect 50 to 100 numerical data. The data can be from published sources or from a survey.
- Enter the observations in one column of an Excel worksheet.
- Sort the data in ascending order.
- Construct a frequency distribution table.
- Construct two (less-than and greater-than) cumulative frequency distribution tables.
- Use the frequency tables to plot a frequency Histogram and two Ogives.
- Calculate the Mean, Median, Third Quartile, and the Standard Deviation of the distribution.
- Print your results.
- Prepare a report summarizing all the steps.

PROCEDURE TO DO THE ASSIGNMENT

For the purpose of demonstrating this assignment, assume you are asked to conduct a survey to evaluate the amount of rainfall in California in the previous year. You obtain the average rainfall in the last twelve months for 60 randomly selected cities in California. The results of the survey are summarized in Table 13.1.

Table 13.1. Survey Results (inches of rain in 60 cities in California)									
5.9	7.7	8.9	5.2	7.3	7.7	6.3	7.3	5.7	5.6
5.6	6.7	6.9	7.0	7.3	6.2	6.5	6.5	9.2	7.1
4.1	4.9	7.5	7.5	9.6	7.9	5.3	5.5	6.1	6.1
8.3	8.1	8.1	4.5	7.3	9.4	5.8	6.7	6.7	6.9
6.9	7.1	6.9	7.7	7.7	8.1	8.7	6.5	6.7	9.1
7.1	6.3	5.1	7.3	8.3	8.9	9.3	5.7	6.0	5.9

$$\text{Suggested class width} = \frac{\text{Highest} - \text{Lowest}}{1 + 3.322 \cdot \text{Log}_{10} \text{ (total \# of observations)}}$$

or

$$\text{Suggested class width} = \frac{\text{Highest} - \text{Lowest}}{1 + 3.322 \cdot \text{Ln}_e \text{ (total \# of observations)}}$$

$$\text{Suggested class width} = \frac{9.6 - 4.1}{1 + 1.4427 \cdot \text{Ln} (60)} = \frac{5.5}{1 + 1.4427 \cdot (4.0943446)}$$

$$= \frac{5.5}{6.906911} = 0.796 \approx 1.0$$

By using the suggested class width, we can construct a tally table, as in Table 13.2.

Table 13.2. Tally Table	
Class Interval	**Tally Marks**
4.0 – 5.0	|||
5.0 – 6.0	₩₩ ₩₩	
6.0 – 7.0	₩₩ ₩₩ ₩₩ ||
7.0 – 8.0	₩₩ ₩₩ ₩₩	
8.0 – 9.0	₩₩ |||
9.0 – 10.0	₩₩

The results of the tally table can be summarized in a frequency distribution table, as in Table 13.3.

Table 13.3. Frequency Distribution				
Class Interval		**Frequency**	**Relative Freq.**	**Percentage Freq.**
4.0	– 5.0	3	0.050	5.0%
5.0	– 6.0	11	0.183	18.3
6.0	– 7.0	17	0.283	28.3
7.0	– 8.0	16	0.267	26.7
8.0	– 9.0	8	0.133	13.3
9.0	– 10.0	5	0.083	8.3
		60	1.000	100.0%

Next, we can construct a cumulative frequency distribution table, as in Table 13.4.

Table 13.4. Cumulative Frequency Distribution		
Class Limit	Less Than Cum. Freq.	Greater Than Cum. Freq.
4.0	0.0%	100.0%
5.0	5.0	95.0
6.0	23.3	76.7
7.0	51.7	48.3
8.0	78.3	21.7
9.0	91.7	8.3
10.0	100.0	0.0

Finally, the results of the frequency distribution and cumulative frequency distribution tables can be plotted, as in Figures 13.1 and 13.2.

Figure 13.1. Histogram

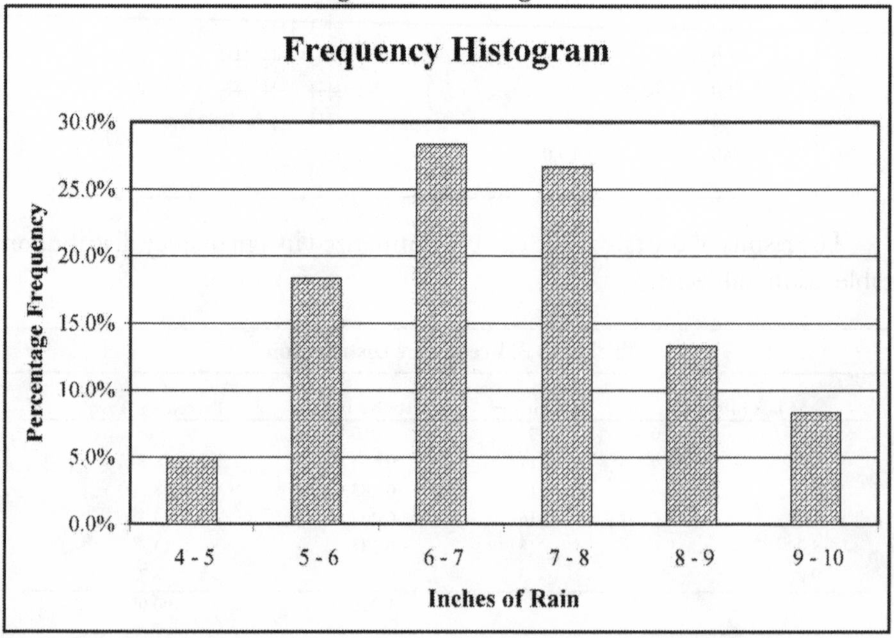

Figure 13.2. Ogives

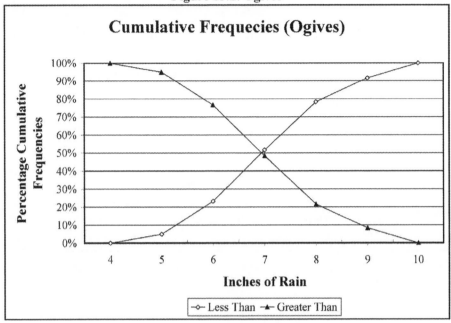

Next, we need to calculate some descriptive summary measures such as mean, median, standard deviation, and quartiles. The first step is to set up a table as in Table 13.5.

Table 13.5. Descriptive Summary Measures of Grouped Data

Class Interval			Frequency f_i	Midpoint m_i	$f_i \cdot m_i$	$(m_i - \bar{x})^2 \cdot f_i$	
4.0	–	5.0	3	4.5	13.5	18.75	
5.0	–	6.0	11	5.5	60.5	24.75	
6.0	**–**	**7.0**	**17**	**6.5**	**110.5**	**4.25**	<== Median class
7.0	**–**	**8.0**	**16**	**7.5**	**120.0**	**4.00**	<== Q3 class
8.0	–	9.0	8	8.5	68.0	18.00	
9.0	–	10.0	5	9.5	47.5	31.25	
			60		$\sum f_i \cdot m_i = 420.0$	$\sum (m_i - \bar{x})^2 \cdot f_i = 101.0$	

MEAN:

$$\bar{X} \approx \frac{420}{60} = 7$$

MEDIAN:

Step 1. Determine the median class by determining the value of n/2, 60 / 2
= 30
Step 2. Use the following formula to calculate the median:

$$Md \approx L + \frac{(n/2 - F)}{f} \cdot W$$

L = Lower limit of median class
F = Cumulative frequency before the median class
F = Frequency of the median class
W = Class width

$$Md \approx 6 + \frac{30 - 14}{17} \cdot 1 = 6 + 0.94 = 6.94$$

THIRD QUARTILE:

Step 1. Determine the median class by determining the value of 3n / 4, (3
* 60) / 4 = 45.
Step 2. Use the following formula to calculate the third quartile:

$$Q3 \approx L + \frac{(3n/4 - F)}{f} \cdot W$$

L = Lower limit of Q3 class
F = Cumulative frequency before the Q3 class
f = Frequency of the Q3 class
W = Class width

$$Q3 \approx 7 + \frac{43 - 31}{16} \cdot 1 = 7 + 0.875 = 7.875$$

VARIANCE AND STANDARD DEVIATION:

$$\text{VAR} \approx \frac{101}{60 - 1} = 1.712, \quad \text{STD} = 1.308$$

SOLVING THE PROBLEM USING EXCEL

Enter the raw data into the worksheet. In our problem we choose cells A7 through A66. Next, sort the data in ascending order so that cell A7 contains the smallest number, 4.1, and cell A66 contains the largest number, 9.6. You can now use Sturges' formula to calculate an approximate class width. This can be done anywhere in your worksheet (Table 13.6). The cell locations are irrelevant.

	Table 13.6. Sturges' Formula			
	D	**E**	**F**	**G**
2	**STURGES' FORMULA**			
3	**Approx. Class**	=(Hi - Lo) / [1 + 3.322 . Log (n)]		
4	**Class Width:**	0.796	rounded	1.000
5				0.999

The formula used in cell A67 is =COUNT(A7:A66), and the formula in E4 is =(A66-A7)/(1+3.322*LOG(A67)).

To create the frequency distribution table in Excel, we need to construct a column of "BIN" numbers. The "BIN" numbers are essentially the class intervals. This is demonstrated in Table 13.7.

Table 13.7. Bin #	
	C
9	**Bin**
10	4.000
11	4.999
12	5.000
13	5.999
14	6.000
15	6.999
16	7.000
17	7.999
18	8.000
19	8.999
20	9.000
21	9.999

To continue in Excel, make sure Analysis ToolPak, which is an Add-in program, has been installed. After the installation is complete, follow the steps below:

- Click on "TOOLS" and choose "DATA ANALYSIS".
- Click on "HISTOGRAM".
- The dialogue box in Figure 13.3 will appear.

Figure 13.3. Histogram Dialogue Box

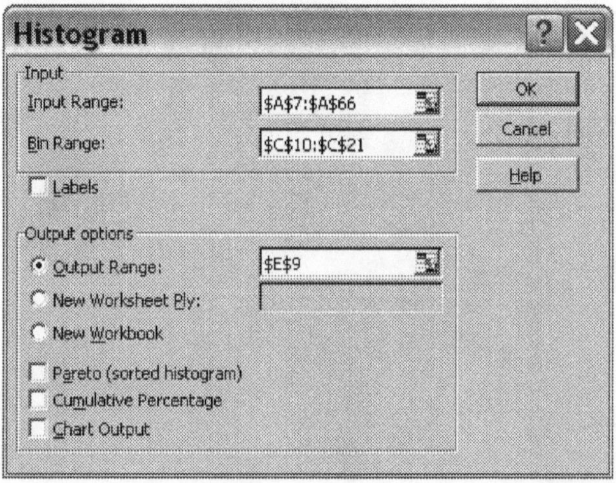

- Enter the "INPUT RANGE", cellsA7:A66.
- Enter the "BIN RANGE", cells C10:C21.
- Specify the OUTPUT RANGE, cell E9.
- Click on OK and Table 13.8 will appear.

Table 13.8. Frequency Numbers	
E	**F**
9 *Bin*	*Frequency*
10 4.000	0
11 4.999	3
12 5.000	0
13 5.999	11
14 6.000	1
15 6.999	16
16 7.000	1
17 7.999	15
18 8.000	0
19 8.999	8
20 9.000	0
21 9.999	5
22 more	0

We can use the numbers from the BIN table to construct a Relative Frequency Distribution table. This is done in Table 13.9.

Table 13.9. Cell Formulas for Frequency Distribution Table				
D	**E**	**F**	**G**	**H**
26	FREQUENCY DISTRIBUTION TABLE			
27	Classes		Freq. (f$_i$)	% Freq.
28 4	=D28+$G$4		=F10+F11	=G28/$G$34
29 =D28+$G$4	=D29+$G$4		=F12+F13	=G29/$G$34
30 =D29+$G$4	=D30+$G$4	Median class	=F14+F15	=G30/$G$34
31 =D30+$G$4	=D31+$G$4	Q$_3$ class	=F16+F17	=G31/$G$34
32 =D31+$G$4	=D32+$G$4		=F18+F19	=G32/$G$34
33 =D32+$G$4	=D33+$G$4		=F20+F21	=G33/$G$34
34		n =	=SUM(G28:G33)	=SUM(H28:H33)

The results of the frequency distribution table are displayed in Table 13.10.

Table 13.10. Frequency Distribution Table				
	D	**E**	**F**	**G**	**H**
26	FREQUENCY DISTRIBUTION TABLE				
27	Classes			Freq. (f$_i$)	% Freq.
28	4	5		3	5.0%
29	5	6		11	18.3%
30	6	7	Median class	17	28.3%
31	7	8	Q$_3$ class	16	26.7%
32	8	9		8	13.3%
33	9	10		5	8.3%
34			n =	60	100.0%

Similarly, we can build a Cumulative Frequency Distribution Table (Table 13.11).

Table 13.11. Cell Formulas for Cumulative Frequency			
	D	**E**	**F**	**G**
36	CUMULATIVE DISTRIBUTION TABLE			
37	Observation	Less Than		Greater Than
38	4	0		1
39	=D38+$G$4	=E38+H28		=G38-H28
40	=D39+$G$4	=E39+H29		=G39-H29
41	=D40+$G$4	=E40+H30		=G40-H30
42	=D41+$G$4	=E41+H31		=G41-H31
43	=D42+$G$4	=E42+H32		=G42-H32
44	=D43+$G$4	=E43+H33		=G43-H33

The results of the cumulative frequency distribution table are displayed in Table 13.12.

Table 13.12. Cumulative Frequency Table			
	D	**E**	**F**	**G**
36	CUMULATIVE DISTRIBUTION TABLE			
37	Observation	Less Than		Greater Than
38	4	0.0%		100.0%
39	5	5.0%		95.0%
40	6	23.3%		76.7%
41	7	51.7%		48.3%
42	8	78.3%		21.7%
43	9	91.7%		8.3%
44	10	100.0%		0.0%

The calculations of Mean, Standard Deviation, Median, and Third Quartile are demonstrated in Table 13.13.

Table 13.13. Cell Formula for Descriptive Summary Measures			
	J	**K**	**L**
25	DESCRIPTIVE SUMMARY MEASURES OF GROUPED DATA		
26	Midpoint		
27	m_i	$f_i \cdot m_i$	$(m_i - mean)^2 \cdot f_i$
28	=(E28+D28)/2	=J28*G28	=(J28-$K$35)^2*G28
29	=(E29+D29)/2	=J29*G29	=(J29-$K$35)^2*G29
30	=(E30+D30)/2	=J30*G30	=(J30-$K$35)^2*G30
31	=(E31+D31)/2	=J31*G31	=(J31-$K$35)^2*G31
32	=(E32+D32)/2	=J32*G32	=(J32-$K$35)^2*G32
33	=(E33+D33)/2	=J33*G33	=(J33-$K$35)^2*G33
34	Sum:	=SUM(K28:K33)	=SUM(L28:L33)
35	Mean:	=K34/G34	
36	Sand. Dev.:	=SQRT(L34/(G34-1))	
37	Median:	=D30+(G34/2-SUM(G28:G29))/G30*(E30-D30)	
38	Third Quartile:	=D31+(G34*3/4-SUM(G28:G30))/G31*(E31-D31)	

The results of the descriptive summary measures are displayed in Table 13.14.

Table 13.14. Descriptive Summary Measures		
J	K	L
25 DESCRIPTIVE SUMMARY MEASURES OF GROUPED DATA		
26 Midpoint		
27 m_i	$f_i \cdot m_i$	$(m_i - mean)^2 \cdot f_i$
28 4.5	13.50	18.75
29 5.5	65.50	24.75
30 6.5	110.50	4.25
31 7.5	120.00	4.00
32 8.5	68.00	18.00
33 9.5	47.50	31.25
34 Sum:	420.00	101
35 Mean:	7.000	
36 Sand. Dev.:	1.308	
37 Median:	6.941	
38 Third Quartile:	7.875	

CHAPTER 14

Resource Allocation Using Linear Programming

T HE ALLOCATION OF scarce resources among competing activities is one of the most fundamental problems in the successful management of an organization. Virtually all organizations are faced with making decisions regarding the allocation of limited resources such as raw materials, labor, machinery, money, and the like among competing projects. The objective of these organizations is to obtain the maximum possible outcome given the available resources. Linear programming is a mathematical technique designed to assist an organization in allocating its scarce resources. In this technique, the desired outcome is expressed as a mathematical formula which is the objective function. The available limited resources, also expressed in terms of mathematical relationships, are the constraints of the problem. The general idea is to maximize or minimize the objective function subject to the constraints.

All linear programming models have certain common components. These components include decision variables, an objective function, and structural constraints. The decision variables depend on the type of linear programming problem being solved. These variables represent levels of activities by an organization. They are the quantities of the limited resources to be allocated, or the number of units to be produced.

The objective function is a mathematical relationship that represents the objective of the organization in terms of the decision variables. It is the function that the linear programming model attempts to optimize. The objective function always involves maximizing or minimizing some value.

The constraints are relationships of the decision variables that represent the restrictions placed on the firm. They are mathematical inequalities that indicate the availability of scarce resources.

The term linear means that all mathematical relationships, the objective function and all the constraints, are linear. Models with linear objective functions and linear constraints are called linear programming models.

Mathematically, the linear programming model can be stated as

$$\textit{Maximize:} \quad Z = c_1 X_1 + c_2 X_2 + \dots + c_n X_n$$

or

$$\textit{Maximize:} \quad Z = \sum_{j=1}^{n} c_j X_j$$

subject to the linear constraints:

$$a_{11} X_1 + a_{12} X_2 + \dots + a_{1n} X_n \le b_1$$
$$a_{21} X_1 + a_{22} X_2 + \dots + a_{n2} X_n \le b_2$$

. .
. .
. .

$$a_{m1} X_1 + a_{m2} X_2 + \dots + a_{mn} X_n \le b_m$$

and the nonnegativity constraints:

$$X_1 \ge 0, \qquad X_2 \ge 0, \quad \dots \quad X_n \ge 0$$

or

$$\sum_{j=1}^{n} a_{ij} X_j \le b_j$$

and

$$X_j \ge 0, \qquad \textit{for } j = 1, 2, \dots, n$$

where:

c_j = *coefficient of the jth variable in the objective function*
X_j = *j^{th} decision variable*
a_{ij} = *coefficient of the jth variable in the ith constraint*
b_j = *right-hand-side constant for the ith constraint*
n = *number of decision variables*
m = *number of constraints*

PROCEDURE

The simplex method, developed by George Dantzig, is a technique used to find the optimal solution of a linear programming problem. It involves going from one solution to another in such a way that the objective function is successively improved until the optimal solution is achieved. The technique requires a number of steps. The first step is to set up the problem in the form of a table, known as the simplex tableau. The second step is to perform operations to the tableau reach the optimal solution. The method is summarized as follows.

1. To begin the simplex method, the constraints are converted from inequalities to linear equations by adding a nonnegative variable, called a slack variable, to each constraint.
2. The coefficients of the variables and the constants from the constraints are written in the form of an augmented matrix, called a simplex tableau.
3. The largest positive number in the bottom row is located. This number establishes the pivot column.
4. The ratios of the right-hand-side to the numbers in the pivot column are obtained. The smallest nonnegative quotient establishes the pivot row. If all quotients are negative, no maximum solution exists.
5. The intersection of the pivot row and column determines the pivot element.
6. By performing row operations, the tableau is transformed so that the pivot element becomes 1 and all other numbers in the pivot column become 0.
7. This is done until a tableau is obtained with no negative numbers in the bottom row.
8. The optimum solution is given by the entries in the last column and the optimum value of the objective function is given by the number in the lower right corner of the final simplex tableau.

SIMPLEX TABLEAU

It is convenient to write the linear programming problem in tableau form. The tableau form, shown in Table 14.1, combines the objective function and the constraints and provides a structure for solving the linear programming problem.

TABLE 14.1. SIMPLEX TABLEAU								
	X_1	X_2	...	X_n	S_1	S_2	...	S_m	RHS
S_1	a_{11}	a_{12}	...	a_{1n}	1	0	...	0	$b1$
S_2	a_{21}	a_{22}	...	a_{2n}	0	1	...	0	b_2
.	.		.	.	.		.	.
.	.		.	.	.		.	.
.	.		.	.	.		.	.
S_m	a_{m1}	a_{m2}	...	a_{mn}	0	0	...	1	b_m
	c_1	c_2	...	c_n	0	0	...	0	Z

MINIMIZATION PROBLEM

For every maximizing linear programming problem, there is a minimizing problem, called the dual problem, and vice versa. The dual of the above maximizing problem is written as:

Minimize: $W = b_1Y_1 + b_2Y_2 + ... + b_mY_m$
Subject to:

$$a_{11}Y_1 + a_{21}Y_2 + ... + a_{m1}Y_m \geq c_1$$
$$a_{12}Y_1 + a_{22}Y_2 + ... + a_{m2}Y_m \geq c_2$$
$$.$$
$$.$$
$$.$$
$$a_{1n}Y_1 + a_{2n}Y_2 + ... + a_{mn}Y_m \geq c_n$$

and the nonnegativity constraints:

$$Y_1 \geq 0 \, Y_2 \geq 0 ... Y_m \geq 0$$

where:

$$Y_i = i^{th} \text{ decision variable}$$

The minimization problems can also be solved using the simplex method. The steps required are summarized in the following:

1. The dual maximizing problem is constructed.
2. The maximizing problem is solved using the simplex method.
3. The minimum value of the objective function W is equal to the maximum value of the objective function Z.
4. The optimal solution is given by the last-row entries in the columns corresponding to the slack variables.

EXERCISE 14.1
RESOURCE ALLOCATION PROBLEMS

1. A firm makes two products, type A and type B. Each product requires
    10 hours in Department I. Each unit of product A requires 4 hours in
    Department II, and each unit of product B requires 8 hours in Department
    II. The maximum hours of labor available are 160 hours in Department
    I and 80 hours in Department II per day. The firm earns a profit of $3
    per unit of product A and a profit of $4 per unit of product B. Assume
    that it is possible to sell all units produced each day. Find the levels of
    production that will maximize profit.

2. A company produces two types of USB devices, a standard model and an
    advanced model. The profit per unit of the standard model is $5 and the
    profit per unit of the advanced model is $8. The marketing department
    estimates that, at most, 1000 devices per week can be sold by the sales
    staff. Because of the rapid growth of the industry, there is a shortage of
    both skilled labor and electronic circuits necessary to assemble these
    devices. Each regular device requires 3 of these electronic circuits and 3
    hours of labor for assembly. Each advanced model requires 6 electronic
    circuits and 2 hours of labor for assembly. There is only a weekly supply
    of 5000 electronic circuits available. Furthermore, the company has only
    2500 hours of skilled labor available per week. How many devices of each
    type should be made each week in order to maximize total profit?

EXERCISE 14.2
TRANSPORTATION PROBLEM

Grain Warehouse	*Supply*	*Mill*	*Demand*
1. Kansas City	160 Tons	1. Chicago	220 Tons
2. Omaha	180	2. St. Louis	110
3. Tulsa	260	3. Cincinnati	270

Table 14.2. Transportation Costs Per Ton			
	Chicago	St. Louis	Cincinnati
Kansas City	$6	$7	$9
Omaha	8	9	10
Tulsa	5	6	11

Write this problem as a linear programming problem (DO NOT SOLVE) to minimize the total transportation cost and satisfy all demand and supply constraints.

EXERCISE 14.3
PRODUCTION PROBLEMS

1. An ice making company is planning for a demand of 3000 hours of labor in May, 5000 hours in June, 5500 hours in July, and 4000 hours in August. The company has 50 experienced workers available on May 1. Each worker averages 160 hours of productive work per month. Newly hired employees must be trained for one month, so that during their first month they do not provide any productive time. Furthermore, training reduces an experienced worker's productive time by 30 hours a month. There is a turnover of 10 percent among the experienced workers, and all new employees give at least one month of productive service. There are no layoffs. An experienced service person is paid $2,500 a month, while a new employee is paid $1,500 a month. Formulate (**do not solve**) a linear programming model to determine the number of new employees that must be hired in May, June, and July.

2. A company manufactures 10-inch LCD color television sets and has received orders for 1700 units to be delivered in the first quarter and 2100 units to be delivered in the second quarter. Each unit requires a circuit board that is produced "in house" or can be purchased from a subcontractor. The cost to manufacture in house is $500.00 and remains the same for the next quarter. Subcontracting costs are currently $550 for units produced in the first quarter, and will increase to $650 for the second quarter. Due to obsolescence, the inventory cost to keep a circuit board from the first quarter to the second quarter is high and is estimated to be $120.00. The company's production capacity is 1900 units per quarter. The Subcontractor can provide 350 units in the first quarter and 425 in the second quarter. Formulate a linear programming model (**do not solve**) to plan production for the two quarters. Assume no beginning or ending inventory levels.

COMPUTER ASSIGNMENT

1. A company manufactures two products, A and B. Each unit of product A requires 5 hours of assembly and 2 hours of finishing. Each unit of product B requires 3 hours for assembly and 4 hours for finishing. The company has 105 hours available per week on the assembly line and 70 hours available in the finishing department. The profit per unit is $200 for product A and $160 for product B. Assuming that the company can sell all the products that it can produce in a week, find the number of units of each type that should be produced per week to maximize the total profit?

2. A company is designing a plant for producing two types of product, X and Y. After extensive marketing research, the company has decided that the plant must be capable of producing at least 100 units of X and 420 units of Y per day. Two possible machines are to be included in the plant, machine A and B. Each machine A costs $600,000 and is capable of producing 10 units of X and 20 units of Y per day; machine B is a lower-price design, costing $300,000 and capable of producing 4 units of X and 30 units of Y per day. Because of operating costs, it is necessary to have at least 4 of each machine in the plant. How many units of machine A and machine B should be included in the plant to minimize the cost of construction and still meet the required production plan?

3. A company sells two different types of health beverage. The lower cost brand contains 80 % orange juice and 20 % grapefruit juice, and the more expensive brand contains 50% of each type of juice. Each week the company can obtain up to 1800 gallons of orange juice and up to 1200 gallons of grapefruit juice. The profit per gallon is 10¢ for the lower cost brand and 15¢ for the more expensive brand. How many gallons of each beverage should be produced in order to maximize total profit?

4. A manufacturer makes two products, A and B, each of which requires time in three different departments. Each unit of A requires 2 hours in department I, 4 hours in department II, and 3 hours in department III. Each unit of product B requires 5 hours in department I, 1 hour in department II, and 2 hours in department III. The company makes profits of $250 per unit of product A and $300 per unit of product B. The hours available in each department per month are 200, 240, and 190, respectively. Find how many units of each product must be produced to maximize total profit.

SOLVING LINEAR PROGRAMMING PROBLEMS WITH EXCEL

In a resource allocation problem, our intention is to either maximize a variable (e.g., Profits or sales) or minimize a variable (e.g., costs). We will use Problem 1 from the Computer Assignment section to demonstrate the solution to a linear programming problem using Excel. The procedure consists of four steps:

1. Define the problem in terms of variables.
2. Summarize the given information in a table.
3. Translate the information into mathematical equations: an objective function and several constraints.
4. Solve the problem with "SOLVER", which is an add-in program in Excel and requires installation.

In this problem, product A requires 5 hours for assembly and 2 hours for finishing. Product B requires 3 hours for assembly and 4 hours for finishing. There are 105 hours of assembly and 70 hours of finishing time available per week. The firm makes profits of $200 per unit of A and $160 per unit of B.

To solve the problem in Excel, we need to follow the steps described below:

1. We set up the problem as follows:

$$\text{Max} \quad Z = 200X_1 + 160X_2$$
$$\text{S.T.}$$
$$5X_1 + 3X_2 <= 105$$
$$2X_1 + 4X_2 <= 70$$

2. We then enter the coefficients of the objective function and the constraints into an Excel worksheet, as in Table 14.3.

Table 14.3. Problem #1			
B	**C**	**D**	**E**
7	Product A	Product B	Max Available
8 Assembly	5	3	105
9 Finishing	2	4	70
10 Profit per Unit	$200	$160	

3. Then we need to enter the formulas for the objective and constraints into cells D16, D18, and D19, as in Table 14.4.

    •   The objective function in D16 will be:
        =$C$10*D13+$D$10*D14.

    •   The constraints in cells D 18 and D 19 will be given by:
        D18: =$C$8*D13+$D$8*D14 and D19:
        =$C$9*D13+$D$9*D14

Table 14.4. Cell Formulas for the Linear Programming Problem			
B	**C**	**D**	**E**
1	Solving Linear Programming Problems Using Excel "Solver"		
2			
3	Max	Z = 200 X1 + 160 X2	
4	S.T.	5 X1 + 3 X2 <= 105	
5		2 X1 + 4 X2 <= 70	
6			
7	**Product A**	**Product B**	**Max Available**
8 Assembly:	5	3	105
9 Finishing:	2	4	70
10 Profit:	200	160	
11			
12			
13	x1 =	0	
14	x2 =	0	
15			
16 Objective Function:		=$C$10*D13+$D$10*D14	
17			
18 Constraint 1:		=$C$8*D13+$D$8*D14	
19 Constraint 2:		=$C$9*D13+$D$9*D14	

4. Under Tools in Excel, select Solver. The dialogue box in Figure 14.1 will appear.

Figure 14.1. Solver Dialogue Box

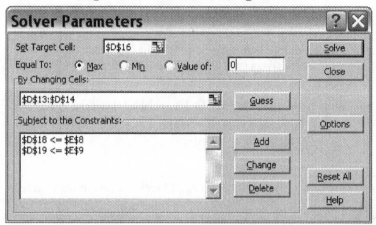

5. "SET TARGET CELL": click on cell containing the objective function formula, $D$16

6. "EQUAL TO": Max

7. "BY CHANGING CELLS": click/drag across the cells containing the decision variables, $D13:$D14

8. "SUBJECT TO THE CONSTRAINTS": enter the constraints by first clicking the 'Add . . .' button and enter the following:

$D$18 <= $E$8
$D$19 <= $E$9

9. Having added all the constraints, click "OK" and then click on "SOLVE."

The results of the linear programming problem will appear, as in Table 14.5.

Table 14.5. Solution to the Linear Programming Problem

	B	C	D	E
1		Solving Linear Programming Problems Using Excel "Solver"		
2				
3			Max $Z = 200\,X1 + 160\,X2$	
4			S.T. $5\,X1 + 3\,X2 <= 105$	
5			$2\,X1 + 4\,X2 <= 70$	
6				
7		Product A	Product B	Max Available
8	Assembly:	5	3	105
9	Finishing:	2	4	70
10	Profit:	$200	$160	
11				
12				
13		x1 =	15	
14		x2 =	10	
15				
16	Objective Function:		$4,600	
17				
18	Constraint 1:		105	
19	Constraint 2:		70	

CHAPTER 15

Simple Linear Regression and Correlation Analysis

S IMPLE REGRESSION ANALYSIS is a technique used to determine the relationship between two variables. The goal is to develop a statistical equation that can predict the value of one variable, the dependent variable, given the value of the other variable, the independent variable. By employing regression analysis, we can also find the direction and amount of change that can be expected in one variable when another variable changes by a given amount.

Correlation analysis, on the other hand, is used to compute the coefficient of correlation, a measure of the strength of the linear relationship between the two variables.

PROCEDURE

A simple linear regression model can be expressed as:

$$Y_i = B_0 + B_1 X_i + E_i$$

where:

Y_i = *value of the dependent variable for the ith observation*
X_i = *value of the independent variable for the ith observation*
B_0 = *true value of the intercept for the population*
B_1 = *true value of the slope for the population*
E_i = *random error for the ith observation*

The four general assumptions of linear regression are:

1. The error terms are normally distributed.
2. The error terms have a mean of zero.
3. The variance of the error terms is constant (homoscedasticity).
4. The error terms are independent of one another.

The regression parameters, B_0 and B_1, are estimated by sample intercept, b_0, and sample slope, b_1. The sample regression equation may be written as:

$$\hat{Y}_i = b_0 + b_1 X_i$$

where:

$$\hat{Y}_i = \text{\textit{predicted value of Y for the } } i^{th} \text{ \textit{observation}}$$

The values of b_0 and b_1 are determined by the method of least-squares. The least-squares method produces the line for which the sum of squared vertical distances of the observations from the line is a minimum. The least-squares method yields the following results:

$$b_1 = \frac{\displaystyle\sum_{i=1}^{n} X_i Y_i - \frac{\left(\displaystyle\sum_{i=1}^{n} X_i\right)\left(\displaystyle\sum_{i=1}^{n} Y_i\right)}{n}}{\displaystyle\sum_{i=1}^{n} X_i^2 - \frac{\left(\displaystyle\sum_{i=1}^{n} X_i\right)^2}{n}}$$

and

$$b_0 = \bar{Y} - b_1 \bar{X} = \frac{\displaystyle\sum_{i=1}^{n} Y_i}{n} - \frac{\displaystyle\sum_{i=1}^{n} X_i}{n}$$

The variance and standard deviation of the error term may be estimated by the following formulas:

$$S^2 = \frac{\sum_{i=1}^{n} (Y_i - \hat{Y}_i)^2}{n - 2}$$

and

$$S = \sqrt{\frac{\sum_{i=1}^{n} (Y_i - \hat{Y}_i)^2}{n - 2}}$$

where:

$\hat{Y}_i$ = *predicted value of Y for a given* X_i
Y_i = *true value of Y for a given* X_i
S = *standard error of estimate*
n = *number of observations in the sample*

It can easily be proven that

$$\sum_{i=1}^{n} (Y_i - \hat{Y}_i)^2 = \sum_{i=1}^{n} Y_i^2 - b_0 \sum_{i=1}^{n} Y_i - b_1 \sum_{i=1}^{n} X_i Y_i$$

Thus

$$S = \sqrt{\frac{\sum_{i=1}^{n} Y_i^2 - b_0 \sum_{i=1}^{n} Y_i - b_1 \sum_{i=1}^{n} X_i Y_i}{n - 2}}$$

The following test is used to check whether the relationship between X and Y is statistically significant:

$$t = \frac{b_1}{S_{b_1}}, \qquad n - 2 \ degrees \ of \ freedom$$

where S_{b1}, the estimate of the standard error of the slope, is obtained by:

$$S_{b_1} = \frac{S}{\sqrt{\sum_{i=1}^{n} X_i^2 - \frac{(\sum_{i=1}^{n} X_i)^2}{n}}}$$

Often analysis of variance (ANOVA) is used to analyze the quality of the estimated regression line. Conventionally, the total variation in Y is subdivided into components:

$$SST \quad = \quad SSR + SSE$$

where:

$$SST \quad = \quad \textit{total sum of squares}$$
$$SSR \quad = \quad \textit{regression sum of squares}$$
$$SSE \quad = \quad \textit{sum of squares error}$$

The sums of squares are computed as follows:

$$SST = \sum_{i=1}^{n} (Y_i - \bar{Y})^2$$

$$SSR = \sum_{i=1}^{n} (\hat{Y}_i - \bar{Y})^2$$

$$SSE = \sum_{i=1}^{n} (Y_i - \hat{Y}_i)^2$$

The goodness of the regression equation is determined by the coefficient of determination, R^2 (R is the coefficient of correlation), and the significance of the entire model is determined by the F test:

$$R^2 = \frac{SSR}{SST} \qquad and \qquad F = \frac{MSR}{MSE}$$

where:

$$MSR = \frac{SSR}{1} \qquad and \qquad MSE = \frac{SSE}{n-2}$$

The results of the sum of squares may be summarized in an analysis of variance (ANOVA) table, as shown in Table 15.1.

Table 15.1. Analysis of Variance Table for Simple Regression				
Source of Variation	Sum of Squares	Degrees of Freedom	Mean Square	F-Ratio
Regression:	SSR	1	MSR	F=MSR / MSE
Error:	SSE	n - 2	MSE	
Total:	SST	n - 1		

The aptness of the fitted equation can also be determined with the help of residual plots. The residual may be defined as the difference between the observed value and predicted value of the dependent variable for given values of the independent variable:

$$e_i = Y_i - \hat{Y}_i$$

The residual is usually plotted on the vertical axis against both the dependent and independent variables. If the hypothesized model is appropriate, no pattern will be apparent in the residual plot.

If residuals in a time series analysis are correlated, it is said that there is the problem of autocorrelation of the residuals. If autocorrelation is present, the regression equation should not be used to make forecasts. The Durbin-Watson test is a widely-used test to determine whether autocorrelation exits. The Durbin-Watson statistic is computed as follows.

$$D = \frac{\sum_{i=1}^{n} (e_t - e_{t-1})}{\sum_{i=1}^{n} e_t^2}$$

where: D =   *Durbin-Watson test statistics*
          e_t =   *residuals at time period t*
          e_{t-1} =   *residual at time period t-1*

The creators of this test have provided tables to examine, for specified significance levels, sample sizes, and numbers of independent variables, the null hypothesis that no serial correlation exists.

COMPUTER ASSIGNMENT

The percentage of people unemployed and the interest rate on treasury bills offered by the federal government are given in Table 15.2.

| Table 15.2. Initial Data ||
Unemployment Rate (%)	Treasury Bill Interest Rate (%)
4.4	8.1
7.8	9.8
4.7	8.2
5.0	8.4
3.9	7.9
5.1	8.3
9.5	10.2
8.8	10.0
4.5	8.4
5.0	8.5
10.2	10.2
9.0	10.1
6.0	8.8
5.0	8.3
9.5	10.1
13.4	10.7
15.0	11.4
4.0	7.8

1. Develop a linear regression model with unemployment rate as the dependent variable and treasury rate as the dependent variable. Can it be concluded that the linear regression model is statistically significant? Test at the alpha level of 0.05.
2. Plot the results. Describe the regression line.
3. Determine what appropriate transformation should be made to the independent variable to improve the regression results. Make this transformation and compute the new regression equation. Perform any necessary statistical tests using an alpha level of 0.05
4. Write a short report explaining the regression results obtained in part 1 with those obtained in part 3.

REGRESSION SOLUTION USING EXCEL

Enter the dependent and independent variables into Excel worksheet, as in Table 15.3.

Table 15.3. Data for Regression Problem	
B	**C**
LINEAR REGRESSION	
Unemployment Rate (%)	Treasury Bill Rate (%)
Y	X
4.4	8.1
7.8	9.8
4.7	8.2
5.0	8.4
3.9	7.9
5.1	8.3
9.5	10.2
8.8	10.0
4.5	8.4
5.0	8.5
10.2	10.2
9.0	10.1
6.0	8.8
5.0	8.3
9.5	10.1
13.4	10.7
15.0	11.4
4.0	7.8

In order to get the solution to this regression problem in Excel, we need to do the following steps:

- Click on "TOOLS".
- Click on "DATA ANALYSIS" from the menu.
- Click on "REGRESSION".
- The dialogue box in Figure 15.1 will appear.

Figure 15.1. Regression Dialogue Box

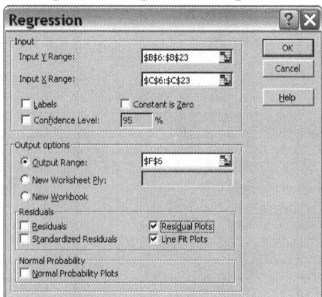

- Specify the values of the independent variable (X), cells C6:C23.
- Specify the values of dependent variable (Y), cells B6:B23.
- It is also a good idea to specify where you want the output to appear. If you do not specify the output area, Excel will put it on top of your input area and erase your input.
- After you are finished, click "OK". The results in Tables 15.4, 15.5, and 15.6 will be displayed.
- Perform a square transformation on the independent variable (X) and repeat the above procedure for the new regression line.

Table 15.4. Regression Results	
SUMMARY OUTPUT	
Regression Statistics	
Multiple R	0.973125087
R Square	0.946972434
Adjusted R Square	0.943658212
Standard Error	0.788972329
Observations	18

Table 15.5. ANOVA Table

ANALYSIS OF VARIANCE (ANOVA) TABLE				
	df	*SS*	*MS*	*F*
Regression	1	177.8603626	177.8603626	285.7298611
Residual	16	9.959637368	0.622477336	
Total	17	187.82		
	Coefficients	*Standard Error*	*t Stat*	*P-value*
Intercept	-19.37255789	1.586888679	-12.20788714	1.60358E-09
X Variable 1	2.902578947	0.171714206	16.90354582	1.25777E-11

Table 15.6. Residual Results		
RESIDUAL OUTPUT		
Observation	Predicted Y	Residuals
1	4.138331579	0.261668421
2	9.072715789	-1.272715789
3	4.428589474	0.271410526
4	5.009105263	-0.009105263
5	3.557815789	0.342184211
6	4.718847368	0.381152632
7	10.23374737	-0.733747368
8	9.653231579	-0.853231579
9	5.009105263	-0.509105263
10	5.299363158	-0.299363158
11	10.23374737	-0.033747368
12	9.943489474	-0.943489474
13	6.170136842	-0.170136842
14	4.718847368	0.281152632
15	9.943489474	-0.443489474
16	11.68503684	1.714963158
17	13.71684211	1.283157895
18	3.267557895	0.732442105

SCATTER AND RESIDUAL PLOTS

In addition to the tables, we can get a scatter plot of dependent variable versus independent variable (Figure 15.2) and a residual plot (Figure 15.3).

Figure 15.2. Simple Regression Scatter Plot

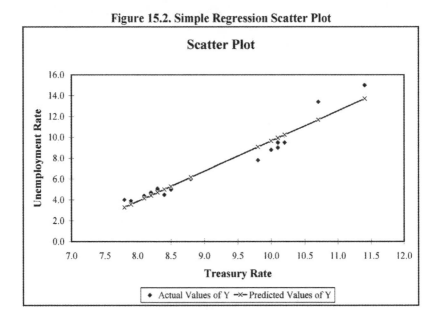

Figure 15.3. Residual Plot Versus Independent Variable

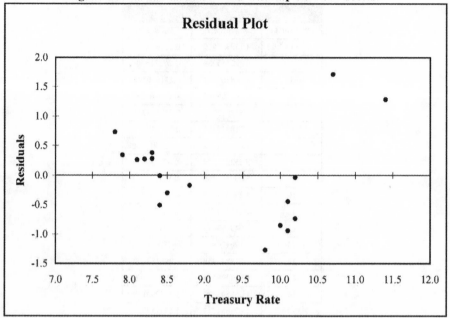

CHAPTER 16

Multiple Regression Analysis

IN PRACTICAL PREDICTION problems, usually more than one independent variable is needed in the prediction of a dependent variable. Adding appropriate additional independent variables to the model reduces the standard error of the estimate and thus enables us to do a better job of predicting values of the dependent variable.

The multiple regression analysis is a natural extension of the simple regression method studied in chapter 15. The difference is that more independent variables are included. The assumptions of the model, estimation procedures, and testing of the model are quite similar to simple regression analysis. However, the computations required in multiple regression analysis are quite complex and require the use of matrix algebra. In practice, computers are always used to solve multiple regression problems.

PROCEDURE

Let a dependent variable Y be a linear function of k independent variables. The multiple regression model can then be specified by the following:

$$\hat{Y}_i = b_0 + b_1 X_{i1} + b_2 X_{i2} + \dots b_k X_{ik}$$

where:

$\hat{Y}_i$ = *value of the dependent variable for the ith observation*
X_{i1} = *value of the 1st independent variable for the ith observation*
X_{i2} = *value of the 2nd independent variable for the ith observation*
X_{ik} = *value of the kth independent variable for the ith observation*
b_0 = *regression constant*

b_1 = *regression coefficient for variable 1*
b_2 = *regression coefficient for variable 2*
b_k = *regression coefficient for variable k*
k = *the number of independent variables*

The basic difference between this model and the one in chapter 15 is that the simple regression model represents a straight line in two dimensions, whereas the multiple regression model represents a plane in multidimensional space.

In matrix form, the equation can be written as

$$Y = X \cdot B$$

where:

$$Y = \begin{bmatrix} Y_1 \\ Y_2 \\ \cdot \\ \cdot \\ \cdot \\ Y_n \end{bmatrix}, \qquad B = \begin{bmatrix} b_0 \\ b_1 \\ \cdot \\ \cdot \\ \cdot \\ b_k \end{bmatrix}$$

and

$$Y = \begin{bmatrix} 1 & X_{11} & X_{12} & \cdots & X_{1k} \\ 1 & X_{21} & X_{22} & \cdots & X_{2k} \\ \cdot & \cdot & \cdot & & \cdot \\ 1 & X_{n1} & X_{n2} & \cdots & X_{nk} \end{bmatrix}$$

The matrix of regression coefficients is determined by the method of least-squares:

$$B = (X' \, X)^{-1} \, X' \, Y$$

where:

$$X' = \text{transpose of matrix } X$$

Variances of the error term and regression coefficients are computed by the following formulas:

$$Var\ (e_j)\ =\ S^2\ =\ \frac{SSE}{n - (k + 1)}\ =\ \frac{\mathbf{Y'Y} - \mathbf{B'X'Y}}{n - (k + 1)}$$

and

$$Var\ (\mathbf{B})\ =\ S^2\ \cdot\ (\mathbf{X'X})^{-1}$$

where, apart from S^2, the matrix $(\mathbf{X'X})^{-1}$ represents the variance-covariance matrix of the regression coefficients. For example, if we write

$$\mathbf{Y} = \begin{bmatrix} C_{100} & C_{01} & \cdots & C_{0k} \\ C_{10} & C_{11} & \cdots & C_{1k} \\ . & . & & . \\ . & . & & . \\ C_{k0} & C_{k1} & \cdots & C_{kk} \end{bmatrix}$$

then

$$Var\ (B_j)\ =\ S^2_{b_j}\ =\ C_{jj}\ \cdot\ S^2, \qquad for\ j\ =\ 0, 1, ..., k$$

and

$$Cov\ (B_j, B_h)\ =\ C_{jh}\ \cdot\ S^2, \qquad for\ j \neq h$$

The following test statistic, with (n-k-1) degrees of freedom, can be used to test the significance of the regression coefficients:

$$t\ =\ \frac{b_j}{S_{b_j}}\ =\ \frac{b_j}{S\sqrt{C_{jj}}}$$

Analysis of variance can also be performed in matrix form:

$$SST = \mathbf{Y'Y} - \frac{(\sum_{i=1}^{n} Y_j)^2}{n}$$

$$SSE = \mathbf{Y'Y} - \mathbf{B'X'Y}$$

$$SSR = SST - SSE = \mathbf{B'X'Y} - \frac{(\sum_{i=1}^{n} Y_j)^2}{n}$$

The analysis of variance table for multiple regression is similar to the table for simple regression model and is displayed in Table 16.1.

Table 16.1. Analysis of Variance Table for Multiple Regression				
Source of Variation	Sum of Squares	Degrees of Freedom	Mean Square	F-Ratio
Regression:	SSR	1	MSR	F=MSR / MSE
Error:	SSE	n - (k+1)	MSE	
Total:	SST	n - 1		

The aptness of the fitted equation can also be determined with the help of residual plots. The residual may be defined as the difference between the observed value and predicted value of the dependent variable for given values of the independent variables:

$$e_i = Y_i - \hat{Y}_i$$

The residual is usually plotted on the vertical axis against both the dependent and independent variables. If the hypothesized model is appropriate, no pattern will be apparent in the residual plot.

If residuals in a time series analysis are correlated, it is said that there is the problem of autocorrelation of the residuals. Most of the tests of significance for a regression equation are based on the assumption that there is no autocorrelation. If autocorrelation is present, the regression equation should not be used to make forecasts. The Durbin-Watson test is a widely-used test to determine whether autocorrelation exits. The test was explained in chapter 15.

COMPUTER ASSIGNMENT

In order to predict the net income of a corporation based on sales and assets, a random sample of 25 corporations was selected for the year 1980 with the results shown in Table 16.2.

1. Use the least-squares method to perform a multiple linear regression analysis.
2. Interpret the meaning of the slopes in this problem.
3. Determine whether there is a significant relationship between net income and the two independent variables (sales and assets) at the 0.05 level of significance.
4. Compute the coefficient of multiple determination, R^2, and interpret its meaning in this problem.
5. Predict the net income for a corporation that has sales of $1 billion end has assets of $1 billion.
6. Perform a residual analysis on your results and determine the adequacy of the fit of the model.

Table 16.2. Example Problem		
Net Income ($ millions)	Sales ($ millions)	Assets ($ millions)
$104.2	$1,521.7	$1,136.3
55.3	1,299.7	1,930.6
38.6	695.5	478.1
45.4	603.5	738.1
83.8	3,706.7	3,446.7
98.3	1,081.6	1,130.0
201.2	3,143.0	2,793.0
29.0	595.6	433.6
43.1	559.1	353.1
145.9	1,789.6	1,848.6
87.9	1,409.9	1,150.6
21.5	671.1	332.2
193.0	3,962.9	2,301.2
52.1	543.3	578.5
422.1	5,912.6	3406.0
11.4	5441.5	257.6
114.0	2,485.2	1,889.7
28.1	1,000.1	583.0
11.9	474.2	387.3
155.4	2,876.4	2,271.7
77.4	1,430.1	1,047.0
315.3	8,011.3	7,147.6
45.2	795.7	368.0
32.3	737.9	743.4
72.5	2,199.8	1,608.5

Source: Fortune Magazine, May 4, 1981

SOLVING MULTIPLE REGRESSION PROBLEMS USING EXCEL

To solve this problem using Excel, we can follow the exact procedure as explained in Chapter 15. The main difference between this problem and the problem in Chapter 15 is that in here we have two independent variables, sales and assets. The steps are summarized below:

1. Enter the dependent and independent variables into an Excel worksheet (Table 16.3).

Table 16.3. Initial Data		
B	**C**	**D**
Net Income	**Sales**	**Assets**
$104.2	$1,521.7	$1,136.3
55.3	1,299.7	1,930.6
38.6	695.5	478.1
45.4	603.5	738.1
83.8	3,706.7	3,446.7
98.3	1,081.6	1,130.0
201.2	3,143.0	2,793.0
29.0	595.6	433.6
43.1	559.1	353.1
145.9	1,789.6	1,848.6
87.9	1,409.9	1,150.6
21.5	671.1	332.2
193.0	3,962.9	2,301.2
52.1	543.3	578.5
422.1	5,912.6	3406.0
11.4	5441.5	257.6
114.0	2,485.2	1,889.7
28.1	1,000.1	583.0
11.9	474.2	387.3
155.4	2,876.4	2,271.7
77.4	1,430.1	1,047.0
315.3	8,011.3	7,147.6
45.2	795.7	368.0
32.3	737.9	743.4
72.5	2,199.8	1,608.5

2. Now click on TOOLS, DATA ANALYSIS, and REGRESSION. The dialogue box in Figure 16.1 will appear.

Figure 16.1 Regression Dialogue Box

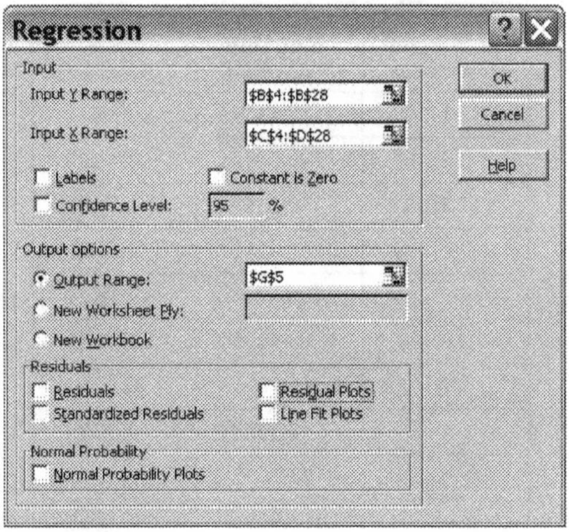

3. Enter the independent variable (Y), cells B4:B28.
4. Enter the independent variables (X1 and X2), cells C4:D28.
5. Enter the output range, G5. The output range can be anywhere.
6. Click OK.

The results of the multiple regression output are displayed in Table 16.4, starting in cell G5.

Table 16.4. Multiple Regression Results								
SUMMARY OUTPUT								
Regression Statistics								
Multiple R	0.8162							
R Square	0.6661							
Adjusted R	0.6357							
Standard Error	59.0701							
Observations	25							
ANOVA								
	df	*SS*	*MS*	*F*	*Significance F*			
Regression	2	153139.9691	76569.9846	21.9443	0.000006			
Residual	22	76764.2005	3489.2818					
Total	24	229904.1696						
	Coefficients	*Standard Error*	*t Stat*	*P-value*	*Lower 95%*	*Upper 95%*	*Lower 95%*	*Upper 95%*
Intercept	12.6666	17.7932	0.7119	0.4840	-24.2343	49.5676	-24.2343	49.5676
X Variable 1	0.0160	0.0107	1.4947	0.1492	-0.0062	0.0381	-0.0062	0.0381
X Variable 2	0.0345	0.0138	2.4943	0.0206	0.0058	0.0632	0.0058	0.0632

If a check mark is put in the residual checkbox in the regression dialogue box (Figure 16.1), Excel will calculate the residuals as in Table 16.5.

Table 16.5. Residual Output		
RESIDUAL OUTPUT		
Observation	*Predicted Y*	*Residuals*
1	76.1479	28.0521
2	100.0027	-44.7027
3	40.2582	-1.6582
4	47.7581	-2.3581
5	190.7141	-106.9141
6	68.9065	29.3935
7	159.1691	42.0309
8	37.1288	-8.1288
9	33.7695	9.3305
10	104.9932	40.9068
11	74.8568	13.0432
12	34.8362	-13.3362
13	155.2911	37.7089
14	41.2921	10.8079
15	224.5168	197.5832
16	108.3993	-96.9993
17	117.5128	-3.5128
18	48.7380	-20.6380
19	33.5942	-21.6942
20	136.9328	18.4672
21	71.6057	5.7943
22	387.0723	-71.7723
23	38.0597	7.1403
24	50.0859	-17.7859
25	103.2582	-30.7582

RESIDUAL PLOTS

In addition to the tables, we can get residual plots versus the predicted values (Figure 16.2) as well as residual plots versus both independent variables (Figures 16.3 and 16.4).

Figure 16.2. Residual Plot Versus Predicted Values

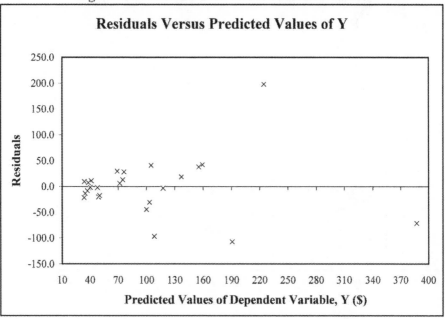

Figure 16.3. Residual Plot Versus the First Independent Variable

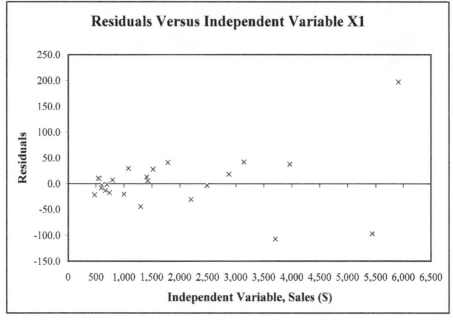

Figure 16.4. Residual Plot Versus the Second Independent Variable

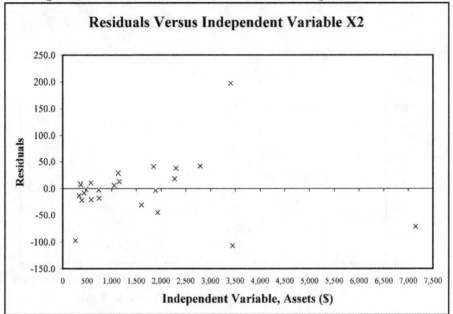

CHAPTER 17

Time Series Analysis
(Annual Data)

A TIME SERIES IS a set of quantitative observations that are obtained at equally spaced points in time. Time series analysis is the process by which the set of data obtained over time is analyzed. The basic assumption is that those factors that have influenced the observations in the past will continue to do so in the future. Thus, the primary goal of time series analysis is to isolate these factors for the purpose of forecasting.

All time series data contain all or only one of four components. These components are long-term trend (T), cyclical component (C), seasonal component (S), and irregular or random fluctuations (I). One of the most widely used models of a time series is the classical multiplicative model, in which the time series is assumed to be a product of these four factors. This model is described by the following formula:

$$Y_t = T_t \cdot C_t \cdot S_t \cdot I_t$$

For annual data, the classical multiplicative model may be written as in the following:

$$Y_t = T_t \cdot C_t \cdot I_t$$

MEASURING THE TREND COMPONENT

SIMPLE REGRESSION

Simple linear regression can be used to measure the long-term trend of annual data. The regression model may be written as

$$T_t = b_0 + b_1 X_t$$

where:

T_t = *trend values for period t*

X_t = *time periods measured in years (X's are numerical codes denoting periods 1, 2, . . . , t)*

The regression coefficients are computed by the method of least-squares. The equation provides values of the trend component, T, over time. If the observed values of the time series are then divided by these trend values, a measure of the cyclical component, with some irregular component, is obtained. The new values are referred to as cyclical-irregular relatives:

$$\frac{Y_t}{T_t} = \frac{T_t \cdot C_t \cdot I_t}{T_t} = C_t \cdot I_t$$

When the time series change at a constant rate over time, a straight-line trend is used. If the series change at an increasing rate over time, an exponential trend equation may be more appropriate. The exponential trend model may be expressed as in the following:

$$T_t = b_0 \cdot b_1{}^{X_t}$$

Using LOG transformations yields a linear equation that can be solved by the method of least-squares:

$$LOG(T_t) = LOG(b_0) + LOG(b_1) \cdot X_t$$

SMOOTHING THE SERIES

Smoothing attempts to remove the effect of unwanted irregular fluctuations in the data. Eliminating the unwanted fluctuations gives a better picture of the underlying movement in the time series. The two most common techniques of smoothing data are the method of moving averages and the method of exponential smoothing.

MOVING AVERAGES

A moving average of a time series eliminates the cyclical or irregular fluctuations by taking successive averages of sequences of observations and replacing each sequence by the average of that sequence. For example, to compute 5-year moving averages, a series of 5-year moving totals is obtained and then the results are divided by 5. The period selected for constructing the averages should be an integer value corresponding to the average length of a cycle in a time series.

EXPONENTIAL SMOOTHING

The method of exponential smoothing is another technique for studying the long-term trend. This method provides us with an exponentially weighted moving average of the time series sequence. The following expression is used for exponential smoothing:

$$F_t = wY_t + (1 - w)F_{t-1}$$

where:

F_t = *smoothed (forecasted) value of the time series in period t*
Y_t = *observed value of the series in period t*
F_{t-1} = *exponentially smoothed value of time series in period t− 1*
w = *weight or smoothing constant ($0 < w < 1$)*

Exponential smoothing starts by setting the smoothed value in time period 1 equal to the observed value in time period 1. Thus in time period 1,

$$F_1 = Y_1$$

and in time period 2,

$$F_2 = wY_2 + (1-w)F_1 = wY_2 + (1-w)Y_1$$

For the third and fourth periods the smoothed values are

$$F_3 = wY_3 - w(1-w)Y_2 + (1-w)^2 Y_1 \text{ and}$$
$$F_4 = wY_4 + w(1-w)Y_3 + w(1-w)^2 Y_2 + (1-w)^3 Y_1$$

As can be seen, the weights change exponentially as the smoothing process moves forward in time. The exponential smoothing procedure reduces the irregular fluctuations in the time series.

The choice of the weight, w, is an important consideration. If the purpose of exponential smoothing is to eliminate the cyclical or irregular components, a small value for w (closer to 0) should be chosen. On the other hand, if the purpose is forecasting, a larger value for w (closer to 1) should be chosen.

COMPUTER ASSIGNMENT

The annual sales of a company are given in Table 17.1. Perform time-series analysis on the data.

Table 17.1. Annual Sales of a Company	
Years	Annual Sales (Thousands of $)
1	68
2	56
3	70
4	77
5	79
6	94
7	87
8	75
9	89
10	83
11	65
12	87
13	89
14	96
15	75
16	68

SOLVING ANNUAL TIME SERIES PROBLEMS USING EXCEL

The first step is to calculate the trend values. This can be done by using simple regression analysis. In this problem the independent variables (X_t) are Years and the dependent variables (T_t) are Sales. The regression coefficients and the predicted values can be computed using the procedure explained in chapter 15. The results are summarized in Table 17.2.

$$b_0 = 71.7, \qquad b_1 = .8147, \qquad T_t = 71.7 + .8147X_t$$

Table 17.2. Predicted Values of T	
	C
3	Predicted T
4	72.515
5	73.329
6	74.144
7	74.959
8	75.774
9	76.588
10	77.403
11	78.218
12	79.032
13	79.847
14	80.662
15	81.476
16	82.291
17	83.106
18	83.921
19	84.735

Once the trend values are calculated, the cyclical and smoothed values can also be computed by using the formulas in Table 17.3.

	A	B	C	D	E
Table 17.3. Cell Formulas for Annual Time Series Analysis					
2					Exponential
3	Y_t / T_t	3-Y Average	5-Y Average	7-Y Average	w = 0.2
4	=B4/C4	0	0	0	=B4
5	=B5/C5	=AVERAGE(B4:B6)	0	0	=$H$3*B5+(1-$H$3)*H4
6	=B6/C6	=AVERAGE(B5:B7)	=AVERAGE(B4:B8)	0	=$H$3*B6+(1-$H$3)*H5
7	=B7/C7	=AVERAGE(B6:B8)	=AVERAGE(B5:B9)	=AVERAGE(B4:B10)	=$H$3*B7+(1-$H$3)*H6
8	=B8/C8	=AVERAGE(B7:B9)	=AVERAGE(B6:B10)	=AVERAGE(B5:B11)	=$H$3*B8+(1-$H$3)*H7
9	=B9/C9	=AVERAGE(B8:B10)	=AVERAGE(B7:B11)	=AVERAGE(B6:B12)	=$H$3*B9+(1-$H$3)*H8
10	=B10/C10	=AVERAGE(B9:B11)	=AVERAGE(B8:B12)	=AVERAGE(B7:B13)	=$H$3*B10+(1-$H$3)*H9
11	=B11/C11	=AVERAGE(B10:B12)	=AVERAGE(B9:B13)	=AVERAGE(B8:B14)	=$H$3*B11+(1-$H$3)*H10
12	=B12/C12	=AVERAGE(B11:B13)	=AVERAGE(B10:B14)	=AVERAGE(B9:B15)	=$H$3*B12+(1-$H$3)*H11
13	=B13/C13	=AVERAGE(B12:B14)	=AVERAGE(B11:B15)	=AVERAGE(B10:B16)	=$H$3*B13+(1-$H$3)*H12
14	=B14/C14	=AVERAGE(B13:B15)	=AVERAGE(B12:B16)	=AVERAGE(B11:B17)	=$H$3*B14+(1-$H$3)*H13
15	=B15/C15	=AVERAGE(B14:B16)	=AVERAGE(B13:B17)	=AVERAGE(B12:B18)	=$H$3*B15+(1-$H$3)*H14
16	=B16/C16	=AVERAGE(B15:B17)	=AVERAGE(B14:B18)	=AVERAGE(B13:B19)	=$H$3*B16+(1-$H$3)*H15
17	=B17/C17	=AVERAGE(B16:B18)	=AVERAGE(B15:B19)	0	=$H$3*B17+(1-$H$3)*H16
18	=B18/C18	=AVERAGE(B17:B19)	0	0	=$H$3*B18+(1-$H$3)*H17
19	=B19/C19	0	0	0	=$H$3*B19+(1-$H$3)*H18

After inserting all the formulas, the final results will look like Table 17.4.

	A	B	C	D	E	F	G	H
Table 17.4. Completed Results for Annual Time Series								
1	Time Series Analysis (Annual Data)							
2								
3	X_t	Y_t	T_t	Y_t / T_t	3-Y	5-Y	7-Y	w = 0.2
4	1	68	72.52	0.938	0.00	0.00	0.00	68.00
5	2	56	73.33	0.764	64.67	0.00	0.00	65.60
6	3	70	74.14	0.944	67.67	70.00	0.00	66.48
7	4	77	74.96	1.027	75.33	75.20	75.86	68.58
8	5	79	75.77	1.043	83.33	81.40	76.86	70.67
9	6	94	76.59	1.227	86.67	82.40	81.57	75.33
10	7	87	77.40	1.124	85.33	84.80	83.43	77.67
11	8	75	78.22	0.959	83.67	85.60	81.71	77.13
12	9	89	79.03	1.126	82.33	79.80	82.86	79.51
13	10	83	79.85	1.039	79.00	79.80	82.14	80.21
14	11	65	80.66	0.806	78.33	82.60	83.43	77.16
15	12	87	81.48	1.068	80.33	84.00	83.43	79.13
16	13	89	82.29	1.082	90.67	82.40	80.43	81.11
17	14	96	83.11	1.155	86.67	83.00	0.00	84.08
18	15	75	83.92	0.894	79.67	0.00	0.00	82.27
19	16	68	84.74	0.802	0.00	0.00	0.00	79.41

GRAPHING THE RESULTS

The results can be plotted using Excel's XY (Scatter) graph option (Figures 17.1., 17.2, 17.3, 17.4, 17.5, and 17.6). The procedure to plot a graph was explained in previous chapters.

Figure 17.1. Graph of Trend Values

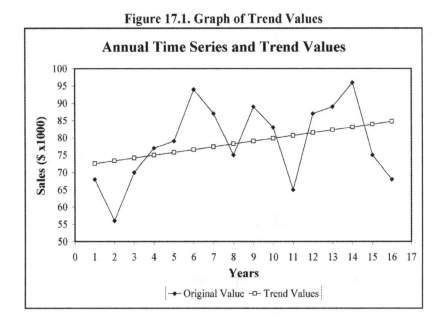

Figure 17.2. Graph of Cyclical-Irregular Relatives

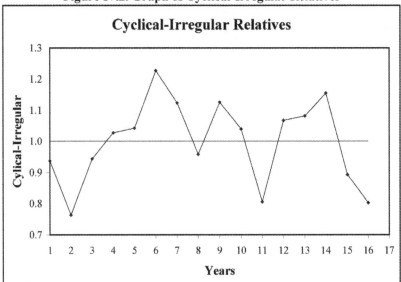

Figure 17.3. Graph of 3-Year Moving Averages

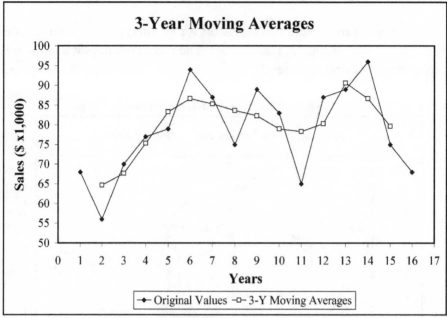

Figure 17.4. Graph of 5-Year Moving Averages

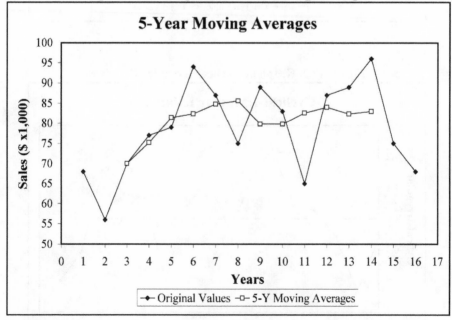

Figure 17.5. Graph of 7-Year Moving Averages

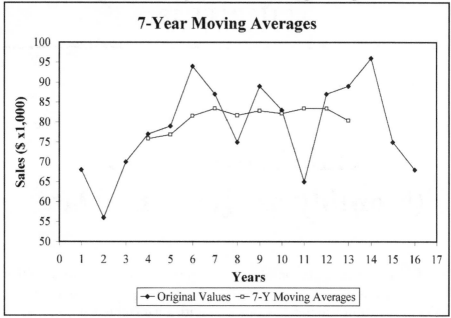

Figure 17.6. Graph of Exponentially Smoothed Series

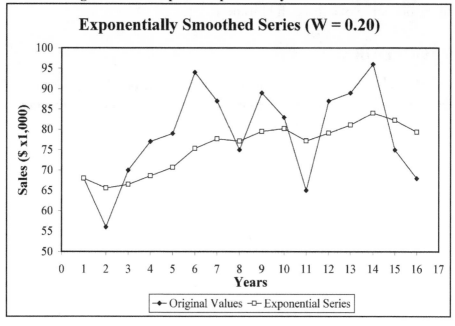

CHAPTER 18

Time Series Analysis (Monthly or Quarterly Data)

IN THE CASE of monthly or quarterly time-series data, we are either interested in making short-term forecasts, or in decomposing the time series by removing the trend, seasonal, and irregular components so that we may determine whether a particular series is a leading indicator, coinciding, or lagging indicator of the overall economic activity. The forecasting of short-term and long-term levels of economic activity is of fundamental importance in the operation of a successful business.

PROCEDURE

The study of monthly or quarterly data is divided into seasonal and cyclical analysis. The analysis begins with the classical multiplicative model for monthly or quarterly data:

$$Y_t = T_t \cdot C_t \cdot S_t \cdot I_t$$

where:

Y_t = *values of the time series*
T_t = *trend component*
C_t = *cyclical component*
S_t = *seasonal component*
I_t = *irregular component*

Seasonal Analysis

The seasonal component is measured by the method of ratio-to-moving-average.

7. Smooth the series by taking centered 4-month moving averages (for quarterly data), or centered 12-month moving averages (for monthly data). The smoothed values reflect the trend-cyclical ($T_t \cdot C_t$) component.
8. Divide the original series by the smoothed values to obtain the seasonal-irregular (or specific seasonal relatives), $S_t \cdot I_t$, component.

$$\frac{Y_t}{T_t \cdot C_t} = \frac{T_t \cdot C_t \cdot S_t \cdot I_t}{T_t \cdot C_t} = S_t \cdot I_t$$

9. Average out the irregular effect in the seasonal-irregular component to isolate the seasonal component (seasonal indices). This is done by averaging out the specific seasonal relatives for each quarter (quarterly data) or for each month (monthly data). An average such as the median is used instead of the mean in order to avoid the effect of extreme irregulars.
10. A final adjustment is needed to make sure that seasonal indices average out to one (or 100 percent) over a year. Thus, the seasonal indices for all quarters (quarterly data) or for all months (monthly data) are added to find the total sum, and then each index is multiplied by 4/Sum (quarterly data) or 12/Sum (monthly data).
11. The observed value for each time period is divided by the seasonal index for that time period in order to remove the effects of seasonal influences. The result is called the seasonally adjusted value for that time period.

$$\frac{Y_t}{S_t} = \frac{T_t \cdot C_t \cdot S_t \cdot I_t}{S_t} = T_t \cdot C_t \cdot I_t$$

Cyclical Analysis

2. The seasonally adjusted value for each period is divided by the trend value (from the regression equation) for that period in order to obtain the cyclical-irregular relatives:

$$\frac{T_t \cdot C_t \cdot I_t}{T_t} = C_t \cdot I_t$$

2. The irregular effect may be eliminated by using 3-month weighted moving averages in which the weight assigned to the middle value is two (2) while the end values are assigned a weight of one (1):

$$\frac{C_t \cdot I_t}{I_t} = C_t$$

COMPUTER ASSIGNMENT

The quarterly sales of a company over a period of 5 years are given in Table 18.1. Compute the seasonal index for each quarter. Then deseasonalize the data, estimate the linear trend, and compute the cyclical relatives for this company.

Table 18.1. Quarterly Sales		
Year	Quarter	Sales
1	Winter	$419
	Spring	495
	Summer	531
	Fall	690
2	Winter	504
	Spring	611
	Summer	590
	Fall	635
3	Winter	466
	Spring	559
	Summer	529
	Fall	582
4	Winter	484
	Spring	527
	Summer	546
	Fall	645
5	Winter	457
	Spring	532
	Summer	518
	Fall	636

SOLVING QUARTERLY OR MONTHLY TIME SERIES USING EXCEL

1. The first step is to calculate the trend values. This can be done by using simple regression analysis. In this problem, the independent variables (X_t) are Quarters (1, 2, . . . , 20) and the dependent variables (T_t) are Sales. The regression coefficients and the predicted values can be computed using the procedure explained in chapter 15. The regression coefficients are summarized below, and the predicted trend values are given in Table 18.2.

$$b_o = 535.2632, \qquad b_1 = 1.19398, \qquad T_t = 535.2632 + 1.19398X_t$$

Table 18.2. Predicted Values of T
Predicted T
536.457142857143
537.651127819549
538.845112781955
540.039097744361
541.233082706767
542.427067669173
543.621052631579
544.815037593985
546.009022556391
547.203007518797
548.396992481203
549.590977443609
550.784962406015
551.978947368421
553.172932330827
554.366917293233
555.560902255639
556.754887218045
557.948872180451
559.142857142857

2. The next step is to calculate centered 4-year moving averages to eliminate the seasonal-irregular factors. This series appears in column E. In column F, the original time series data are divided by the centered 4-year moving averages to isolate $S_t \cdot I_t$. This series is called the ratio-to-moving-average.

3. Third, the irregular effect is removed by grouping all the available ratios from column F by quarter and finding the median ratio for each quarter, as in Table 18.3.
4. The median ratios in Table 18.3 are adjusted so that they average to 1.00, or 100 percent, over the course of a year; thus their sum is equal to 4. Therefore, each median is multiplied by 4/Sum to compute the seasonal index, as in the following:

Winter: .8481 * 4 / (0.8481 + 1.0116 + 0.9922 + 1.1504)
          = 0.8476 or 84.76%
Spring: 1.0116 * 4 / (0.8481 + 1.0116 + 0.9922 + 1.1504)
          = 1.0110 or 101.10%
Summer: 0.9922 * 4 / (0.8481 + 1.0116 + 0.9922 + 1.1504)
          = 0.9916 or 99.16%
Fall: 1.1504 * 4 / (0.8481 + 1.0116 + 0.9922 + 1.1504)
          = 1.1497 or 114.97%

Table 18.3. Removal of Irregular Effects				
	Quarter			
Year	Winter	Spring	Summer	Fall
1	—	—	0.975	1.212
2	0.852	1.032	1.017	1.116
3	0.840	1.034	0.986	1.089
4	0.909	0.971	0.998	1.185
5	0.844	0.991	—	—
Median Ratio for Each Quarter (Unadjusted):	0.8481	1.0116	0.9922	1.1504

Tables 18.4 and 18.5 demonstrate the above procedure in Excel format.

Table 18.4. Cell Formulas for Quarterly Time Series Analysis

	E	F	G
1	$T_t . C_t$	$S_t . I_t$	Median for Each
2	4-Y Mov. Ave.	$Y_t / 4$-Y	Quarter
3	Centered	Ratio to Moving	
4	-----	-----	=MEDIAN($F$8,$F$12,$F$16,$F$20)
5	-----	-----	=MEDIAN($F$9,$F$13,$F$17,$F$21)
6	=(AVERAGE(D4:D7)+AVERAGE(D5:D8))/2	=D6/E6	=MEDIAN($F$6,$F$10,$F$14,$F$18)
7	=(AVERAGE(D5:D8)+AVERAGE(D6:D9))/2	=D7/E7	=MEDIAN($F$7,$F$11,$F$15,$F$19)
8	=(AVERAGE(D6:D9)+AVERAGE(D7:D10))/2	=D8/E8	=MEDIAN($F$8,$F$12,$F$16,$F$20)
9	=(AVERAGE(D7:D10)+AVERAGE(D8:D11))/2	=D9/E9	=MEDIAN($F$9,$F$13,$F$17,$F$21)
10	=(AVERAGE(D8:D11)+AVERAGE(D9:D12))/2	=D10/E10	=MEDIAN($F$6,$F$10,$F$14,$F$18)
11	=(AVERAGE(D9:D12)+AVERAGE(D10:D13))/2	=D11/E11	=MEDIAN($F$7,$F$11,$F$15,$F$19)
12	=(AVERAGE(D10:D13)+AVERAGE(D11:D14))/2	=D12/E12	=MEDIAN($F$8,$F$12,$F$16,$F$20)
13	=(AVERAGE(D11:D14)+AVERAGE(D12:D15))/2	=D13/E13	=MEDIAN($F$9,$F$13,$F$17,$F$21)
14	=(AVERAGE(D12:D15)+AVERAGE(D13:D16))/2	=D14/E14	=MEDIAN($F$6,$F$10,$F$14,$F$18)
15	=(AVERAGE(D13:D16)+AVERAGE(D14:D17))/2	=D15/E15	=MEDIAN($F$7,$F$11,$F$15,$F$19)
16	=(AVERAGE(D14:D17)+AVERAGE(D15:D18))/2	=D16/E16	=MEDIAN($F$8,$F$12,$F$16,$F$20)
17	=(AVERAGE(D15:D18)+AVERAGE(D16:D19))/2	=D17/E17	=MEDIAN($F$9,$F$13,$F$17,$F$21)
18	=(AVERAGE(D16:D19)+AVERAGE(D17:D20))/2	=D18/E18	=MEDIAN($F$6,$F$10,$F$14,$F$18)
19	=(AVERAGE(D17:D20)+AVERAGE(D18:D21))/2	=D19/E19	=MEDIAN($F$7,$F$11,$F$15,$F$19)
20	=(AVERAGE(D18:D21)+AVERAGE(D19:D22))/2	=D20/E20	=MEDIAN($F$8,$F$12,$F$16,$F$20)
21	=(AVERAGE(D19:D22)+AVERAGE(D20:D23))/2	=D21/E21	=MEDIAN($F$9,$F$13,$F$17,$F$21)
22	0	-----	=MEDIAN($F$6,$F$10,$F$14,$F$18)
23	0	-----	=MEDIAN($F$7,$F$11,$F$15,$F$19)

Table 18.5. Cell Formulas for Quarterly Time Series Analysis

	H	I	J	K	L
1	S_t	$T_t . C_t . I_t$	T_t	$C_t . I_t$	C_t
2	Adjusted Median	Deseasonalized	Predicted Values	Cyclical	3-Y Moving Average
3	Seasonal Index	Data	Trend	Irregular Rel.	Cyclical Relatives
4	=4*G4/SUM($G$4:$G$7)	=D4/H4	536.457142857143	=I4/J4	-----
5	=4*G5/SUM($G$4:$G$7)	=D5/H5	537.651127819549	=I5/J5	=AVERAGE(K4:K6)
6	=4*G6/SUM($G$4:$G$7)	=D6/H6	538.845112781955	=I6/J6	=AVERAGE(K5:K7)
7	=4*G7/SUM($G$4:$G$7)	=D7/H7	540.039097744361	=I7/J7	=AVERAGE(K6:K8)
8	=4*G8/SUM($G$4:$G$7)	=D8/H8	541.233082706767	=I8/J8	=AVERAGE(K7:K9)
9	=4*G9/SUM($G$4:$G$7)	=D9/H9	542.427067669173	=I9/J9	=AVERAGE(K8:K10)
10	=4*G10/SUM($G$4:$G$7)	=D10/H10	543.621052631579	=I10/J10	=AVERAGE(K9:K11)
11	=4*G11/SUM($G$4:$G$7)	=D11/H11	544.815037593985	=I11/J11	=AVERAGE(K10:K12)
12	=4*G12/SUM($G$4:$G$7)	=D12/H12	546.009022556391	=I12/J12	=AVERAGE(K11:K13)
13	=4*G13/SUM($G$4:$G$7)	=D13/H13	547.203007518797	=I13/J13	=AVERAGE(K12:K14)
14	=4*G14/SUM($G$4:$G$7)	=D14/H14	548.396992481203	=I14/J14	=AVERAGE(K13:K15)
15	=4*G15/SUM($G$4:$G$7)	=D15/H15	549.590977443609	=I15/J15	=AVERAGE(K14:K16)
16	=4*G16/SUM($G$4:$G$7)	=D16/H16	550.784962406015	=I16/J16	=AVERAGE(K15:K17)
17	=4*G17/SUM($G$4:$G$7)	=D17/H17	551.978947368421	=I17/J17	=AVERAGE(K16:K18)
18	=4*G18/SUM($G$4:$G$7)	=D18/H18	553.172932330827	=I18/J18	=AVERAGE(K17:K19)
19	=4*G19/SUM($G$4:$G$7)	=D19/H19	554.366917293233	=I19/J19	=AVERAGE(K18:K20)
20	=4*G20/SUM($G$4:$G$7)	=D20/H20	555.560902255639	=I20/J20	=AVERAGE(K19:K21)
21	=4*G21/SUM($G$4:$G$7)	=D21/H21	556.754887218045	=I21/J21	=AVERAGE(K20:K22)
22	=4*G22/SUM($G$4:$G$7)	=D22/H22	557.948872180451	=I22/J22	=AVERAGE(K21:K23)
23	=4*G23/SUM($G$4:$G$7)	=D23/H23	559.142857142857	=I23/J23	-----

The final results are displayed in Tables 18.6 and 18.7.

			Table 18.6. Final Results for Quarterly Time Series Analysis			
A	**B**	**C**	**D**	**E**	**F**	**G**
			$T_t \cdot C_t \cdot S_t \cdot I_t$	$T_t \cdot C_t$	$S_t \cdot I_t$	Median for Each
			Y_t	4-Y Mov. Ave.	$Y_t / 4$-Y	Quarter
Period	Year	Quarter	Raw Data	Centered	Ratio to Mov. Ave.	Unadjusted
1	1	Win.	419	----	----	0.8481
2	1	Spr.	495	----	----	1.0116
3	1	Sum.	531	544.375	0.975	0.9922
4	1	Fall	690	569.500	1.212	1.1504
5	2	Win.	504	591.375	0.852	0.8481
6	2	Spr.	611	591.875	1.032	1.0116
7	2	Sum.	590	580.250	1.017	0.9922
8	2	Fall	635	569.000	1.116	1.1504
9	3	Win.	466	554.875	0.840	0.8481
10	3	Spr.	559	540.625	1.034	1.0116
11	3	Sum.	529	536.250	0.986	0.9922
12	3	Fall	582	534.500	1.089	1.1504
13	4	Win.	484	532.625	0.909	0.8481
14	4	Spr.	527	542.625	0.971	1.0116
15	4	Sum.	546	547.125	0.998	0.9922
16	4	Fall	645	544.375	1.185	1.1504
17	5	Win.	457	541.500	0.844	0.8481
18	5	Spr.	532	536.875	0.991	1.0116
19	5	Sum.	518	---	---	0.9922
20	5	Fall	636	----	----	1.1504

	Table 18.7. Final Results for Quarterly Time Series Analysis			
H	**I**	**J**	**K**	**L**
S_t	$T_t \cdot C_t \cdot I_t$	T_t	$C_t \cdot I_t$	C_t
Adjusted Median	Deseasonalized	Predicted Values	Cyclical	3-Y Moving Average
Seasonal Index	Data	Trend	Irregular Relatives	Cyclical Relatives
84.76%	494.335	536.457	0.921	0.000
101.10%	489.603	537.651	0.911	0.942
99.16%	535.482	538.845	0.994	1.005
114.97%	600.134	540.039	1.111	1.068
84.76%	594.617	541.233	1.099	1.108
101.10%	604.339	542.427	1.114	1.102
99.16%	594.980	543.621	1.094	1.074
114.97%	552.297	544.815	1.014	1.038
84.76%	549.785	546.009	1.007	1.010
101.10%	552.906	547.203	1.010	0.997
99.16%	533.465	548.397	0.973	0.968
114.97%	506.200	549.591	0.921	0.977
84.76%	571.021	550.785	1.037	0.967
101.10%	521.254	551.979	0.944	0.992
99.16%	550.609	553.173	0.995	0.984
114.97%	560.994	554.367	1.012	0.993
84.76%	539.167	555.561	0.970	0.976
101.10%	526.200	556.755	0.945	0.951
99.16%	522.372	557.949	0.936	0.957
114.97%	553.167	559.143	0.989	0.000

PREDICTING FUTURE VALUES OF SALES

To make predictions about the Winter quarter of year 6 (future year), use the quarterly trend equation

$$T_t = 535.2632 + 1.19398X_t$$

where X = 1 was located at the middle of the winter quarter of year 1. On the basis of this equation the value of X for the winter quarter of year 6 will be 21. Using the above trend equation will predict

$$T_{21} = 535.2632 + 1.19398 * (21) = \$560.33684.$$

By applying the seasonal index of 0.8476 for the winter quarter, the forecast can be adjusted to

$$560.33684 * 0.8476 = \$474.944.$$

GRAPHING THE RESULTS

The final results can be plotted using XY graphs (Figures 18.1., 18.2, 18.3, and 18.4). The procedure to plot a graph was explained in previous chapters.

Figure 18.1. Graph of Trend Values

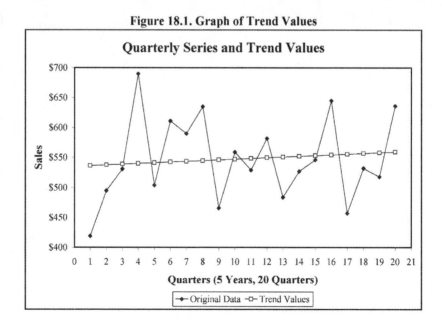

Figure 18.2. Graph of 4-Year Moving Averages

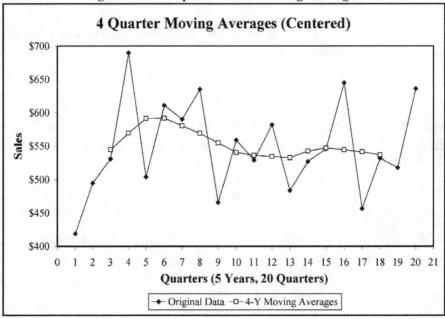

Figure 18.3. Graph of Deseasonalized Data

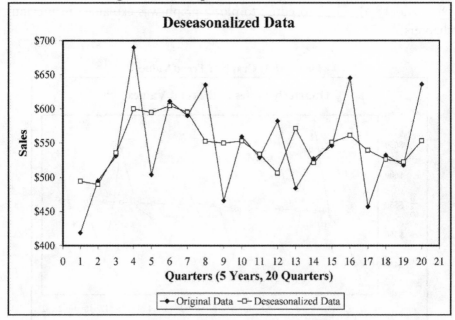

Figure 18.4. Graph of Cyclical-Irregular Relatives

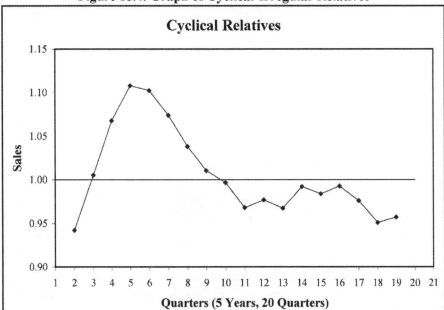

Cyclical Relatives

CHAPTER 19

Chi-Square Test of Independence

THE CHI-SQUARE TEST can be used to test the hypothesis of independence of two random variables. This is a natural extension of the goodness-of-fit test. The null and alternative hypotheses in this case can be stated as follows:

H_o: The variables are independent
H_a: The variables are not independent

PROCEDURE

Consider a population that is classified according to two attributes, A and B. Suppose there are r categories for attribute A and c categories for attribute B. To test the independence of the two attributes, a random sample is taken from the population and the observed frequencies are tabulated in a cross-classification (contingency) table, shown in Table 19.1, with r rows and c columns.

Table 19.1. Test-of-Independence Data Layout					
		Attribute B			
		1	2	. . .	c	Total
Attribute A	1	O_{11}	O_{12}	. . .	O_{1c}	R_1
	2	O_{21}	O_{22}	. . .	O_{2c}	R_2
	. . .	.	.	.	.	.
	r	O_{r1}	O_{r2}		O_{rc}	R_r
	Total	C_1	C_2		C_c	T

where:

O_{ij} = *observed frequency in each cell*
r = *number of rows*
c = *number of columns*
R_i = *total of each row*
C_j = *total of each column*
T = *grand total i = 1, 2, . . . , r*
j = *1, 2, . . . , c*

To determine whether the variables are independent, the following test statistic is computed:

$$X^2 = \sum_{i=1}^{r} \sum_{j=1}^{c} \frac{(O_{ij} - E_{ij})^2}{E_{ij}}$$

where:

$$E_{ij} = \frac{R_i \cdot C_j}{T} = \text{expected frequency per cell}$$

and

$$\text{Degrees of Freedom} \; = \; (r - 1)(c - 1)$$

Under the null hypothesis, for large sample sizes, X^2 follows a chi-square distribution with $(r - 1)(c - 1)$ degrees of freedom. If X^2 is larger than the value obtained from the table at the appropriate level of significance, the null hypothesis of independence is rejected; otherwise, the null hypothesis is not rejected.

EXERCISE 19.1
CONTINGENCY TABLE

5. Suppose the Department of Motor Vehicles (DMV) is interested in determining whether there is a link between the type of traffic violation and the type of vehicle driven. The contingency table, given in Table 19.2, summarizes traffic violations in the past week. Determine whether these two variables are statistically independent.

Table 19.2. Data for Exercise 19.1			
	B. Type of Vehicle		
A. Type of Violation	**1. Passenger**	**2. Truck**	**Total**
1. Stop Sign	45	25	
2. Red Light	35	15	
3. Failing to Yield	20	11	
4. Speeding	20	10	
5. Tail Gating	75	11	
6. DUI	25	8	
Total			

EXERCISE 19.2
CONTINGENCY PROBLEM USING EXCEL

In a study of the performance of students in a college with respect to their age, 100 students are selected at random and their ages and grades are recorded. The results are shown in Table 19.3. Determine whether age and performance are dependent.

	B	C	D	E	F	G	H
	\multicolumn{7}{c|}{**Table 19.3. Example Problem**}						
	B	**C**	**D**	**E**	**F**	**G**	**H**
3	TABLE OF OBSERVED VALUES						
4			Grade				
5			**A**	**B**	**C**	**D**	**Total**
6		19	10	10	6	6	32
7	Age	20	4	14	20	5	43
8		21	6	11	4	4	25
9		Total	20	35	30	15	100

The first step in solving a chi-square problem is to calculate expected values by using the following formula:

Expected Value = (Row Total) × (Column Total) / Grand Total

This is done in Table 19.4.

	Table 19.4. Cell Formulas for Calculating Expected Values					
	B	**C**	**D**	**E**	**F**	**G**	**H**
11	\multicolumn{7}{c	}{TABLE OF EXPECTED VALUES}
12				Grade			
13			**A**	**B**	**C**	**D**	**Total**
14		19	=$H6*D$9/$H$9	=$H6*E$9/$H$9	=$H6*F$9/$H$9	=$H6*G$9/$H$9	=SUM(D14..G14)
15	Age	20	=$H7*D$9/$H$9	=$H7*E$9/$H$9	=$H7*F$9/$H$9	=$H7*G$9/$H$9	=SUM(D15..G15)
16		21	=$H8*D$9/$H$9	=$H8*E$9/$H$9	=$H8*F$9/$H$9	=$H8*G$9/$H$9	=SUM(D16..G16)
17		Total	=SUM(D14..D16)	=SUM(E14..E16)	=SUM(F14..F16)	=SUM(G14..G16)	=SUM(D17..G17)

After the formulas are completed, the actual expected values will be displayed, as in Table 19.5.

Table 19.5. Expected Values for the Problem						
B	**C**	**D**	**E**	**F**	**G**	**H**
11	TABLE OF EXPECTED VALUES					
12			Grade			Totals
13		A	B	C	D	
14	19	6.40	11.20	9.60	4.80	**32.00**
15 Age	20	8.6	15.05	12.9	6.45	**43.00**
16	21	5.00	8.75	7.50	3.75	**25.00**
17 Totals		**20.00**	**35.00**	**30.00**	**15.00**	**100.00**

The next step is to calculate the chi-square ratio by using the following formula:

$$X^2 = \text{Sum (observed value } - \text{ expected value})^2 \text{ / Expected Value, summed across all cells.}$$

This is performed in Table 19.6, and the actual results are displayed in Table 19.7.

Table 19.6. Cell Formulas for Calculating the Chi-Square Ratio						
B	**C**	**D**	**E**	**F**	**G**	**H**
19	CALCULATION OF CHI SQUARE					
20			Grade			Totals
21		A (4.0)	B (3.0)	C(2.0)	D (1.0)	
22	19	=(D6-D14)^2/D14	=(E6-E14)^2/E14	=(F6-F14)^2/F14	=(G6-G14)^2/G14	=SUM(D22..G22)
23 Age	20	=(D7-D15)^2/D15	=(E7-E15)^2/E15	=(F7-F15)^2/F15	=(G7-G15)^2/G15	=SUM(D23..G23)
24	21	=(D8-D16)^2/D16	=(E8-E16)^2/E16	=(F8-F16)^2/F16	=(G8-G16)^2/G16	=SUM(D24..G24)
25 Totals		=SUM(D22..D24)	=SUM(E22..E24)	=SUM(F22..F24)	=SUM(G22..G24)	=SUM(D25..G25)

Table 19.7. Chi-Square Calculation							
	B	**C**	**D**	**E**	**F**	**G**	**H**
19	CALCULATION OF CHI SQUARE						
20				Grade			Totals
21			A	B	C	D	
22		19	2.02	0.13	1.35	0.30	**3.80**
23	Age	20	2.46	0.07	3.91	0.33	**6.77**
24		21	0.20	0.58	1.63	0.02	**2.43**
25	Totals		**4.69**	**0.78**	**6.89**	**0.64**	**13.00**

$$X^2 = 13.00$$
$$D.F. = (3 - 1)(4 - 1) = 6$$

The null and alternative hypotheses can be written as:

H_0: *Age and grades are independent variables.*
H_a: *Age and grades are dependent variables.*

If the Chi-Square value calculated above is larger than the value in the chi-square table with 6 degrees of freedom, age and grade performance are considered to be independent. Assuming that the level of significance, alpha, is 0.05, the value of chi-square from the table is $X^2_{0.05} = 12.592$.

Since $13.00 > 12.592$, we reject H_0 and conclude that age and grades are statistically dependent.

COMPUTER ASSIGNMENT

The problem in Table 19.8 involves a study of the effect of T.V. advertising on the purchase of the advertised products. A sample of 2,450 people were interviewed in September and then again in December. Each time the people were asked whether they watched a specific T.V. program and whether they purchased the product advertised during the program. Their responses are summarized below:

Table 19.8. Advertising Effectiveness					
The Effect of Advertising on Purchasing Decisions					
		Purchased Product (Sept./Dec.)				Totals
		Yes/Yes	Yes/No	No/Yes	No/No	
Watched Program (Sept./Dec.)	Yes/Yes	462	173	191	351	
	Yes/No	76	53	34	117	
	No/Yes	87	27	53	85	
	No/No	176	104	113	348	
Totals						

1. Enter the above table of observed results into an Excel worksheet.
2. Create a table of expected values: (row total x column total) / grand total.
3. Set up the Null and Alternative hypotheses:

   H_o: There is no relationship between T.V. advertising and purchasing the advertised product.

   H_a: There is a relationship between T.V. advertising and purchasing the advertised product.

4. Calculate the Chi-Square (X^2) coefficient:

   X^2 = Sum (observed value − expected value)^2 / Expected Value, summed across all cells

5. Calculate the degrees of freedom.
6. At $\alpha = 0.05$, test the significance of advertising on purchasing decisions.
7. Write a report explaining all the procedures and conclusions.
8. Print the result.

CHAPTER 20

Breakeven Analysis

B REAKEVEN ANALYSIS IS a means of determining the number of goods and/or services that must be sold at a given price in order to generate sufficient revenue to cover total costs. The breakeven analysis determines at which sales volume your firm will start making money.

The breakeven formula:

Quantity = Fixed Costs / (Revenue per unit − Variable Costs per unit)

$ **Fixed Costs:** Costs that must be paid whether or not any units are produced. These costs are fixed only over a specified period of time or range of production.

$ **Variable Costs:** Costs that vary directly with the number of units produced. (Typically: materials and labor used to produce the desired number of units)

EXAMPLE 20.1. (Determining the Breakeven Point)

Suppose a firm's cost structure is given in Table 20.1. Determine the breakeven point for this firm.

Table 20.1. Cost Structure of a Firm	
Total Fixed Costs (FC):	**$50,000** per year
Variable costs per unit (AVC):	
Materials:	$1.60
Labor:	3.00
Miscellaneous:	0.60
Total Variable Cost per unit:	**$5.20** per unit
Selling Price per unit (P):	**$9.20** per unit
Number of units to break even:	$\dfrac{\$50,000}{\$9.20 - \$5.20}$ = **12,500** units per year

In this example, 12,500 units must be sold at $9.20 before the firm will begin to realize a profit.

DERIVATION OF BREAKEVEN FORMULA

To derive the breakeven formula, we need to define total revenue (TR), total cost (TC), and total variable cost (VC):

$$TR = P \cdot Q$$
$$TC = FC + VC$$
$$VC = AVC \cdot Q$$

where P is the price per unit, Q is the total number of units of output, and AVC is average variable cost or variable cost per unit. In order for a firm to break even, total revenue must equal to total cost.

Breakeven condition: TR = TC

Substituting for all the terms, we get the following results:

$$P \cdot Q = FC + VC$$
$$P \cdot Q = FC + AVC \cdot Q$$
$$P \cdot Q - AVC \cdot Q = FC$$
$$Q = FC / (P - AVC)$$

GRAPHICAL SOLUTION

The breakeven analysis can also be demonstrated graphically. Breakeven occurs at the point where the total revenue line intersects the total cost line. This point corresponds to 12,500 units of output. When you multiply this number by $9.20, you will get the total revenue (cost) at this point:

$$12,500 * 9.20 = \$115,000$$

To do the graphs using Excel, we need to enter the Fixed Cost, Variable Cost per Unit, and price (see Table 20.2).

	Table 20.2. Revenue and Cost Data for Breakeven Analysis						
	B	**C**	**D**	**E**	**F**	**G**	**H**
2	Fixed Cost (FC):	$50,000.00					
3	Variable Cost Per Unit (AVC):	$5.20					
4	Price Per Unit (P):	$9.20					
5							
6	Q	FC	VC	TC	TR	Profit/Loss	
7	0	$50,000.00	$0.00	$50,000.00	$0.00	-$50,000.00	Loss
8	1,250	50,000.00	6,500.00	56,500.00	11,500.00	-45,000.00	Loss
9	2,500	50,000.00	13,000.00	63,000.00	23,000.00	-40,000.00	Loss
10	3,750	50,000.00	19,500.00	69,500.00	34,500.00	-35,000.00	Loss
11	5,000	50,000.00	26,000.00	76,000.00	46,000.00	-30,000.00	Loss
12	6,250	50,000.00	32,500.00	82,500.00	57,500.00	-25,000.00	Loss
13	7,500	50,000.00	39,000.00	89,000.00	69,000.00	-20,000.00	Loss
14	8,750	50,000.00	45,500.00	95,500.00	80,500.00	-15,000.00	Loss
15	10,000	50,000.00	52,000.00	102,000.00	92,000.00	-10,000.00	Loss
16	11,250	50,000.00	58,500.00	108,500.00	103,500.00	-5,000.00	Loss
17	12,500	50,000.00	65,000.00	115,000.00	115,000.00	0.00	Breakeven
18	13,750	50,000.00	71,500.00	121,500.00	126,500.00	5,000.00	Profit
19	15,000	50,000.00	78,000.00	128,000.00	138,000.00	10,000.00	Profit
20	16,250	50,000.00	84,500.00	134,500.00	149,500.00	15,000.00	Profit
21	17,500	50,000.00	91,000.00	141,000.00	161,000.00	20,000.00	Profit
22	18,750	50,000.00	97,500.00	147,500.00	172,500.00	25,000.00	Profit
23	20,000	50,000.00	104,000.00	154,000.00	184,000.00	30,000.00	Profit
24	21,250	50,000.00	110,500.00	160,500.00	195,500.00	35,000.00	Profit
25	22,500	50,000.00	117,000.00	167,000.00	207,000.00	40,000.00	Profit
26	23,750	50,000.00	123,500.00	173,500.00	218,500.00	45,000.00	Profit
27	25,000	50,000.00	130,000.00	180,000.00	230,000.00	50,000.00	Profit
28	26,250	50,000.00	136,500.00	186,500.00	241,500.00	55,000.00	Profit
29	27,500	50,000.00	143,000.00	193,000.00	253,000.00	60,000.00	Profit
30	28,750	50,000.00	149,500.00	199,500.00	264,500.00	65,000.00	Profit
31	30,000	50,000.00	156,000.00	206,000.00	276,000.00	70,000.00	Profit
32	Q:	Quantity of Output					
33	FC:	Total Fixed Cost					
34	AVC:	Average Variable Cost or Variable Cost Per Unit					
35	TC:	Total Cost					
36	TR:	Total Revenue					

Table 20.3 contains the cell formulas for the first 4 rows of Table 20.2. Note the use of absolute and relative addressing.

	B	C	D	E	F	G	H
	Table 20.3. Revenue and Cost Data for Breakeven Analysis						
7	0	=$D$2	=B7*$D$3	=C7+D7	=B7*$D$4	=F7-E7	Loss
8	=B7+1250	=$D$2	=B8*$D$3	=C8+D8	=B8*$D$4	=F8-E8	Loss
9	=B8+1250	=$D$2	=B9*$D$3	=C9+D9	=B9*$D$4	=F9-E9	Loss
10	=B9+1250	=$D$2	=B10*$D$3	=C10+D10	=B10*$D$4	=F10-E10	Loss

The breakeven point is at the point where total revenue just equals total cost (Figure 20.1). In this example, a selling price of $9.20 and average variable cost of $5.20 results in a breakeven point at 12,500 units of output. At this point, total revenue and total cost are equal to $115,000.

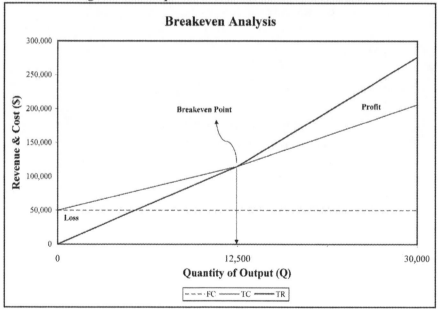

Figure 20.1. Graphical Solution to Breakeven Problem

A breakeven analysis is most clearly illustrated in a chart such as the one shown in Figure 20.1. You may use the breakeven analysis to determine how price changes, sales level changes, or cost increases or decreases will affect profitability.

CHAPTER 21

The Business & Marketing Plans

T HE FIRST STEP in starting a business is to write a business plan. Although there are many different styles of writing such a plan, all business plans should include the following:

I. COVER PAGE

Include:
- Legal name of business.
- Name of document ("Business Plan").
- Date of preparation or modification of the document.
- Name, address and phone number of the business or contact person.
- Optional: A notice advising the reader that the plan is copyrighted and confidential.

II. TABLE OF CONTENTS

- This section is written upon completion of the business plan.

III. EXECUTIVE SUMMARY

Investor's questions:
- Who? What? Why? How?

- Is this the type of business in which I want to invest?
- Will it provide a satisfactory return on investment for me?

Include the following:
- Who is asking for money? Is the business a sole proprietorship (one owner), partnership, or corporation?
- The opportunity: Product or business venture being proposed, and the size and expected growth rate.
- Total financial requirement. Itemize the major uses of money raised.
- From what sources (owner's contribution, loans, etc.) will you obtain funds?
- For a loan: How and when do you plan to repay the money?
- Expected return on investment.

Note: This section is written upon completion of the entire plan. The reader may decide to read the rest of the plan based on the executive summary. Therefore, it must be written in a way that will capture the interest of the reader.

IV. THE BUSINESS

Investor's question:
- Why should I give my money to these people?

Description
- Type: Merchandising, services, etc.
- Form: Sole proprietorship, partnership or corporation.
- Status: Start-up, expansion, etc.
- Size: Sales volume, number of employees, number and size of facilities.

Management
- Owners and the management team: Who are they? What strengths do they bring to the business (experience, expertise, etc.)? Be brief and include resumes in the appendix.
- What is the position of each? Will this be their sole means of employment?
- Name your professional advisors (lawyers, accountants, banker, consultants, etc.).

V. THE OPPORTUNITY AND MARKETING PLAN

Investor's questions:
- Why will people buy this product / service?
- Will enough people buy it?
- Is there a future for it?

4Ps of Marketing
- A good marketing plan must include a thorough explanation of the 4Ps of marketing: Product, Price, Place, and Promotion.

The Product or Service
- What is it? What is it used for?
- Is it a new idea? Has it been protected by patent, copyright, or other legal means?
- Describe unique or innovative features.
- How soon could it be expected to become obsolete? Do you have plans to modify or bring it up-to-date in the future?

Pricing Strategy
- What type of pricing strategy (skimming, penetration, etc.) will be used?
- Why is this pricing strategy beneficial for this product?

The Market
- Who are your potential customers?
- How does your product or service satisfy their needs?
- Size of market. Support this figure with market research data, statistics, etc.
- Market growth potential. Support with local, national, and international data.
- Your market share and the share you hope to obtain in the first year. How will you make a profit, yet remain competitive?
- Sales forecasts for the next five years (pessimistic, optimistic).

Promotion/Sales
- How will your product/service be sold (personal selling, mail-order, etc.)?
- How will it be advertised and promoted?

Competitive Analysis
- Major competitors: names and market shares.
- Are competitors' sales increasing, decreasing, steady? Why?
- Strengths and weaknesses: Compare your company with theirs (size, reputation, location, distribution channels, warranty, quality, price, image, etc.).
- What have you learned from watching their operations?

STP (Segmentation, Targeting, Positioning)
- How will you segment the population to market your product?
- Which segment will you target and why?
- How will you position your product?

VI. STRATEGIES FOR BUILDING THE BUSINESS

Website
- An effective Web site can attract new customers to your business.
- When your Web site has high rankings in the search engines, you have a better chance of receiving inquiries and telephone calls.

E-Mail Marketing
- E-mail campaigns are similar to advertising.
- E-mails with no plan or theme will yield minimal results.
- Make your e-mail messages brief.
- Keep your e-mail database up to date.

Personal Touch
- Technology makes it too easy to get some real impersonal marketing.
- When you have a Web site and use email to contact your customers, you may think there is no reason to contact them personally.
- A Web site or email is never a substitute for a client or prospective customer to hear your voice or seeing your face.
- Many customers will not commit to a purchase without first talking to or seeing the marketer.

VII. PRODUCTION

Investor's question:
- How will this business operate?

Location

- What makes your location suitable (proximity to markets, suppliers, transportation, availability of skilled labor, cost, etc.)?

Facilities

- Are your facilities owned or leased? State the terms.
- Briefly describe your facilities. You may wish to include sketches or floor plans.
- Will renovations be required? At what cost? Include quotes from more than one contractor in the appendix.
- What is your current capacity? What is your current percent usage of plant and equipment? For how long will this be sufficient?

Materials/Supplies

- Describe any risks associated with your materials/supplies. Who are the suppliers? Can any supplies be obtained from only one source? Are your supplies perishable? Do you have adequate storage facilities?

Personnel

- What are your current personnel needs? You may include an organizational chart in the appendix to show how your staff will be organized.
- What skills and training are required? What will be the cost of training?
- List the compensation and benefits that will be provided for each position. Include salaries, wages, overtime, and fringe benefits.

Setup

- What special environmental, municipal or other governmental permits may be required? How long does it take to obtain these permits?
- How long will it take to acquire facilities, equipment, personnel to set up operations?
- For manufacturing companies: How long after the operation has been set up will the first production run be completed?

VIII. FINANCIAL DATA

Investor's question:
- Is this an attractive investment?

Required Investment
- Total amount of funding required?
- List applications of funds (equipment, renovations, inventory, working capital, etc.). A detailed expense breakdown is not required.
- List sources of funds (owner's investment, mortgage loan, term loan, etc.).
- When can investors expect repayment?

Break-Even Analysis
- Include breakeven analysis.
- For detailed explanation of break-even analysis, refer to Chapter 20.

Balance Sheet
- Balance sheet at the start of the business.
- Pro Forma monthly balance sheets for year 1.
- Optional: Pro forma quarterly balance sheets for years 2 and 3.

Pro Forma Income Statement
- Optional: Monthly income statement for year 1.
- Annual income statement for years 1, 2 and 3.

Pro Forma Cash Flow
- Monthly cash flow for year 1.
- Optional: Quarterly cash flow for years 2 and 3.

Historical Financial Reports for Established Business
- Income statement for past year.
- Optional: Income statements for past 3-5 years.
- Balance sheet for past year.
- Optional: Balance sheets for past 3-5 years.

SAMPLE BUSINESS PLAN

A sample business plan is included in the next few pages. It is included only as a guide. This is by no means the only way to write a business plan. The plan is a modified version of a plan suggested by Canada/BC Business Service Centre.

(http://www.sb.gov.bc.ca/smallbus/workshop/download/samplebp.html).

AUTO-SWITCH MANUFACTURING, LTD. BUSINESS PLAN

TABLE OF CONTENTS

- Executive Summary
- The Business Venture
- The Company
- Management
- The Product
- The Market Place
- Market Size
- The Competition
- Auto-Switch's Advantage
- Marketing Opportunities
  - < Products and Services
  - < Research
  - < Competitive Advantage
- Marketing Strategy
  - < Target Markets
- Promotion Strategy
  - < Personal Selling
  - < Advertising
  - < Sales Promotion
  - < Publicity
- Pricing Strategy
- Distribution Strategy
- Sales Plan
- Sales Forecast
- Sources of Market Information
- Product Development
- Production
- Product Costs
- Gross Profit
- Financial Requirements

EXECUTIVE SUMMARY

This business plan has been prepared to obtain financing in the amount of $510,000 to complete the product development, set up manufacturing, and implement an aggressive sales and marketing program.

Auto-Switch Manufacturing Ltd. is a new company that has developed an automatic electronic light control product called Auto-Switch for consumer, commercial and industrial applications.

The potential market for this product is over $150 million over the next 5 years.

Auto-Switch Manufacturing Ltd. will be profitable within the first year of operations and conservatively expects to achieve sales of almost $3 million with net profit of over $1 million by the end of the third year.

The company will be self-sustaining by the end of the first year.

The major markets for the new product are throughout North America.

An extensive market survey has revealed that no other product presently on the market compares with Auto-Switch in terms of features, benefits and low price.

Full production can begin within 3 months after financing, has been arranged and the first 1000 production units will be available for the market within 5 months after financing.

Auto-Switch Manufacturing Ltd. is prepared to offer equity return for investment in the Company. The Company will also consider other arrangements to obtain the necessary finances.

No guarantees are expressed or implied regarding the success of the venture described in this business plan.

THE BUSINESS VENTURE

This business plan has been prepared in order to raise the financing necessary to further develop, manufacture, and distribute a new electronic product that has widespread industrial, commercial and consumer applications.

The new product, called "Auto-Switch", will automatically turn lights on and off when the ambient light in a room reaches a predetermined level.

The increasing concerns about security, personal safety, energy conservation and the general trend toward automation has created a market for devices that reduce or eliminate the problems associated with manual control of lighting systems.

Homes, offices, factories, hospitals, schools, public buildings and construction sites are only a few of the more obvious applications. Auto-Switch will be particularly valuable in remote or unattended locations.

The idea for the product was conceived by Mr. Light as a result of numerous inquiries received by Mr. Light's present employer for a simple, automatic light control device. Mr. Light's employer is not involved in the lighting or light control marketplace and is not interested in developing a product or entering the marketplace because of other commitments and business priorities.

Mr. Light has received permission from his employer to pursue the development of the product as a private venture, provided that the venture does not interfere with the employer's business.

Mr. Light has contacted various prospective users of the product to determine product requirements and develop specifications.

An engineering prototype of the product has already been developed. The prototype was developed by Mr. Light in his spare time with limited resources.

An amount equal to $510,000 is required to complete the development of the product, to set up manufacturing, and to establish a sales and marketing program.

The $510,000 will be supplemented by revenue generated from sales of the product, to cover the total financial requirements for the first year of operation. The business will be self-sustaining by the end of the first year of operation.

Auto-Switch Manufacturing Ltd. is prepared to offer common (voting) shares or other arrangements in return for the investment.

THE COMPANY

Auto-Switch Manufacturing Ltd. was incorporated in the State of California on June 1, 20xx.

The Company's business address is: 220 Innovation Boulevard, Pomona, CA 12345.

Telephone (909) 123-1234, Fax: (909) 123-1234, E Mail: light@Auto Switch.com.

Auto-Switch Manufacturing Ltd. was established to develop and manufacture a specialty electronic light control product.

The product is still under development. At present, the Company does not have any full time employees.

The Company is presently operating out of the residence of one of the principals.

The two principals of the Company are:

- Mr. I. M. Light, President and original developer of the product.
- Mr. N. O. Electric, Secretary of the Company, responsible for production.

Any questions relating to the business plan are to be directed to Mr. I. M. Light.

MANAGEMENT

The current members of the management group are the principals of Auto-Switch Manufacturing Ltd.

Mr. Light is a graduate of Cal. Poly. Pomona with a bachelor's degree in Electrical Engineering. He has 7 years of industrial experience, progressing from a technician to the supervisor of an engineering test laboratory with a local manufacturer of electronic equipment.

Mr. Electric graduated from Cal. Poly. Pomona with a bachelor's degree in Operations Management, and has over 10 years of industrial experience in electrical components and electronics manufacturing. He currently is employed as the production manager with the same electronics firm as Mr. Light.

Mr. Light is responsible for technical development and Mr. Electric will be responsible for production and project management.

Mr. Light and Mr. Electric each own 50% of Auto-Switch Manufacturing Ltd.

The sales and marketing functions will be the responsibility of an individual who is currently employed as a sales manager for a home entertainment distribution company. The sales manager has over 15 years of sales and marketing experience in the home entertainment industry.

All three individuals are prepared to resign their present positions and make a full time commitment to Auto-Switch when financing has been arranged.

Initially, the accounting and financial control functions will be handled on a part-time basis by a senior member of a firm of Certified Public Accountants. The CPA is prepared to work for modest compensation until the product has been developed and is ready for manufacturing.

Detailed resumes of the management team members are in the appendix.

THE PRODUCT

Auto-Switch is an automatic electronic switch for controlling electric lights. The complete assembly is the same size and shape as a standard wall-type electric light switch and is designed to replace the wall switch using the same standard mounting screws and electrical wiring. No modifications to the mounting or wiring is required.

Auto-Switch consists of an optical sensor that detects the amount of light in the room and an electronic circuit that operates a sensitive relay for turning the lights on and off. The sensitivity of the light detecting circuit can be set to one of three preset levels depending on the type of application (i.e. to maintain a minimum acceptable light level for normal vision in an office, to turn the lights on under partially subdued ambient light conditions, or to switch the lights on only under extremely low light levels).

The adjustment control is easily accessible on the face plate of Auto-Switch. A manually operated switch is also available on the face plate of Auto-Switch to disable the automatic control and enable Auto-Switch to be used as a standard manual on/off light switch.

A unique feature in Auto-Switch is the extremely sensitive and reliable light sensing circuit. The Auto-Switch product is not patented. However, a detailed description of the product and design drawings have been witnessed and dated by a notary public and two independent electronic engineers.

THE MARKETPLACE

The primary markets for Auto-Switch at this time which provide the greatest sales potential in a relatively short period of time, are in Canada and the United States.

Consumer, commercial and industrial users are all prospective customers for the product. The major potential market in the consumer sector will be accessed through the large retailers of small appliances, lighting fixtures, and electrical hardware such as:

- Major department stores
- Hardware store chains
- Retail lighting outlets
- Mail order houses

The primary customers in the commercial and industrial sector will be electrical engineering firms, electrical contractors, industrial plant and commercial building maintenance departments, security companies, and public buildings. The target markets are easily accessible and identifiable.

Considerable interest in the product has already been expressed by the following:

- House Depot Chain in the U.S.
- Low's emporium in Canada.
- The Federal, State, and Provincial Governments.
- Electric Generating Companies in Canada and the U.S.
- Southern California Electrical Distributors in the U.S.
- Several large engineering and architectural firms in Canada and the U.S.
- Wally Marty department store chains in Canada and U.S.

All of the above feel that there will be a demand for Auto-Switch because of the practical value of the product, and because there is no other product currently available that provides the features and low price of Auto-Switch.

The product is fully automatic, highly reliable, can be adjusted for different light levels, is CSA approved in Canada and UL approved in the United States, and will have a **retail price** of $128. Letters of intent have been received from three large retailers in the U.S. for trial orders totaling 1500 units. The purchases are subject to the product meeting all specifications. An industrial distributor in Canada has issued a purchase order for 1000 units, subject to successful demonstration of the prototype unit.

MARKET SIZE

Approximately 200,000 products similar to Auto-Switch were sold in 2004, and approximately 280,000 were sold in 2005. The market is expected to grow at an annual rate of 40% over the next 5 years.

The following market values are based on an average **wholesale selling price** by Auto-Switch Manufacturing of $70.

- Estimated size of the total Canadian market over the next 5 years: **200,000** units.
- Total Canadian market sales volume potential over the next 5 years: **$14,000,000 US$).**
- Estimated size of the total U.S. market over the next 5 years: **2,000,000** units.

- Total U.S. market sales volume potential over the next 5 years: **$140,000,000 (US$).**
- The suggested retail price (end user price) will be **$128.**

THE COMPETITION

There are three known competitors in North America for products that are in part, similar to the proposed Auto-Switch product. The three competitors are:

1. Holt Industries
2. Day & Night Enterprises, Inc.
3. Switch-Guard Unlimited, Inc.

1. Holt Industries

Holt Industries is a small manufacturer located in the Midwestern United States which sells primarily to the farming industry. The product is not easily adaptable to other applications. They do not have a distribution network, and they sell directly to the end user. The reported selling price of the product is $220 U.S. Holt Industries currently has approximately 20% of the present market.

2. Day & Night Enterprises, Inc.

Day & Night is located in the Southwestern United States and manufactures a very simple, low cost device that is capable of controlling only external desk or table lamps. The device is plugged into a standard wall outlet and the lamp to be controlled is then plugged into the device. The unit sells for $125 U.S. retail and is widely distributed throughout the United States and Canada. Tests on the product indicate that the device will only sense an extreme change in light conditions (i.e. from very light to very dark). Because of the limited applications and operation of the product, it is not considered to be a serious threat to the marketability of Auto-Switch. Day & Night presently has approximately 30% of the present market.

3. Switch-Guard Unlimited Inc.

Switch-Guard Unlimited is located in eastern Canada and has a product similar to Auto-Switch but which sells for almost twice Auto-Switch's projected retail selling price. The product is sold direct to the end user. They have approximately 40% of the market share.

The balance of the market is shared by 4 or 5 small U.S. manufacturers and 2 imports. None of the products is considered to be reliable, and all are sold only through mail order catalogues.

AUTO-SWITCH'S ADVANTAGE

The production cost of Auto-Switch will be substantially lower than the competitors because of Auto-Switch's superior design and use of more advanced and lower-cost technology.

Auto-Switch combines low-cost, high reliability and adaptability to a wide range of applications. Auto-Switch will be CSA approved for sale in Canada and UL approved for sale in the United States.

Auto-Switch will also be sold through an effective distributor and dealer network, and will be adaptable to a wide range of industrial, commercial, and consumer needs.

MARKETING OPPORTUNITIES

The market for security products is continuously growing, and business and technology changes are certain. Also, familiarity of the companies' names that are in this type of business can be helpful because the added-value of our company would strengthen its competitive position once the potential user has examined the available options and benefits. We are determined to gain a 50% share of the electronic switch market.

It is estimated that half of the expected users would consider switching to a system that offers added-value for first-time users. Although this type of business is not considered a new business, options can be considered new to many who are becoming interested in acquiring particular views toward its usage.

The Company intends to use a combination of employees and distributors for marketing its products. Auto-Switch's founders have extensive understanding and experience in establishing relationships with major prospective distributors, which should facilitate marketing. The Company also has been developing distinctive packaging and logos to achieve brand recognition for its products.

Our basic approach in the development stages of this product includes setting objectives, examining the scope and limitations, conducting a situation and environmental analysis, and selecting strategies while detailing specific programs and activities. Areas of concern include the decision areas in marketing, specifically the product, promotion, pricing, and distribution decisions.

It is vital to provide the marketing people with essential information to coordinate marketing operations once patent controls and licenses are in place.

PRODUCTS AND SERVICES

The overall product strategy was to develop an electronic switch that was of universal appeal to a large population mix. Introducing a new product involves many decisions and preparations to ensure the product has the best chance of acceptance and survival. Planning activities will therefore be coordinated with the development and marketing research personnel to ensure total involvement and commitment to the innovative product.

Our product is not owned by any merchant or retailer. Simplicity and ease of access are common concerns for first-time users. Speed of delivery is critical for experienced users. Consequently, our plan is to market a product that will provide a combination of uses that will accommodate customers' needs and demands.

RESEARCH

Research was limited to the personal experience of the founders and secondary sources. The implementation has no limitations because the use of such devices is widespread and the demand for security extensive. Furthermore, demand for this product has conclusively been established, as exhibited by the willingness of users and their desires to purchase and use such products.

Preliminary New Product Planning and Testing

The planning process is primarily directed at the first stage of the marketing program. It is wise to conduct some form of market test prior to incurring the large expenditure of introducing the product on a full-scale basis.

In our limited market testing, we conducted an experiment on a small scale to learn what to expect when we are ready to market the product on a large scale. Users' reactions to the product were very favorable in general, and to such associated characteristics as performance, desired attributes, reliability, design, etc.

We answered major questions:

1. What applications and usage levels would buyers employ?
2. Are there any high-potential markets where the product fits a real need in the user's operations?
3. Who are the key purchasing influences in high-potential markets?
4. What volume of sales (and market share) and profits can be expected?
5. What are some of the relative effectiveness of various promotional techniques?
6. What are users' responses to various price possibilities?

Members of the test market sample accurately represented characteristics of the universe of potential users identified above. The sample was designed to include the probable preferences and prejudices, wants and needs. The method involved demonstrating to prospective users and learning their reactions. We were satisfied that enough users liked and thoroughly appreciated our product. We further revised the product's design and specifications.

We were able to accomplish the following:

1. Measure general interest and opportunities via actual usage.
2. Forecast probable size and nature of the market.
3. Evaluate alternative solutions.
4. Provide experience before fully expanding the line and offerings.
5. Improve the quality of product performance in actual use.

COMPETITIVE ADVANTAGES

In this multi-billion dollar market, where security concerns are strong, Auto-Switch mounts its confidence based on major differences in its offering. The biggest selling point for our company is our intelligent and innovative product designed to fully integrate and dramatically improve light switching process.

In anticipating competitors' reactions to the introduction of our product, we are prepared to improve the design and increase promotional incentives.

MARKETING STRATEGY

TARGET MARKETS

Users do not have to be technically proficient. We are best prepared to acquire a strong position in the market because our product version is technically advanced yet simple to use with quickness of delivery.

Two main targets toward which promotional activities can be directed:

1. Industries and Governmental agencies.
2. First-time users and existing users who wish to expand their present use of this category of products.

Customer cultivation includes identification of industries, markets, and companies offering the greatest potential. It is important to note that the demand for small electronic devices has increased tenfold since the nineties. The trend is observed by looking at advertisements for such products. These numbers justify our decision to focus on present and future users.

Findings reveal that the market for this type of usage consists primarily of people in the home and in business. Our target market will be the same as our competitors' for the most part, yet, more of value to the more-sophisticated and time-conscious consumer. Increasing familiarity can best be accomplished by implementing the strategy which will be discussed later.

PROMOTION STRATEGY

Promotional strategy consists of personal selling, advertising, sales promotion and publicity, directed toward communicating to the target markets, while stimulating usage and search behavior:

a) Increase attention, interest, desire and action. Stimulate inquiries.
b) Increase the number of users and the frequency of their use.
c) Increase the quality of users, (i.e., users with the greatest probability of repurchase).
d) Increase repurchases—Increase frequency, volume, extend the period of time over which repurchases continue to be made.
e) Increase the quality and the amount of word-of-mouth communications among consumers and increase favorable user feedback.

A percentage of prospective users may have never considered using a light switching device because of the widespread lack of knowledge. However, a trend is noted when observing advertisements for security devices. These numbers confirm our decision to focus on present and future users.

Increase product knowledge by implementing the following:

a) Increase the user's total knowledge about our product.
b) Increase the ratio of favorable knowledge to unfavorable knowledge about our brand.
c) Improve the accessibility of this knowledge in the consumer's mind.
d) Improve the accuracy of knowledge about the product in the consumer's mind (eliminate unfavorable myths).
e) Improve the appropriateness of consumer knowledge—especially on unique points of product differentiation and hidden qualities.
f) Improve the credibility of consumer knowledge.

A potential drawback to our company is its lack of name familiarity at this period of introduction. This will be overcome through the communications strategy.

PERSONAL SELLING

Personal Selling strategies emphasize informing and persuading our users to connect with Auto-Switch, Ltd. Familiarity with our Web site will enable our salespeople to educate users/advertisers and highlight the advantages of our offering and options as compared to those of competitors. An awareness of our brand and site, while encouraging feedback from both advertisers and users, will assist us in maintaining customer satisfaction.

Basic alternatives to consider:

1. Direct sales force (salary plus commission basis).
2. Agents.
3. Distributors (commission basis).

Sales training includes determination of the following:

1. Training objectives in terms of results desired, such as knowledge of products, sales techniques, etc.
2. Timing (during working hours or after hours).
3. Training costs.

Sales territories include a group of existing or potential customers who can readily be called on by one or more channels of distribution. Market potentials are useful in defining sales territories.

ADVERTISING

The starting point in the selection of media is an analysis of the various strengths and weaknesses, and the characteristics as appropriate to the particular strategy. Media choices include home/lifestyle and electronic magazines.

Advertising messages will emphasize the following:

1. Differentiate our offering from our competitors' offerings. This activity is best accomplished by developing a strong image in the customers' mind.
2. Establish our offerings as both easy-to-use and yet advanced for the non-technical user and sophisticated users.

SALES PROMOTION

Primary demand could be stimulated by offering incentives to try our product, in cooperation with advertising sponsors.

Brochure

Informational brochures will be used to complement other promotional strategies. A corporate brochure will be developed outlining our provisions, services, and fee structure. The brochure will highlight our level of expertise. The brochures will be distributed at workshops, seminars, associations, and conferences to key business leaders and prospective users.

PUBLICITY

This effort will support other promotional activities. When information about a company or its offerings is considered newsworthy, the media communicate that information for "free" without payment by a sponsor. Credibility of the party communicating is vital in the delivery of the message.

Publicity of the product takes the form of free editorial space in trade and consumer media. Non-product publicity involves newsworthy reports to the media of activity as related to this industry.

Ways to acquire publicity:

1. Establishing relationships with media people.
2. Preparing and distributing news releases—coordination and timing are key elements.
3. Developing mailing lists.
4. Distributing flyers.

Trade Shows

A trade show is a unique promotional tool because it exposes our company to thousands of potential customers in a matter of days. This vehicle offers selling awareness and selling opportunities. It further allows our marketing and technical people to meet prospective buyers face-to-face. We will focus on clarifying needs by:

a) making the potential buyers conscious of the differences between our product and competitors,
b) demonstrating the nature of this difference,
c) increasing the magnitude of the differences, and
d) making the consumer feel more certain that our product is best for them at present and in the future.

PRICING STRATEGY

Profits are generated through wholesalers and direct sales through the Internet. Therefore, we believe that a primary task is to have a flexible pricing policy. Pricing is determined by the following strategies:

1. Stimulate market growth and capture and hold a satisfactory market share at a profit through low prices.
2. Emphasize value more than costs in pricing.
3. Allow maximum exposure and penetration in a relatively short time.

DISTRIBUTION STRATEGY

These are ways by which goods and services reach the final users. Options to consider:

1. Encourage users to visit our Web site. This would require a substantial investment in upgrading our site.
2. Sell the consumer version of our products in selected retail stores to enable the user to have the product instantly available.
3. Sell a bare-bones version of the product through our Web site at a lower cost. The cost of production would be less because no elaborate packaging will be required.
4. Encourage users to buy the more-advanced version of our product for its superior performance.

The Company's managers have determined that it is in the company's best interest to adopt a policy that combines all of the above mentioned methods. This strategy will have the advantage of meeting the majority of the users' needs and preferences.

SALES PLAN

The sales program for the first year will concentrate on developing the Canadian marketplace. The U.S. sales program will commence within six months after the product is available in Canada.

The sales organization will be divided into two groups: Consumer sales and Commercial/Industrial sales. The consumer sales group will concentrate on developing a dealer network (retailer) that will sell the product directly to the consumer. The initial sales efforts will concentrate on the national department store chains, national lighting outlets, hardware store chains, and a major international mail order house.

In general, each of the above retailers uses a central purchasing department for all outlets in Canada and the United States. The purchasing decisions are generally made by merchandising managers who are responsible for small electrical appliances and other similar hard goods.

Initially, the consumer sales group will require two full time sales people to develop the Canadian consumer market. The commercial/industrial sales group will also require two full time sales people to concentrate initially on developing a wholesale distributor network with at least 6 distributors in Canada and 10 to 12 distributors in the U.S. The distributors will have access to the major electrical contractors, engineering firms, and electrical suppliers in their respective areas.

All sales to Provincial and Federal government departments in Canada will be handled by Auto-Switch Manufacturing Ltd. U.S. government sales will be handled by the U.S. distributors. A secretary and a sales order clerk will provide sales support for both the consumer sales group and the commercial/ industrial sales group.

A simple but effective advertising campaign will be implemented to support the sales efforts. Consumer advertising will consist of monthly advertisements in several magazines. Half-page advertisements will be placed in two monthly trade publications with a large circulation to the electrical contracting and plant maintenance markets in Canada and the U.S.

As mentioned above, there is a variety of ways this product can be made available to generate revenue. With mounting competition and increasing costs in television ads, Internet sites are an appealing way to a narrow but passionate population. As more users spend more time on the Web, advertisers allocate more of their budgets to this medium. We, therefore, expect a rapidly increasing presence for our company.

We recognize and acknowledge that attracting high-end customers must be our key objective in promoting our products. To this end, we plan to do the following.

- Establish a clear-cut brand to distinguish our product from the other products. We believe that doing so establishes a compelling value equation for customers.
- Identify the key elements that bond our products and their users, and what the brand mean to them.
- Promote our brand identity by establishing clear objectives for our site that inform, entertain, and instruct. These objectives will establish the relationship that create customer bond and foster user loyalty.
- By thinking of the media as benefactors rather than necessary evil, we will create opportunities for both ourselves and end users that will greatly enhance and expand the long-term value of our company.

SALES FORECAST

The sales forecast in Table 21.1 is considered to be an estimate based on the responses from the companies surveyed. Additional sales can be anticipated with increased market penetration and product recognition.

Table 21.1. Sales Forecasts			
	Unit Sales	**Price**	**Total Sales**
Year 1	7,000	$70	$490,000
Year 2	17,000	$70	$1,190,000
Year 3	42,000	$70	$2,940,000

Note: Year 1 will commence approximately 5 months after financing has been arranged, and Year 3 sales will represent approximately 30% market share.

The sales over the first year will be divided approximately as follows:

35% to Western Canada
55% to Central and Eastern Canada
10% to the United States

Division of sales over the second and third years will be approximately:

10% to Western Canada
30% to Central and Eastern Canada
60% to the United States

The above estimate of sales is considered to be extremely conservative in view of the wide range of applications, the unique operating features, and the low selling price of the product.

SOURCES OF MARKET INFORMATION

The market and sales data were collected by a combination of a market survey and research of published information. The market survey was conducted primarily in the United States and Eastern Canada. Information also was obtained from the following publications:

- *Home Owners of America*, Issue 38, March 2005.
- *Electrical Contractors Journal*, April 2005.
- *U.S. Government Report*, # 134297-4236A.

PRODUCT DEVELOPMENT

An engineering prototype model of Auto-Switch has been developed to prove the concept and basic design of the product. The engineering prototype satisfactorily demonstrates the technical feasibility and basic operation of the product.

The information in Table 21.2 is a list of estimated additional engineering development work that is required before the product is ready for mass production.

Table 21.2. Number of Hours of Work Required to Complete the Task	
TASK	HOURS
1. Refine design to improve operation and to reduce costs.	60
2. Build two engineering prototypes for tests and evaluation.	60
3. Conduct performance and reliability tests on the engineering	60
4. Modify design and repeat performance tests as required.	40
5. Prepare formal engineering drawings, design packaging and establish projected manufacturing costs.	250

Special engineering test equipment will be required to conduct performance and reliability tests. The test equipment will consist of special light-sensing and measuring equipment and controlled light sources.

No major or critical risks are anticipated during successful completion of the engineering development. The technical feasibility has already been proven on the engineering prototype. The balance of the engineering development program will consist primarily of refining the design to optimize its performance and reliability and to reduce manufacturing costs. A technician will be required to assist Mr. Light with the engineering development.

PRODUCTION

Auto-Switch will be manufactured using standard electronic assembly techniques. All electronic circuitry will be mounted on a printed circuit board which will be installed in a plastic molded case.

The electronic printed circuit board will be manufactured under sub-contract by a local electronics manufacturing company. Auto-Switch Manufacturing will supply all materials to the sub-contractor.

The plastic case will be manufactured by a local plastics manufacturing company. All materials and components for the product are readily available "off-the-shelf" from at least three suppliers. Auto-Switch Manufacturing Ltd. will assemble the electronic printed circuit board in the plastic case and test the product before shipping.

A total of 6 assembly personnel, plus an assembly line supervisor, will be required to assemble the product. Two test technicians will be required to inspect and test the product before shipping. Approximately 4,000 square feet of space will be required to store inventory, assemble the product, and test it. Special semi-automated equipment will be required to test the product after assembly. Each unit will undergo 24 hours of continuous testing before shipping to a customer.

Suitable manufacturing space has been identified. The owners of the property are prepared to enter into a 5-year lease agreement or longer if required.

Three months from the time that financing has been arranged will be required to set up manufacturing and start production of the first 1000 pieces. These production units will be complete within two months after the start of production.

PRODUCT COSTS

The information in Table 21.3 is the projected production costs for one Auto-Switch Unit based on an initial production run of 1,000 pieces.

Table 21.3. Production Costs	
Materials	$15.00
Sub-contractor circuit board assembly	$10.00
Assembly, inspection, testing and packaging for shipping	$10.00
Total Product Cost (per unit)	**$35.00**

GROSS PROFIT

The suggested retail price for Auto-Switch will be $128 excluding taxes. The discount required by the major retail outlets for the consumer market are between 40% and 50% off the list price. A 45% discount has been used for purposes of determining the gross profit (Table 21.4). The selling price to the industrial/commercial wholesale distributor will be the same as to the retail outlets, and will be established at 45% below the retail list price.

Table 21.4. Calculation of Gross Profit	
Net selling price by Auto-Switch Manufacturing:	$70.00
Cost of Sales (Product Cost) per unit:	$35.00
Gross profit per unit:	$35.00
Margin:	50%

FINANCIAL REQUIREMENTS

The design of the Auto-Switch product has been completely financed to date from personal resources by Mr. Light and Mr. Electric. The total investment to date has exceeded $50,000, not including the Principals' time. Additional financing in the amount of $510,000 is required to complete the product development, to set up production, and to establish a marketing program. Table 21.5 is a summary of the projected first year's total costs.

Table 21.5. Projected First-Year Costs	
PROJECTED FIRST YEAR'S TOTAL COSTS	
Production Development Costs	$45,000
Production (including inventory)	477,000
Sales and marketing expenses	106,000
Administration and overhead	72,000
Total financial requirements for first year	**$700,000**

The above costs include all operating expenses, manufacturing labor, materials, and capital equipment for engineering and production. The difference of $190,000 between the total costs ($700,000) and the additional financing required ($ 510,000) will be covered by revenue generated from the sale of the product during the first year. The Auto-Switch Manufacturing operations will be self-sustaining by the end of the first year (see Table 21.6).

Table 21.6. Pro Forma Income Statements			
PRO FORMA INCOME STATEMENTS			
	Year 1	**Year 2**	**Year 3**
Sales	$490,000	$1,190,000	$2,940,000
Cost of Sales	245,000	595,000	1,470,000
Gross Profit	245,000	595,000	1,470,000
Sales Expense	106,000	177,000	248,500
Administration & Overhead	72,000	110,000	130,000
Engineering Expense	35,000	24,000	80,000
Net Profit (Loss)	**$32,000**	**$248,000**	**$1,011,500**

CHAPTER 22

Creating A Web Page

A WEB SITE CAN attract new customers to your business, from your local area to across the globe. A Web site is a hybrid marketing tool, serving both as a resource and as advertising. As a resource, it has the same effect as a one-on-one presentation. As advertising, it is broadcasting your message to a wide audience.

In order to create a Web Page, you are encouraged to use Notepad. While in Notepad, make sure you include all the required HTML tags and save your document with extension "HTM" or "HTML." By default, Notepad adds extension "TXT" to all saved files. You must override it and change it to HTM or HTML. Your Web Page in Notepad should look like the following:

<**HTML**> (This is the beginning of your file).
<HEAD>
<TITLE> Use a title of your choice here</TITLE>
</HEAD>
<BODY>
    All your HTML code will go here (i.e., the body of your document).
</BODY>
</**HTML**> (This is the end of your file).

After completion of your code, make sure you save it as a file on your disk. Don't forget to change the extension. For example, "Lab1.htm" or "WebPage1. html", or any other name as long as the extension is correct.

EXAMPLE 22.1. This example shows how to create a simple Web page. The source code is displayed in Figure 22.1.

Figure 22.1. Source Code for Example 22.1

```
<html>
<head>
<title> First web page </title>
</head>
<body>
Welcome to my first web page. This page only displays text.
</body>
</html>
```

Use Notepad to create the HTML code. Make sure you save it on your disk with extension htm or html. After the file is saved, you can click on this file on your disk to load it in the browser. Your Web page should look like Figure 22.2.

Figure 22.2. Results for Example 22.1

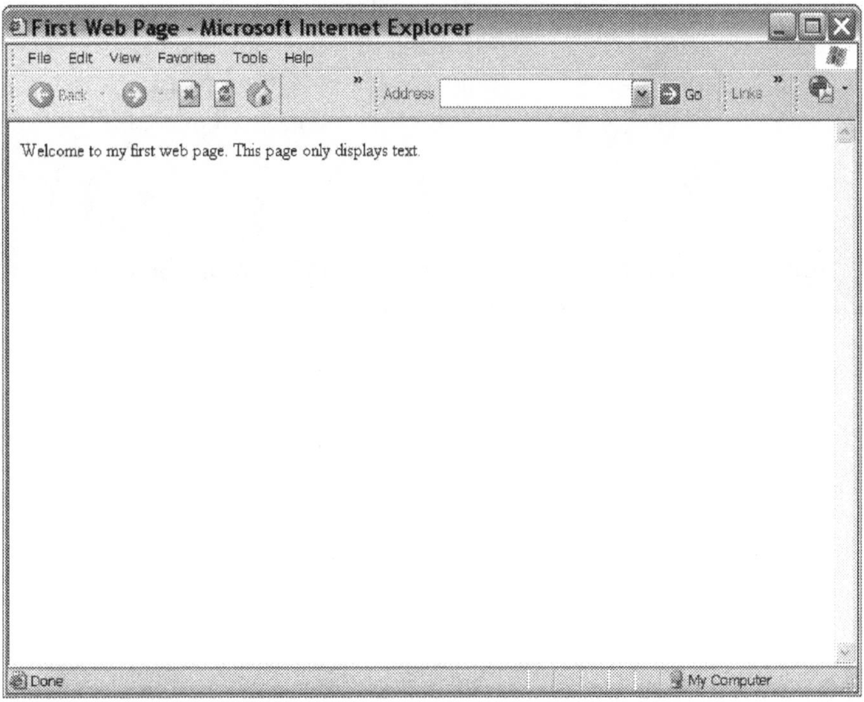

For convenience, some of the most common HTML tags are summarized below:

TAG	**FUNCTION**
<HTML> . . . </HTML>	Encloses the entire HTML document.
<head> . . . </head>	Encloses the head of the HTML document.
<title> . . . </title>	Indicates the title of the document. Used within <head>.
<body> . . . </body>	Encloses the body of the HTML document.
<p> . . . </p>	A paragraph; skips a line between paragraphs.
 	A line break.
<hr>	A horizontal rule line. <hr width="50%" size="6" align="center">
<h1> . . . </h1>	A first-level heading.
<h2> . . . </h2>	A second-level heading.
<h3> . . . </h3>	A third-level heading.
<h4> . . . </h4>	A fourth-level heading (seldom used).
<h5> . . . </h5>	A fifth-level heading (seldom used).
<h6> . . . </h6>	A sixth-level heading (seldom used).
<b> . . . </b>	Bold.
<i> . . . </i>	Italics.

You can use italics within headings (h1, h2, . . .), but boldface usually won't show in headings because they are already bold.

<small> . . . </small>	Small text.
<big> . . . </big>	Big text.
^{. . .}	Superscript Small.
_{. . .}	Subscript Small.
<strike> . . . </strike>	Strikethrough Small (draws a line through text).
<u> . . . </u>	Underline.
<div> . . . </div>	A region of text to be formatted.
	align= ". . ." Align text to center, left, or right. (Can also be used with <p>, <h1>, <h2>, <h3>, and so on)
<OL> . . . </OL>	An ordered (numbered) list.
	type= ". . ." The type of numerals used

<table>
<tbody>
<tr><td></td><td></td><td>to label the list. Possible values are A, a, I, i, 1 ·</td></tr>
<tr><td></td><td>start= ". . ."</td><td>The value with which to start this list.</td></tr>
<tr><td><UL> . . . </UL></td><td></td><td>An unordered (bulleted) list.</td></tr>
<tr><td></td><td>type= ". . ."</td><td>The bullet used to mark list items. Possible values are disc, circle, and square.</td></tr>
<tr><td><Li> . . . </Li></td><td></td><td>A list item for use with <OL> or <UL>.</td></tr>
<tr><td></td><td>type= ". . ."</td><td>The type of bullet or number used to label this item. Possible values are disc, circle, square, a, A, i, I, 1.</td></tr>
<tr><td></td><td>value= ". . ."</td><td>The numeric value this list item should have (affects this item and all below it in <OL> lists).</td></tr>
</tbody>
</table>

Use <UL> and <Li> for unordered lists, <OL> and <Li> for ordered lists.

EXAMPLE 22.2. This example teaches you how to create bullets (lists). There are two types of bullet: ordered (OL) and unordered (UL). The source code in Figure 22.3 demonstrates the format for entering lists. You can create this file with Notepad. Indentation is for clarity and plays no role. Make sure you save the file with extension .htm or .html.

Figure 22.3. Source Code for Example 22.2

```
<html>
<head>
<title>Bullets</title>
</head>
<body>
<h1 align= "center"> Welcome to My Web Page </h1>
The following are the assignments for this course:
<br>
<OL>
        <Li> Financial statements </Li>
        <Li> Sales Forecasting </Li>
        <Li> Regression Analysis </Li>
        <Li> Web Page Design </Li>
</OL>
<br>
<i><b>All the assignments are due at the end of the week.</b></i>
</body>
</html>
```

After you have saved the file, you can click on it and the results, as displayed in Figure 22.4, will appear.

Figure 22.4. Results for Example 22.2

NESTED LISTS

Both ordered and unordered lists can be nested within each other. This is shown in Example 22.3. In here, the problem in Example 22.2 is modified by nesting an ordered list within the first list and then nesting an unordered list within the second one. Again, you can create this file with Notepad. Make sure you save it with extension .htm or .html.

EXAMPLE 22.3. This example demonstrates how nested lists are created. The source code is displayed in Figure 22.5.

Figure 22.5. Source Code for Example 22.3

```
<html>
<head>
<title>Nested Bullets</title>
</head>
<body>
<h1 align= "center"> Nested Bullets </h1>
The following are the assignments for this course:
<br>
<OL>
        <Li> Financial statements </Li>
        <Li> Sales Forecasting </Li>
        <Li> Regression Analysis </Li>
        <Li> Web Page Design </Li>

        <OL TYPE="a">
                <LI>Make sure source code is included</LI>
                <LI>Submit Your Disk</LI>

                <UL type= "circle">
                        <LI>3.5" Floppy Disk</LI>
                        <LI>Compact Disk (CD)</LI>
                        <LI>DVD</LI>
                </UL>
        <OL>
</OL>

</body>
</html>
```

After the source code is saved, you can click on it and the results, displayed in Figure 22.6, will appear.

Figure 22.6. Results for Example 22.3

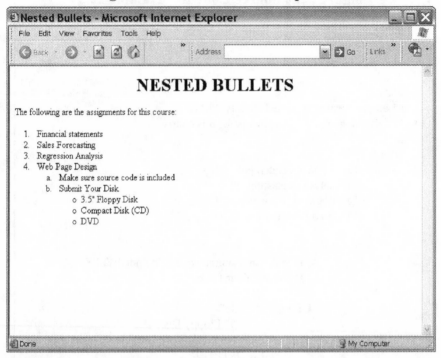

LINKING TO OTHER WEB PAGES

The tag to create a link is called <a>, which stands for anchor. You put the address of the page to link to in quotes after href=, like the following:

<a href = "http://www.csupomona.edu">click here to go to Cal Poly Pomona's Web page</a>

LINKING BETWEEN YOUR OWN PAGES

When you create a link from one page to another page on the same computer, it isn't necessary to specify a complete Internet address. If the two pages are in the same directory folder, you can simply use the name of the HTML file:

<a href = "pagetwo.htm">click here to go to page 2.</a>

LINKING BETWEEN DIFFERENT PARTS OF THE SAME WEB PAGE

Put this command on top of your Web page:

<a name = "top"> </a>

Put this command in the bottom of your Web page:

<a href = "#top"> Click here to return to the top.</a>

CREATING A TABLE

<TABLE border = "6" Bordercolor = "red" cellpadding = "5" cellspacing = "4" width= "500">
    <TR> Create table row
        <TH> Table heading (optional)
        </TH>
    </TR>
    <TR>
        <TD> Table details (columns)
        </TD>
    </TR>
</TABLE>

EXAMPLE 22.4. This example teaches you how to create a table. The source code is displayed in Figure 22.7.

Figure 22.7. HTML Code for Example 22.4

```
<html>
<head>
<title> My First Table </title>
</head>
<body>
<br>
<b> The due dates are subject to change: </b>
<br><br>
<center><font size= "4" color= "blue">ASSIGNMENT TABLE
</font></center>
<br>
<table align= "center" width= "45%"  border= "2"  bordercolor="red"
cellpadding= "3">
        <tr>
                <th> Assignment  </th>
                <th> Topic </th>
                <th> Due Date </th>
        </tr>
        <tr>

                <td align = "center"> #1 </td>
                <td> Spreadsheets </td>
                <td> March 15 </td>
        </tr>
        <tr>

                <td align = "center"> #2 </td>
                <td> Market Research </td>
                <td> April 10 </td>
        </tr>
</table>
</body>
</html>
```

The results are displayed in Figure 22.8.

Figure 22.8. Results for Example 22.4

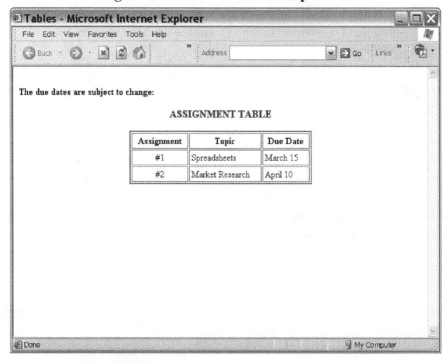

PUTTING GRAPHICS ON A WEB PAGE

<img src = "picture.gif" width = "put a number here" height = "put a number here" align = "center, right, top, middle">

CHANGING THE BACKGROUND

<body background = "picture.jpg" text = "white"> or
<body bgcolor = "purple" text = "yellow">

PRESERVING SPACES AND LINE BREAKS

<pre> </pre>

CHANGING FONT SIZE AND COLORS

<font size = "5" color = "blue"> </font> size can be from 1 (smallest) to 7 (largest)

MARQUEES

<marquee>
     put text or picture here
</marquee>
<marquee loop = "   " behavior = "   " direction = "   " Bgcolor = "   " Height = "   " Width = "   ">
     Loop can be any number. The default value is "infinite".
     Behavior can be "scroll", "slide" or "alternate"
     Direction can be "left", "right", "up", or "down"
</marquee>

EXAMPLE 22.5. This example teaches you how to create Marquees. Some of the browsers do not support Marquees.

Figure 22.9. HTML Code for Example 22.5

```
<html>
<head>
<title>Marquee</title>
</head>
<body>
<font size = "5">
<marquee>

        This is the <big><u><b>scroll</b></u></big> (default)

</marquee>

<br><br>

<marquee behavior = "slide">

        This is the <big><u><b>slide</b></u></big>

</marquee>

<br><br>

<marquee behavior = "alternate">

        This is the <big><u><b>alternate</b></u></big>

</marquee>

</font>
</body>
</html>
```

The results of Example 22.5 are displayed in Figure 22.10.

Figure 22.10. Results for Example 22.5

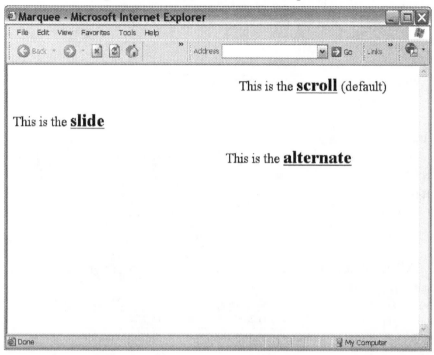

FORMS

<form method = "post" action = "mailto: put e mail address here">

Text

Enter your name: <input type = "text" name = "Lastname" size = "15" maxlength = "40">

Checkbox

<input type = "checkbox" name = "Like it"> I really like this class.
<input type = "checkbox" name = "best" checked = "checked"> This class is the best.

Radio

<input type = "radio" name= "card" value= "v" checked> Visa
<input type = "radio" name= "card" value= "m">Master Card

Select

```
<select size = "1" name = "family">
<option> 1 or 2 </option>
<option selected > 3 or 4 </option>
</select>
```

Textarea

```
<textarea name = "comments" rows = "3" cols = "65">
</textarea>
```

Submit

```
<input type = "submit" value = "Click here to submit this form">
```

Reset

```
<input type = "reset" value = "Erase and start over">
</form>
```

EXAMPLE 22.6. This example demonstrates how to use some of the most common Forms.

Figure 22.11. Source Code for Example 22.6

```
<html>
<head>
<title>Forms</title>
</head>
<body >
<font size="5">
<form method= "post" action = "mailto:put email address here">

        Enter your last name: <input type = "text" name = "last" size = "15" maxlength = "50">
        <br><br>
        Enter your first name: <input type = "text" name = "first" size= "15" maxlength = "50">
        <br><br>
        Enter your e mail: <input type = "text" name = "email" size= "25">
        <br><br>
        How did you hear about us? Check all that apply. <br>
        <input type = "checkbox"  Name = "a."> a. Friends. <br>
        <input type = "checkbox"  name = "b."> b. Magazine/Newspaper. <br>
        <input type = "checkbox"  name = "c."  checked> c. T.V./Radio <br>
        <input type = "checkbox"  name = "d." > d. Internet. <br>
        <br> <br>
        Type of credit card?<br>
        <input type ="radio" name="card" value="V" checked>Visa<br>
        <input type ="radio" name="card" value="M">Master Card<br>
        <input type ="radio" name="card" value="X">American Express<br>
        <input type ="radio" name="card" value="D">Discover<br>
        <br><br>
        <div align = "center">
                <textarea name = "comments" rows = "3" cols = "65">

                </textarea>
        </div>
        <br><br>
        <input type= "submit"  value = "Click here to submit this form">
        <input typ e= "reset"  value = "Erase and start over">
</form>
</font>
</body>
</html>
```

The results of Example 22.6 are displayed in Figure 22.12.

Figure 22.12. Results for Example 22.6

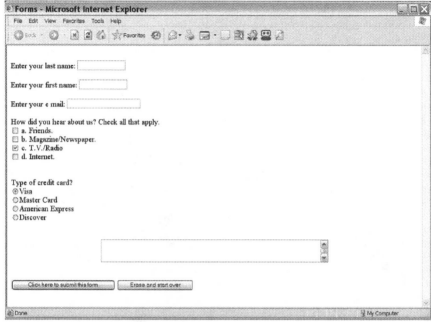

COLORS

For color names and color codes, check the following Web addresses:

http://www.htmlgoodies.com/tutorials/colors/article.php/3478921
http://www.w3schools.com/html/html_colors.asp

APPENDIX A

COMPUTER ACRONYMS

FOR COMPLETE LIST and description of computer acronyms, check the following sources:

1. Jeff Prosise, A Guide to Computer Acronyms, PC Magazine (*www.pcmag.com*), January 9, 1995, p. 259, p.262, p.266 and January 23, 1996, p.211, p.212, p.217.
2. *http://www.computer-dictionary-online.org/.*
3. *http://www.geocities.com/SiliconValley/Park/9104/.*
4. *http://www.textfiles.com/magazines/BTW/compacro.300.*
5. *http://www.su.edu/instcomp/Virtual_HelpDesk/glossary.htm.*
6. *http://www.jimspages.com/Acronyms2.html*
7. *http://www.acronymsonline.com/*
8. *http://www.acronyms.ch.*

CHRONOLOGICAL HISTORY OF COMPUTERS

For a brief chronological history of computers, check the following sources:

1. "Computing Through the Ages," PC World, 2001.
2. Metz, Cade, "A History of Personal Computing," PC MAGAZINE (*www.pcmag.com*), September 4, 2001, pp.186-191, as compiled by Nancy Sirapyan.
3. *http://www.cyberstreet.com/hcs/museum/chron.htm.*
4. *http://www.maxmon.com/history.htm.*
5. http://www2.fht-esslingen.de/studentisches/Computer_Geschichte/fold1.html.
6. *http://history.acusd.edu/gen/recording/computer2.html.*
7. *http://www.islandnet.com/~kpolsson/comphist/.*

APPENDIX B

Solutions to Select Exercises and Computer Assignments

CHAPTER 1
EXERCISE 1.1
TECHNOLOGY ACRONYMS ANSWER SHEET

AI   (Artificial Intelligence): The use of computers for specific work traditionally considered to require human intelligence.

ANSI   (American National Standards Institute): A group made up of people from government, universities, and business which is responsible for developing standards.

ASCII   (American Standard Code for Information Interchange): A standard developed by the American National Standards Institute (ANSI) describing how characters can be represented on a computer.

ATM   (Automatic Teller Machine): A computer that electronically functions as a bank teller and processes banking transactions.

CAD   (Computer Aided Design): A system which uses graphics and plotting tools to create mechanical and architectural designs and drafts.

CCD   (Charged Coupled Device): A scanner with light sensitive diodes that read intensity of light. It is used in devices such as digital cameras, video cameras, and scanners.

CMOS   (Complementary Metal Oxide Semiconductor): RAM memory that stores a PC's configuration information (such as time, date, number & capacity of disk drives, the amount of RAM installed, etc.). It is backed by battery.

CPU (Central Processing Unit): A computer chip that controls the entire operation of a computer system. It is considered to be the brain of a computer.

CRT (Cathode Ray Tube): The tube of a television or computer monitor in which rays of electrons are beamed onto a screen to display text, pictures, or graphics.

DLP (Digital Light Processing): DLP was developed by Texas Instruments and is used in projectors and projection televisions. In DLP sets, the image is created by microscopically small mirrors laid out in a matrix on a semiconductor chip, known as a Digital Micromirror Device (DMD). Each mirror represents one pixel in the image.

DOS (Disk Operating System): An operating system on a disk for the IBM and compatible personal computers. PC-DOS refers to the version created for IBM machines; MS-DOS is the generic version created by Microsoft for compatible machines.

DSP (Digital Signal Processor): A microprocessor-like device designed to process electrical signals very quickly. DSPs are used in a variety of devices such as personal computers, modems, sound boards, and audio/video devices such as receivers.

ECR (Electronic Cash Register): A point-of-sale terminal that operates independently of other terminals.

EFT (Electronic Funds Transfer): A computerized process by which money is transferred electronically.

ESL (Electronic Shelf Labeling): Small liquid crystal screens that display product price and other relevant information on the shelves in retail stores.

FAT (File Allocation Table): The file system used by DOS and 16-bit versions of Windows to store and manage files on floppy disks, hard disks, and other disk media.

I/O (Input/Output): Refers generally to devices that read input data, produce output information, or both. GIGO means "Garbage In", "Garbage Out"

LAN (Local Area Network): The network communications system by which computers and terminals are linked in relatively close to each other.

MIPS (Million of Instructions Per Second): The standard of measuring the speed of a processor. Faster computers have higher MIPS.

MIS (Management Information System): An integrated system designed to provide information to the managers and decision-makers.

MPEG (Motion Picture Experts Group): A standard that allows digital video to be compressed. There are several MPEG standards. The two most popular standards are MPEG-1, which supports a playback quality roughly equal to that of a VCR, and MPEG-2, which supports high-quality digital video of DVD players.

OCR (Optical Character Recognition): A program that converts the text images read by a scanner into characters that can be used by a word processor.

OEM (Original Equipment Manufacturer): A manufacturer who sells his/her products to other vendors, who then may supply custom configurations to end users.

PC (Personal Computer): A microcomputer that is used mainly in homes, small businesses, schools, or as a professional workstation in large businesses. The two most common type of PCs are desktop and laptop.

PCI (Peripheral Component Interface): A 32/64bit local bus architecture developed by DEC, IBM. Intel, and others that is used in Pentium-based PCs. A PCI bus provides a high-bandwidth data channel between the CPU and peripheral devices such as hard disks, modems, and video adapters.

PIN (Personal Identification Number): The personal codes (consisting of letters and numbers) that people use to access their accounts on an ATM machine or other computers.

PLU (Price Lookup): A process by which a point-of-sale terminal automatically finds the corresponding price of a product through the SKU number.

PnP (Plug and Play): The technology that allows the operating system such as Windows automatically detect and configure most of the devices and peripherals connected to a PC.

POS (Point-of-Sale): Refers to the use of computer/cash registers that immediately update sales and inventory data.

RAM (Random-Access Memory): Temporary computer memory used for storing programs and data that can be erased or altered. Information in Ram is volatile and must be saved on disk. RAM is also called primary memory.

ROM (Read-Only Memory): The computer chip on a motherboard that has been programmed to start a computer. These programs are permanent and cannot be altered.

SKU   (Stock Keeping Unit): SKU is a number used for managing inventory of items in a merchandising business. Every product is assigned an SKU by the merchant. This number is then used to order, locate and manage the inventory of a product.

UNIX   (Doesn't stand for anything): It's a play on words that refers to MULTICS, an old Honeywell operating system. Where MULTICS implied multiple, UNIX implies unified. UNIX is a powerful operating system developed by Bell Labs and used primarily with servers.

UPC   (Universal Product Code): The standard bar code developed for the retail industry since 1973. They look like vertical lines of different widths and appear on boxes, cans, and all packages of retail goods.

CHAPTER 3
EXERCISE 3.1
SPREADSHEET ADDRESSING

1. Describe the type of addressing and the meaning of the following:

    a. =J5 + I8
        relative addressing, has no meaning since the formula does not specify its location
    b. Cell H6 contains the formula =J5 + I8
        relative addressing, the formula means 2 cols right, 1 row up + 1 col right, 2 rows down
    c. Cell K10 contains the formula =J5 + I8
        relative addressing, the formula means 1 col left, 5 rows up + 2 col left, 2 rows up
    d. Cell A4 contains the formula =$J5 + I$8
        mixed addressing (both relative and absolute), the formula means col J, 1 row down + 8 cols right, row 8

2. Suppose B4, B5, B6 contain the numbers 3, 2, 4, respectively.

    a. Calculate the result in A7 if it contains the formula =STDEV(B4: B6)?

        Mean = (3 + 2+ 4) / 3 = 9 / 3 = 3

Table B3.1			
i	X_i	X_i - Mean	$(X_i - Mean)^2$
1	3	3 - 3 = 0	$(0)^2 = 0$
2	2	2 - 3 = -1	$(-1)^2 = 1$
3	4	4 - 3 = +1	$(+1)^2 = 1$
Sum:	9	0	2

STDEV = SQRT [2 / (3-1)] = 1

b. If cell A7 is copied to cell E20, what formula will be displayed in E20?

*The formula in A7 means: STDEV(1 col right, 3 rows up : 1 col
    right, 1 row up)
When it is copied to E20, it will translate to STDEV(F17:F19).*

CHAPTER 3
EXERCISE 3.2
LOGICAL STATEMENTS

1. Assume cells B7, B8, and B9 contain numbers 76, 83, and 78.

    !   Write a command in cell H10 to find the highest of these numbers.

        H10: =MAX(B7,B8,B9)

    !   Write another command in cell H11 to find the lowest of these three
        numbers.

        H11: =MIN(B7,B8,B9)

    !   Write an IF statement in cell H12 to find the second highest number.

Pseudo Code:
    *IF (first # > min AND first # < max) THEN
        first # is the answer*

> *ELSE IF (second # > min AND second # < max) THEN*
> > *second # is the answer*
> *ELSE IF (third # > min AND third # < max) THEN*
> > *third # is the answer*
> *ELSE IF (first # = second #) THEN*
> > *either first # or second # is the answer*
> *ELSE IF (first # = third #) THEN*
> > *either first # or third # is the answer*
> *ELSE (by default it means second # = third #)*
> > *either second # or third # is the answer*

Computer (Excel) Code:

> = IF(AND(B7>H11,B7<H10),B7,IF(AND(B8>H11,B8<H10),
> B8, IF(AND(B9>H11,B9<H10),B9,IF(B7=B8,B7,IF(B7=B9,
> B7,B8)))))

2. Suppose K = 4 and L = 8. Determine the values for K and L after the following commands are executed.

If K < L then let K = L + 1,	*K = 9,*	*L = 8*
Let L = K + 3,	*K = 9,*	*L = 12*
If K < 7 then let L = L + 2,	*K = 9,*	*L = 12*
Let K = L – 2,	*K = 10,*	*L = 12*

CHAPTER 4
COMPUTER ASSIGNMENT
INCOME STATEMENT SOLUTION

A2:   XYZ COMPANY
A3:   Income Statement
A4:   For the Year Ended December 31, 20—
A6:   Gross sales . . . .
E6:   1500000
A7:   Less: Sales returns and allowances . . . .
D7:   36000
A8:   Sales discounts . . . .

D8:   23000
E8:   =D7+D8
A9:   Net sales . . . .
E9:   =E6-E8
A10:   Cost of goods sold:
A11:   Inventory, Jan. 1 . . . .
D11:   125000
A12:   Purchases . . . .
C12:   885000
A13:   Less: Purchase returns & allowances . . . .
B13:   42000
A14:   Purchase discounts . . . .
B14:   31000
C14:   =B13+B14
A15:   Net purchases . . . .
C15:   =C12-C14
A16:   Add: Transportation-in . . . .
C16:   62000
A17:   Cost of goods purchased . . . .
D17:   =C15+C16
A18:   Cost of goods available for sale . . . .
D18:   =D11+D17
A19:   Less: Inventory, Dec. 31 . . . .
D19:   180000
A20:   Cost of goods sold . . . .
E20:   =D18-D19
A21:   Gross profit on sales . . . .
E21:   =E9-E20
A22:   Operating expenses:
A23:   Selling expenses:
A24:   Sales salaries . . . .
C24:   232000
A25:   Advertising . . . .
C25:   41400
A26:   Depreciation: building . . . .
C26:   9000
A27:   Depreciation: store equipment . . . .
C27:   10400

A28: Depreciation: delivery equipment . . . .

C28: 8500

A29: Insurance . . . .

C29: 4000

A30: Miscellaneous . . . .

C30: 1500

A31: Total selling expenses . . . .

D31: =SUM(C24:C30)

A32: General and administrative expenses:

A33: Office salaries . . . .

C33: 147800

A34: Dues and subscriptions . . . .

C34: 1080

A35: Depreciation: building . . . .

C35: 5000

A36: Insurance . . . .

C36: 2600

A37: Miscellaneous . . . .

C37: 700

A38: Total general and administrative expenses . . . .

D38: =SUM(C33:C37)

A39: Total operating expenses . . . .

E39: =D31+D38

A40: Income from operations . . . .

E40: =E21-E39

A41: Interest earned on investments . . . .

E41: 7500

A42: Net income . . . .

E42: =E40+E41

CHAPTER 4
COMPUTER ASSIGNMENT
BALANCE SHEET SOLUTION

A2: XYZ COMPANY

A3: Balance Sheet December 31, 20—

A5: Assets

A7: Current assets:

A8:   Cash . . . .

E8:   253000

A9:   Government bonds . . . .

E9:   110000

A10:   Notes receivable . . . .

E10:   135000

A11:   Accounts receivable . . . .

E11:   252000

A12:   Inventory . . . .

E12:   365000

A13:   Prepaid expenses . . . .

E13:   32000

A14:   Total current assets . . . .

E14:   =SUM(E8..E13)

A16:   Plant and equipment:

A17:   Land . . . .

D17:   215000

A18:   Building . . . .

C18:   345000

A19:   Less: Accumulated depreciation . . . .

C19:   29200

D19:   =C18-C19

A20:   Store equipment . . . .

C20:   104000

A21:   Less: Accumulated depreciation . . . .

C21:   28800

D21:   =C20-C21

A22:   Delivery equipment . . . .

C22:   38000

A23:   Less: Accumulated depreciation . . . .

C23:   9000

D23:   =C22-C23

A24:   Total plant and equipment . . . .

E24:   =SUM(D17,D19,D21,D23)

A26:   Other assets:

A27:   Land (future building site) . . . .

E27:   152000

A28:   Total assets . . . .

E28:   =SUM(E14,E24,E27)
A30:   Liabilities & Owner's Equity
A32:   Current liabilities:
A33:   Notes payable . . . .
E33:   146000
A34:   Accounts payable . . . .
E34:   290000
A35:   Salaries payable . . . .
E35:   24500
A36:   Unearned revenue . . . .
E36:   31000
A37:   Total current liabilities . . . .
E37:   =SUM(E33..E36)
A39:   Long-term liabilities:
A40:   Mortgage payable (due in 15 years) . . . .
E40:   276000
A41:   Total liabilities . . . .
E41:   =E37+E40
A43:   Owner's equity:
A44:   XYZ, capital . . . .
E44:   =E28-E41
A45:   Total liabilities & owner's equity . . . .
E45:   =E41+E44

CHAPTER 5
EXERCISE 5.1
LOANS AND AMORTIZATION TABLES

1. a) Assume $30,000 is borrowed for 3 years at 10% interest. The loan is to be repaid in three (3) annual payments. Find the annual payment.

$$PV \quad = \quad PMT \cdot [\, 1 - 1\,/\,(1+k)^n\,]\,/\,k$$
$$PMT \quad = \quad PV\,/\,\{[1 - 1/(1+k)\wedge n]\,/\,k\}$$
$$PMT \quad = \quad 30{,}000\,/\,\{[1 - 1/(1+.10)^3]/.10\}$$
$$PMT \quad = \quad \$12{,}063.44$$

    b) Construct an amortization table for this loan.

Table B5.1				
Period	Payment	Interest	Principal	Balance
0	—	—	—	$30,000.00
1	$12,063.44	$3,000.00	$9,063.44	20,936.56
2	12,063.44	2,093.66	9,969.79	10,966.77
3	12,063.44	1,096.68	10,966.77	0.00

CHAPTER 5
COMPUTER ASSIGNMENT

C2:   LOANS AND AMORTIZATION TABLES
C4:   Loan Amount:
D4:   50000
C5:   Rate:
D5:   0.09
E5:   Per Year
F5:   =D5/12
G5:   Per Month
C6:   Term:
D6:   3
E6:   Years
F6:   =D6*12
G6:   Months
C8:   PMT:
D8:   =D4/((1-1/(1+F5)^F6)/F5)
E8:   Per Month
F8:   =PMT(F5,F6,E4)
C10:   Period
D10:   PMT
E10:   Interest
F10:   Principal

G10: Balance
C11: 0
D11: —
E11: —
F11: —
G11: =D4
C12: =C11+1
D12: =$D$8
E12: =G11*$F$5
F12: =D12-E12
G12: =G11-F12
C13: =C12+1
D13: =$D$8
E13: =G12*$F$5
F13: =D13-E13
G13: =G12-F13
C14: =C13+1
D14: =$D$8
E14: =G13*$F$5
F14: =D14-E14
G14: =G13-F14
C15: =C14+1
D15: =$D$8
E15: =G14*$F$5
F15: =D15-E15
G15: =G14-F15
C16: =C15+1
D16: =$D$8
E16: =G15*$F$5
F16: =D16-E16
G16: =G15-F16
C17: =C16+1
D17: =$D$8
E17: =G16*$F$5
F17: =D17-E17
G17: =G16-F17
C18: =C17+1
D18: =$D$8

```
E18:    =G17*$F$5
F18:    =D18-E18
G18:    =G17-F18
C19:    =C18+1
D19:    =$D$8
E19:    =G18*$F$5
F19:    =D19-E19
G19:    =G18-F19
C20:    =C19+1
D20:    =$D$8
E20:    =G19*$F$5
F20:    =D20-E20
G20:    =G19-F20
C21:    =C20+1
D21:    =$D$8
E21:    =G20*$F$5
F21:    =D21-E21
G21:    =G20-F21
C22:    =C21+1
D22:    =$D$8
E22:    =G21*$F$5
F22:    =D22-E22
G22:    =G21-F22
C23:    =C22+1
D23:    =$D$8
E23:    =G22*$F$5
F23:    =D23-E23
G23:    =G22-F23
C24:    =C23+1
D24:    =$D$8
E24:    =G23*$F$5
F24:    =D24-E24
G24:    =G23-F24
C25:    =C24+1
D25:    =$D$8
E25:    =G24*$F$5
F25:    =D25-E25
G25:    =G24-F25
```

C26:   =C25+1
D26:   =$D$8
E26:   =G25*$F$5
F26:   =D26-E26
G26:   =G25-F26
C27:   =C26+1
D27:   =$D$8
E27:   =G26*$F$5
F27:   =D27-E27
G27:   =G26-F27
C28:   =C27+1
D28:   =$D$8
E28:   =G27*$F$5
F28:   =D28-E28
G28:   =G27-F28
C29:   =C28+1
D29:   =$D$8
E29:   =G28*$F$5
F29:   =D29-E29
G29:   =G28-F29
C30:   =C29+1
D30:   =$D$8
E30:   =G29*$F$5
F30:   =D30-E30
G30:   =G29-F30
C31:   =C30+1
D31:   =$D$8
E31:   =G30*$F$5
F31:   =D31-E31
G31:   =G30-F31
C32:   =C31+1
D32:   =$D$8
E32:   =G31*$F$5
F32:   =D32-E32
G32:   =G31-F32
C33:   =C32+1
D33:   =$D$8
E33:   =G32*$F$5

```
F33:    =D33-E33
G33:    =G32-F33
C34:    =C33+1
D34:    =$D$8
E34:    =G33*$F$5
F34:    =D34-E34
G34:    =G33-F34
C35:    =C34+1
D35:    =$D$8
E35:    =G34*$F$5
F35:    =D35-E35
G35:    =G34-F35
C36:    =C35+1
D36:    =$D$8
E36:    =G35*$F$5
F36:    =D36-E36
G36:    =G35-F36
C37:    =C36+1
D37:    =$D$8
E37:    =G36*$F$5
F37:    =D37-E37
G37:    =G36-F37
C38:    =C37+1
D38:    =$D$8
E38:    =G37*$F$5
F38:    =D38-E38
G38:    =G37-F38
C39:    =C38+1
D39:    =$D$8
E39:    =G38*$F$5
F39:    =D39-E39
G39:    =G38-F39
C40:    =C39+1
D40:    =$D$8
E40:    =G39*$F$5
F40:    =D40-E40
G40:    =G39-F40
C41:    =C40+1
```

```
D41:    =$D$8
E41:    =G40*$F$5
F41:    =D41-E41
G41:    =G40-F41
C42:    =C41+1
D42:    =$D$8
E42:    =G41*$F$5
F42:    =D42-E42
G42:    =G41-F42
C43:    =C42+1
D43:    =$D$8
E43:    =G42*$F$5
F43:    =D43-E43
G43:    =G42-F43
C44:    =C43+1
D44:    =$D$8
E44:    =G43*$F$5
F44:    =D44-E44
G44:    =G43-F44
C45:    =C44+1
D45:    =$D$8
E45:    =G44*$F$5
F45:    =D45-E45
G45:    =G44-F45
C46:    =C45+1
D46:    =$D$8
E46:    =G45*$F$5
F46:    =D46-E46
G46:    =G45-F46
C47:    =C46+1
D47:    =$D$8
E47:    =G46*$F$5
F47:    =D47-E47
G47:    =G46-F47
C48:    Total:
D48:    =SUM(D12:D47)
E48:    =SUM(E12:E47)
F48:    =SUM(F12:F47)
```

CHAPTER 6
EXERCISE 6.1
INCOME TAX

a. Complete the Tax on Base column.

Table B6.1		
Income	**Tax Rate**	**Tax on Base**
$0 - $5,000	0%	0
5,000 - 12,000	10%	0*(5,000-0)*0.0=$0
12,000 - 20,000	15%	0+(12,000-5,000)*.10=700
20,000 - 35,000	20%	700+(20,000-12,000)*.15=1,900
35,000 - 60,000	25%	1,900+(35,000-20,000)*.20=4,900
> 60,000	30%	4,900+(60,000-35,000)*.25=11,150

b. Suppose your taxable income is $42,000. Calculate the tax liability.

Tax liability = 4,900 + (42,000 − 35,000) x 0.25 = 4,900 + 1,750 = $6,650

c. Given the level of taxable income, write an IF STATEMENT in pseudo code to calculate the amount of tax liability.

if income < 5,000 then
*0 + (income − 0) * 0.0*
else if income < 12,000 then
*0 + (income − 5,000) * 0.10*
else if income < 20,000 then
*700 + (income − 12,000) * 0.15*
else if income < 35,000 then
*1,900 + (income − 20,000) * 0.20*
else if income < 60,000 then
*4,900 + (income − 35,000) * 0.25*
else
*11,150 + (income − 60,000) * 0.30*

CHAPTER 6
COMPUTER ASSIGNMENT

B3:	INCOME TAX CALCULATION
B6:	TAX TABLE:
B8:	Income
E8:	Tax Rate
F8:	Tax on Base
B9:	0
C9:	—
D9:	5000
E9:	0.05
F9:	0
B10:	5000
C10:	—
D10:	15000
E10:	0.1
F10:	=F9+(D9-B9)*E9
B11:	15000
C11:	—
D11:	20000
E11:	0.15
F11:	=F10+(D10-B10)*E10
B12:	20000
C12:	—
D12:	28000
E12:	0.2
F12:	=F11+(D11-B11)*E11
B13:	28000
C13:	—
D13:	35000
E13:	0.25
F13:	=F12+(D12-B12)*E12
B14:	35000
C14:	—
D14:	50000
E14:	0.3
F14:	=F13+(D13-B13)*E13
C15:	>=

D15: 50000

E15: 0.35

F15: =F14+(D14-B14)*E14

D19: Individual 1

E19: Individual 2

F19: Individual 3

B20: Taxable Income:

D20: 120000

E20: 35000

F20: 2500

B22: Tax Amount:

D22: =IF(D20<$D$9,$F$9+(D20-$B$9)*$E$9,IF(D20<$D$10,$F$1
0+(D20-$B$10)*$E$10,IF(D20<$D$11,$F$11+(D20-$B$11)*$
E$11,IF(D20<$D$12,$F$12+(D20-$B$12)*$E$12,IF(D20<$D
$13,$F$13+(D20-$B$13)*$E$13,IF(D20<$D$14,$F$14+(D20-
$B$14)*$E$14,$F$15+(D20-$D$15)*$E$15))))))

E22: =IF(E20<$D$9,$F$9+(E20-$B$9)*$E$9,IF(E20<$D$10,$F$1
0+(E20-$B$10)*$E$10,IF(E20<$D$11,$F$11+(E20-$B$11)*$
E$11,IF(E20<$D$12,$F$12+(E20-$B$12)*$E$12,IF(E20<$D
$13,$F$13+(E20-$B$13)*$E$13,IF(E20<$D$14,$F$14+(E20-
$B$14)*$E$14,$F$15+(E20-$D$15)*$E$15))))))

F22: =IF(F20<$D$9,$F$9+(F20-$B$9)*$E$9,IF(F20<$D$10,$F$1
0+(F20-$B$10)*$E$10,IF(F20<$D$11,$F$11+(F20-$B$11)*$
E$11,IF(F20<$D$12,$F$12+(F20-$B$12)*$E$12,IF(F20<$D
$13,$F$13+(F20-$B$13)*$E$13,IF(F20<$D$14,$F$14+(F20-
$B$14)*$E$14,$F$15+(F20-$D$15)*$E$15))))))

CHAPTER 9
COMPUTER ASSIGNMENT
SALES AND PROFIT FORECASTING

B1:   PRO FORMA INCOME STATEMENT
B3:   Gross Sales for 2005 (Given Year):
D3:   8100
B4:   Commission Rate:
D4:   0.02
B5:   Tax Rate:
D5:   0.4
B6:   Annual Growth Rate of Sales:
D6:   0.05
B7:   COGS (% of Net Sales):
D7:   0.65
C10:   2005
D10:   =C10+1
E10:   =D10+1
F10:   =E10+1
G10:   =F10+1
B11:   Gross Sales:
C11:   =D3
D11:   =C11*(1+$$D$6)
E11:   =D11*(1+$$D$6)
F11:   =E11*(1+$$D$6)
G11:   =F11*(1+$$D$6)
B12:   Commissions:
C12:   =C11*$$D$4
D12:   =D11*$$D$4
E12:   =E11*$$D$4
F12:   =F11*$$D$4
G12:   =G11*$$D$4
B13:   Net Sales:
C13:   =C11-C12
D13:   =D11-D12
E13:   =E11-E12
F13:   =F11-F12
G13:   =G11-G12
B14:   COGS:

C14:   =C13*$$D$7
D14:   =D13*$$D$7
E14:   =E13*$$D$7
F14:   =F13*$$D$7
G14:   =G13*$$D$7
B15:   Gross Profit:
C15:   =C13-C14
D15:   =D13-D14
E15:   =E13-E14
F15:   =F13-F14
G15:   =G13-G14
B16:   Tax Amount:
C16:   =C15*$$D$5
D16:   =D15*$$D$5
E16:   =E15*$$D$5
F16:   =F15*$$D$5
G16:   =G15*$$D$5
B18:   Net Profit:
C18:   =C15-C16
D18:   =D15-D16
E18:   =E15-E16
F18:   =F15-F16
G18:   =G15-G16

CHAPTER 10
COMPUTER ASSIGNMENT
SALES AND PROFIT FORECASTING IN THE
INTERNATIONAL ARENA

A2:   Pro Forma Income Statement:
A3:   Sales and Profit Forecasting in the International Arena
A4:   (For an American Firm Selling Products in Japan)
A6:   Total Sales for 2005 (in Japan):
C6:   20000000
D6:   Yen
A7:   Exchange Rate ($ vs. Yen):
C7:   110
A8:   Commission Rate:
C8:   0.1

A9:   Tax Rate:
C9:   0.4
A10:   Annual Growth Rate of Sales in Japan:
C10:   0.05
A11:   COGS (% of Net Sales):
C11:   0.65
A13:   Growth of Sales in Japan (in Yen)
B14:   2005
C14:   =B14+1
D14:   =C14+1
E14:   =D14+1
F14:   =E14+1
A16:   Gross Sales:
B16:   =$C$6
C16:   =B16*(1+$$C$10)
D16:   =C16*(1+$$C$10)
E16:   =D16*(1+$$C$10)
F16:   =E16*(1+$$C$10)
A17:   Commissions Paid to Japanese Sales Force:
B17:   =B16*$C$8
C17:   =C16*$C$8
D17:   =D16*$C$8
E17:   =E16*$C$8
F17:   =F16*$C$8
A19:   Net Sales:
B19:   =B16-B17
C19:   =C16-C17
D19:   =D16-D17
E19:   =E16-E17
F19:   =F16-F17
A21:   Growth of Sales in Dollars
B22:   =B14
C22:   =B22+1
D22:   =C22+1
E22:   =D22+1
F22:   =E22+1
A24:   Gross Sales:
B24:   =B16/$C$7
C24:   =C16/$C$7

D24:   =D16/$C$7
E24:   =E16/$C$7
F24:   =F16/$C$7
A25:   —Commissions:
B25:   =B17/$C$7
C25:   =C17/$C$7
D25:   =D17/$C$7
E25:   =E17/$C$7
F25:   =F17/$C$7
A27:   = Net Sales:
B27:   =B24-B25
C27:   =C24-C25
D27:   =D24-D25
E27:   =E24-E25
F27:   =F24-F25
A28:   —COGS:
B28:   =B27*$$C$11
C28:   =C27*$$C$11
D28:   =D27*$$C$11
E28:   =E27*$$C$11
F28:   =F27*$$C$11
A30:   = Gross Profit:
B30:   =B27-B28
C30:   =C27-C28
D30:   =D27-D28
E30:   =E27-E28
F30:   =F27-F28
A31:   —Tax:
B31:   =B30*$$C$9
C31:   =C30*$$C$9
D31:   =D30*$$C$9
E31:   =E30*$$C$9
F31:   =F30*$$C$9
A33:   = Net Profit:
B33:   =B30-B31
C33:   =C30-C31
D33:   =D30-D31
E33:   =E30-E31
F33:   =F30-F31

CHAPTER 11
COMPUTER ASSIGNMENT
EXPENSE REPORTS AND ADVANCED GRAPHING

A2:	CONSULTING SERVICE
B3:	Jan
C3:	Feb
D3:	Mar
E3:	Apr
F3:	May
G3:	Y.T.D.
A4:	Sales:
B4:	1600
C4:	1600
D4:	1600
E4:	1800
F4:	1700
G4:	=SUM(B4..F4)
A5:	Expenses:
A6:	Rent
B6:	400
C6:	400
D6:	400
E6:	400
F6:	400
G6:	=SUM(B6..F6)
A7:	Supplies
B7:	300
C7:	270
D7:	340
E7:	295
F7:	210
G7:	=SUM(B7..F7)
A8:	Utilities
B8:	130
C8:	130
D8:	120
E8:	85
F8:	75

G8:   =SUM(B8..F8)
A9:   Travel
B9:   120
C9:   90
D9:   160
E9:   100
F9:   120
G9:   =SUM(B9..F9)
A10:   Total Expenses:
B10:   =SUM(B6..B9)
C10:   =SUM(C6..C9)
D10:   =SUM(D6..D9)
E10:   =SUM(E6..E9)
F10:   =SUM(F6..F9)
G10:   =SUM(G6..G9)
A11:   Monthly Profits:
B11:   =B4-B10
C11:   =C4-C10
D11:   =D4-D10
E11:   =E4-E10
F11:   =F4-F10
G11:   =G4-G10
A13:   Y.T.D. Profits:
B13:   =B11
C13:   =B13+C11
D13:   =C13+D11
E13:   =D13+E11
F13:   =E13+F11

CHAPTER 13
EXERCISE 13.1
UNGROUPED DATA

1. For the following observations:

    97 93 92 89 87 85 85 84 82 79
    78 78 76 76 76 76 75 72 70 69
    67 67 67 67 67 66 66 66 66 65
    64 63 63 63 63 62 61 60 60 60
    57 57 56 55 53 50 47 45 43 35

    a. Calculate the median.

    $$M_d = (X_{25} + X_{26}) / 2 = (66 + 67) / 2 = 66.5$$

    b. Calculate the mode.

    $$Mode_1 = 67, Mode_2 = 76, Mode_3 = 66, Mode_4 = 63$$

    c. Calculate the first, second, and third quartiles.

    $$Q_1 = X_{(n+1)/4} = X_{51/4} = X_{12.75} = 60$$
    $$Q_2 = M_d = 66.5$$
    $$Q3 = X_{3(n+1)/4} = X_{(3)(51)/4} = X_{38.25} = 77$$

2. Calculate the standard deviation of the following numbers: 5, 8, 12, 15, 20.

Table B13.1				
i	X_i	Mean	X_i - Mean	$(X_i$ - Mean$)^2$
1	5	12	-7	49
2	8	12	-4	16
3	12	12	0	0
4	15	12	3	9
5	20	12	8	64
Total:	60		0	138
	Mean = 60 / 5 = 12		Std = SQRT[138/(5-1)] = 5.87	

CHAPTER 13
EXERCISE 13.2
GROUPED OBSERVATIONS

Given the following table:

Table B13.2				
Age	Freq (f$_i$)	Midpoints (m$_i$)	f$_i$. m$_i$	(m$_i$-Mean)^2 . f$_i$
20 - 30	10	25	250	2,152.089
30- 40	20	35	700	436.178
40 - 50	22	45	990	624.9958
50 - 60	8	55	440	1,880.0712
Totals:	60		2,380	5,093.334

a. Calculate the mean.

   Mean = 2,380 / 60 = 39.67

b. Calculate the standard deviation.

   STD = SQRT[5,093.334 / (60-1)] = SQRT[86.32769] = 9.29

c. Calculate the median.

   Identify the median class: n/2 = 60/2 = 30
   Md ≈ L + [(n/2 – F) / f] · W = 30 + [(30 – 10) / 20] · (10) = 40

d. Calculate the third quartile.

   Identify the third quartile class: 3(n) / 4 = 3 (60) / 4 = 45
   Q$_3$ ≈ 40 + [(45 – 30) / 22] · (10) = 40 + 6.818 = 46.82

e. Calculate the 20th percentile.

   Identify the 20th percentile class: 20(n) / 100 = (20)(60) / 100 = 12
   P$_{20}$ ≈ 30 + [(12 – 10) / 20] · (10) = 31

f. Calculate the 90th percentile.

Identify the 90th percentile class: $90n / 100 = (90)(60) / 100 = 54$
$P_{90} \approx 50 + [(54 - 52) / 9] \cdot (10) = 52.5$

CHAPTER 14
EXERCISE 14.1
RESOURCE ALLOCATION PROBLEMS

1. A firm makes two products, type A and type B. Each product requires 10 hours in Department I. Each unit of product A requires 4 hours in Department II, and each unit of product B requires 8 hours in Department II. The maximum number of labor hours available are 160 hours in Department I and 80 hours in Department II per day. The firm earns a profit of $3 per unit of product A and a profit of $4 per unit of product B. Assume that it is possible to sell all units produced each day. Find the levels of production that will maximize profit.

Maximize $Z = 3X_1 + 4X_2$ $X_1 = 12$
S.T. $10X_1 + 10X_2 <= 160$ $X_2 = 4$
              $4X_1 + 8X_2 <= 80$ $Z = \$52$
                   $X_1, X_2 >= 0$

2. A company produces two types of USB devices, a standard model and an advanced model. The profit per unit of the standard model is $5 and the profit per unit of the advanced model is $8. The marketing department estimates that, at most, 1000 devices per week can be sold by the sales staff. Because of the rapid growth of the industry, there is a shortage of both the skilled labor and electronic circuits necessary to assemble these devices. Each regular device requires 3 of these electronic circuits and 3 hours of labor for assembly. Each advanced model requires 6 electronic circuits and 2 hours of labor for assembly. There is only a weekly supply of 5000 electronic circuits available. Furthermore, the company has only 2500 hours of skilled labor available per week. How many devices of each type should be made each week in order to maximize total profit?

Maximize $Z = 5X_1 + 8X_2$
S.T. $3X_1 + 6X_2 <= 5000$ $X1 = 333$
              $3X_1 + 2X_2 <= 2500$ $X2 = 667$
               $X_1 + X_2 <= 1000$ $Z = \$7000$

CHAPTER 14
EXERCISE 14.2
TRANSPORTATION PROBLEM

Grain Warehouse	*Supply*	*Mill*	*Demand*
1. Kansas City	160 Tons	1. Chicago	220 Tons
2. Omaha	180	2. St. Louis	110
3. Tulsa	260	3. Cincinnati	270

Table B14.1			
	Chicago (1)	St. Louis (2)	Cincinnati (3)
Kansas City (1)	$6	$7	$9
Omaha (2)	8	9	10
Tulsa (3)	5	6	11

Write this problem as a linear programming problem (DO NOT SOLVE) to minimize the total transportation cost and satisfy all demand and supply constraints.

$Let\ X_{ij}$ = *Total amount transported from source i to destination j*

Minimize Z = $6X_{11} + 7X_{12} + 9X_{13} + 8X_{21} + 9X_{22} + 10X_{23} + 5X_{31} + 6X_{32} + 11X_{33}$

S.T.

$$X_{11} + X_{12} + X_{13} = 160$$
$$X_{21} + X_{22} + X_{23} = 180 \quad \textit{Supply Constraints}$$
$$X_{31} + X_{32} + X_{33} = 260$$

$$X_{11} + X_{21} + X_{31} = 220$$
$$X_{12} + X_{22} + X_{32} = 110 \quad \textit{Demand Constraints}$$
$$X_{13} + X_{23} + X_{33} = 270$$

CHAPTER 14
EXERCISE 14.3
PRODUCTION PROBLEMS

3. An ice making company is planning for a demand of 3000 hours of labor in May, 5000 hours in June, 5500 hours in July, and 4000 hours

in August. The company has 50 experienced workers available on May 1. Each worker averages 160 hours of productive work per month. Newly hired employees must be trained for one month, so that during their first month they do not provide any productive time. Furthermore, training reduces an experienced worker's productive time by 30 hours a month. There is a turnover of 10 percent among the experienced workers, and all new employees give at least one month of productive service. There are no layoffs. An experienced service person is paid $2,500 a month, while a new employee is paid $1,500 a month. Formulate (**do not solve**) a linear programming model to determine the number of new employees that must be hired in May, June, and July.

Let X_i = # of new people hired in month i (i = 1, 2, 3)
Let Y_i = # of experienced workers available in month i (i = 1, 2, 3, 4)
Minimize $Z = 2500Y_1 + 2500Y_2 + 2500Y_3 + 2500Y_4 + 1500X_1 + 1500X_2 + 1500X_3$

S.T.

May:	$Y_1 = 50,$		$160Y_1 - 30X_1 >= 3000$
June:	$Y_2 = .90Y_1 + X_1,$		$160Y_2 - 30X_2 >= 5000$
July:	$Y_3 = .90Y_2 + X_2$		$160Y_3 - 30X_3 >= 5500$
August:	$Y_4 = .90Y_3 + X_3,$		$160Y_4 >= 4000$
	$X_i, Y_i >= 0$		

2. A company manufactures 10-inch LCD color television sets and has received orders for 1700 units to be delivered in the first quarter and 2100 units to be delivered in the second quarter. Each unit requires a circuit board that is produced "in house" or can be purchased from a subcontractor. The cost to manufacture in house is $500.00 and remains the same for the next quarter. Subcontracting costs are currently $550 for units produced in the first quarter, and will increase to $650 for the second quarter. Due to obsolescence, the inventory cost to keep a circuit board from the first quarter to the second quarter is high and is estimated to be $120.00. The company's production capacity is 1900 units per quarter. The Subcontractor can provide 350 units in the first quarter and 425 in the second quarter. Formulate a linear programming model (**do not solve**) to plan production for the two quarters. Assume no beginning or ending inventory levels.

Let X_{11} = # of units produced in the first quarter, in-house

X_{12} = # of units produced in the first quarter, subcontract
X_{21} = # of units produced in the second quarter, in-house
X_{22} = # of units produced in the second quarter, subcontract
I = Inventory carried over from the first quarter to the second quarter

Minimize $Z = 500X11 + 500X_{21} + 550X_{12} + 650X_{22} + 120_I$
S.T.

$$X_{11} <= 1900$$
$$X_{21} <= 1900$$
$$X_{12} <= 350$$
$$X_{22} <= 425$$
$$X_{11} + X_{12} - I = 1700$$
$$I + X_{21} + X_{22} = 2100$$
$$X_{ij}, I >= 0$$

CHAPTER 14
COMPUTER ASSIGNMENT

1. A company manufactures two products, A and B. Each unit of product A requires 5 hours of assembly and 2 hours of finishing. Each unit of product B requires 3 hours for assembly and 4 hours for finishing. The company has 105 hours available per week on the assembly line and 70 hours available in the finishing department. The profit per unit is $200 for product A and $160 for product B. Assuming that the company can sell all the products that it can produce in a week, find the number of units of each type that should be produced per week to maximize the total profit?

Max. $Z = 200X_1 + 160X_2$ $X_1 = 15$
S.T. $5X_1 + 3X_2 <= 105$ $X_2 = 10$
      $2X_1 + 4X_2 <= 70$ $Z = \$4,600$

2. A company is designing a plant for producing two types of product, X and Y. After extensive marketing research, the company has decided that the plant must be capable of producing at least 100 units of X and 420 units of Y per day. Two possible machines are to be included in the plant, machine A and B. Each machine A costs $600,000 and is capable of producing 10 units of X and 20 units of Y per day; machine B is a

lower priced design costing $300,000 and capable of producing 4 units of X and 30 units of Y per day. Because of operating costs it is necessary to have at least 4 units of each machine in the plant. How many units of machine A and how many units of machine B should be included in the plant to minimize the cost of construction and still meet the required production plan?

$$Min.\ Z = 600,000X_1 + 300,000X_2 \qquad X_1 = 6$$
$$S.T.\ 10X_1 + 4X_2 >= 100, \qquad X_2 = 10$$
$$20X1 + 30X_2 >= 420, \qquad Z = \$6,600,000$$
$$X_1 >= 4$$
$$X_2 >= 4$$

3. A company sells two different types of health beverage. The lower cost brand contains 80 % orange juice and 20 % grapefruit juice, while the more expensive brand contains 50% of each type of juice. Each week the company can obtain up to 1800 gallons of orange juice and up to 1200 gallons of grapefruit juice. The profit per gallon is 10¢ for the lower cost brand and 15¢ for the more expensive brand. How many gallons of each beverage should be produced in order to maximize total profit?

$$Max.\ Z = 0.10X_1 + 0.15X_2 \qquad X_1 = 1000$$
$$S.T.\ 0.80X_1 + 0.50X_2 <= 1800 \qquad X_2 = 2000$$
$$0.20X_1 + 0.50X_2 <= 1200 \qquad Z = \$400$$

4. A manufacturer makes two products, A and B, each of which requires time in three different departments. Each unit of A requires 2 hours in department I, 4 hours in department II, and 3 hours in department III. Each unit of product B requires 5 hours in department I, 1 hour in department II, and 2 hours in department III. The company makes profits of $250 per unit of product A and $300 per unit of product B. The number of hours available in each department per month are 200, 240, and 190, respectively. Find how many units of each product must be produced to maximize total profit.

$$Max.\ Z = 250X_1 + 300X_2 \qquad X_1 = 50$$
$$S.T.\ 2X_1 + 5X_2 <= 200 \qquad X_2 = 20$$
$$4X_1 + 1X_2 <= 240 \qquad Z = \$18,500$$
$$3X_1 + 2X_2 <= 190$$

CHAPTER 19
EXERCISE 19.1
CONTINGENCY TABLES

1. Suppose the Department of Motor Vehicles (DMV) is interested in determining whether there is a link between the type of traffic violation and type of vehicle driven. The following contingency table summarizes the traffic violations in the past week. Determine whether these two variables are statistically independent.

Table B19.1			
	B. Type of Vehicle		
A. Type of Violation	**1. Passenger**	**2. Truck**	**Total**
1. Stop Sign	45	25	**70**
2. Red Light	35	15	**50**
3. Failing to Yield	20	11	**31**
4. Speeding	20	10	**30**
5. Tail Gating	75	11	**86**
6. DUI	25	8	**33**
Total	**220**	**80**	**300**

The expected frequencies are calculated as

$$expected\ frequency,\ f_e = (row\ total \times column\ total)\ /\ sample\ size$$

Table B19.2			
	B. Type of Vehicle		
A. Type of Violation	**1. Passenger**	**2. Truck**	**Total**
1. Stop Sign	(70)(220)/300 = 51.33	(70)(80)/300 = 18.67	**70**
2. Red Light	(50)(220)/300 = 36.67	(50)(80)/300 = 13.33	**50**
3. Failing to Yield	(31)(220)/300 = 22.73	(31)(80)/300 = 8.27	**31**
4. Speeding	(30)(220)/300 = 22.00	(30)(80)/300 = 8.00	**30**
5. Tail Gating	(86)(220)/300 = 63.07	(86)(80)/300 = 22.93	**86**
6. DUI	(33)(220)/300 = 24.20	(33)(80)/300 = 8.80	**33**
Total	**220**	**80**	**300**

The chi-square statistic can be calculated as

$$X^2 = \Sigma (f_o - f_e)^2 / f_e$$

Table B19.3			
	B. Type of Vehicle		
A. Type of Violation	**1. Passenger**	**2. Truck**	**Total**
1. Stop Sign	$(45-51.33)^2/51.33 = 0.78$	$(25-18.67)^2/18.67 = 2.15$	**2.93**
2. Red Light	$(35-36.67)^2/36.67 = 0.08$	$(15-13.33)^2/13.33 = 0.21$	**0.29**
3. Failing to Yield	$(20-22.73)^2/22.73 = 0.33$	$(11-8.27)^2/8.27 = 0.90$	**1.23**
4. Speeding	$(20-22.00)^2/22.00 = 0.18$	$(10-8.00)^2/8.00 = 0.50$	**0.68**
5. Tail Gating	$(75-63.07)^2/63.07 = 2.26$	$(11-22.93)^2/22.93 = 6.21$	**8.47**
6. DUI	$(25-24.20)2/24.20 = 0.03$	$(8-8.80)^2/8.80 = 0.07$	**0.10**
Total	**3.66**	**10.04**	**13.70**

H_0: *Traffic violation and type of vehicle are independent variables.*
H_a: *Traffic violation and type of vehicle are dependent variables.*

$X^2 = 13.70$ *with degrees of freedom = (rows − 1)(cols − 1) = (6 − 1)(2 − 1) = 5*

At $\Sigma = .05$ level of significance and 5 degrees of freedom, the value of $X^2_{.05}$ = 11.07. Since 13.07 >11.07, we conclude that traffic violation and type of vehicle are statistically dependent variables.

CHAPTER 19
COMPUTER ASSIGNMENT
ADVERTISING EFFECTIVENESS

1. The problem in Table B19.4 involves a study of the effect of T.V. advertising on the purchase of the advertised products. A sample of 2,450 people were interviewed in September and then again in December. Each time the people were asked whether they watched a specific T.V. program and whether they purchased the product advertised during the program. Their responses are summarized below:

<table>
<tr><th colspan="7">Table B19.4</th></tr>
<tr><th rowspan="2" colspan="2"></th><th colspan="4">Purchased Product (Sept./Dec.)</th><th rowspan="2">Totals</th></tr>
<tr><th>Yes/Yes</th><th>Yes/No</th><th>No/Yes</th><th>No/No</th></tr>
<tr><td rowspan="4">Watched Program (Sept./Dec.)</td><td>Yes/Yes</td><td>462</td><td>173</td><td>191</td><td>351</td><td></td></tr>
<tr><td>Yes/No</td><td>76</td><td>53</td><td>34</td><td>117</td><td></td></tr>
<tr><td>No/Yes</td><td>87</td><td>27</td><td>53</td><td>85</td><td></td></tr>
<tr><td>No/No</td><td>176</td><td>104</td><td>113</td><td>348</td><td></td></tr>
<tr><td colspan="2">Totals</td><td></td><td></td><td></td><td></td><td></td></tr>
</table>

2. Enter the above table of observed results into an Excel worksheet.

<table>
<tr><th colspan="7">Table B19.5</th></tr>
<tr><th>A</th><th>B</th><th>C</th><th>D</th><th>E</th><th>F</th><th>G</th></tr>
<tr><td>2</td><td colspan="6">The Effect of Advertising on Purchasing Decisions</td></tr>
<tr><td>3</td><td></td><td>Purchased</td><td></td><td></td><td></td><td>Totals</td></tr>
<tr><td>4</td><td></td><td>Yes/Yes</td><td>Yes/No</td><td>No/Yes</td><td>No/No</td><td></td></tr>
<tr><td>5</td><td rowspan="4">Watched Program (Sept./Dec.)</td><td>Y/Y</td><td>462</td><td>173</td><td>191</td><td>351</td></tr>
<tr><td>6</td><td>Y/N</td><td>76</td><td>53</td><td>34</td><td>117</td></tr>
<tr><td>7</td><td>N/Y</td><td>87</td><td>27</td><td>53</td><td>85</td></tr>
<tr><td>8</td><td>N/N</td><td>176</td><td>104</td><td>113</td><td>348</td></tr>
<tr><td>9</td><td>Totals</td><td>=SUM(C5:C8)</td><td>=SUM(D5:D8)</td><td>=SUM(E5:E8)</td><td>=SUM(F5:F8)</td><td>=SUM(G5:G8</td></tr>
</table>

Note: The G column in rows 5-8 contains the formulas =SUM(C5:F5), =SUM(C6:F6), =SUM(C7:F7), =SUM(C8:F8).

	A	B	C	D	E	F	G
				Table B19.6			
2			The Effect of Advertising on Purchasing Decisions				
3			**Purchased Product (Sept./Dec.)**				**Totals**
4			Yes/Yes	Yes/No	No/Yes	No/No	
5		**Yes/Yes**	462	173	191	351	**1177**
6	**Watched Program (Sept./Dec.)**	**Yes/No**	76	53	34	117	**280**
7		**No/Yes**	87	27	53	85	**252**
8		**No/No**	176	104	113	348	**741**
9	**Totals**		**801**	**357**	**391**	**901**	**2450**

3. Create a table of expected values: (row total x column total) / grand total.

	A	B	C	D	E	F	G
				Table B19.7			
12			The Effect of Advertising on Purchasing Decisions				
13			**Purchased Product (Sept./Dec.)**				**Totals**
14			Yes/Yes	Yes/No	No/Yes	No/No	
15	**Watched Program Sep/Dec**	Y/Y	=G5*$C$9/$G$9	=G5*$D$9/$G$9	=G5*$E$9/$G$9	=G5*$F$9/$G$9	=SUM(C15:F15)
16		Y/N	=G6*$C$9/$G$9	=G6*$D$9/$G$9	=G6*$E$9/$G$9	=G6*$F$9/$G$9	=SUM(C16:F16)
17		N/Y	=G7*$C$9/$G$9	=G7*$D$9/$G$9	=G7*$E$9/$G$9	=G7*$F$9/$G$9	=SUM(C17:F17)
18		N/N	=G8*$C$9/$G$9	=G8*$D$9/$G$9	=G8*$E$9/$G$9	=G8*$F$9/$G$9	=SUM(C18:F18)
19	Totals		=SUM(C15:C18)	=SUM(D15:D18)	=SUM(E15:E18)	=SUM(F15:F18)	=SUM(G15:G18)

	A	B	C	D	E	F	G
				Table B19.8			
12			The Effect of Advertising on Purchasing Decisions				
13			**Purchased Product (Sept./Dec.)**				**Totals**
14			Yes/Yes	Yes/No	No/Yes	No/No	
15		**Yes/Yes**	384.81	171.51	187.84	432.85	1177
16	**Watched Program (Sept./Dec.)**	**Yes/No**	91.54	40.80	44.69	102.97	280
17		**No/Yes**	82.39	36.72	40.22	92.67	252
18		**No/No**	242.26	107.97	118.26	272.51	741
19	**Totals**		801	357	391	901	2450

4. Set up the Null and Alternative hypotheses:

> H_0: *There is no relationship between T.V. advertising and purchasing the advertised product*
>
> H_a: *There is a relationship between T.V. advertising and purchasing the advertised product*

5. Calculate the Chi-Square (X^2) coefficient.

> X^2 = *Sum (observed value – expected value)^2 / Expected Value, summed across all cells.*

			Table B19.9			
A	**B**	**C**	**D**	**E**	**F**	**G**
22			The Effect of Advertising on Purchasing Decisions			
23			Purchased Product (Sept./Dec.)			Totals
24		Yes/Yes	Yes/No	No/Yes	No/No	
25	Y/Y	=(C5-C15)^2/C15	=(D5-D15)^2/D15	=(E5-E15)^2/E15	=(F5-F15)^2/F15	=SUM(C25:F25)
26 Watched	Y/N	=(C6-C16)^2/C16	=(D6-D16)^2/D16	=(E6-E16)^2/E16	=(F6-F16)^2/F16	=SUM(C26:F26)
27 Program Sept./Dec.	N/Y	=(C7-C17)^2/C17	=(D7-D17)^2/D17	=(E7-E17)^2/E17	=(F7-F17)^2/F17	=SUM(C27:F27)
28	N/N	=(C8-C18)^2/C18	=(D8-D18)^2/D18	=(E8-E18)^2/E18	=(F8-F18)^2/F18	=SUM(C28:F28)
29 Totals		=SUM(C25:C28)	=SUM(D25:D28)	=SUM(E25:E28)	=SUM(F25:F28)	=SUM(G25:G28)

		Table B19.10				
A	**B**	**C**	**D**	**E**	**F**	**G**
22		The Effect of Advertising on Purchasing Decisions				
23		Purchased Product (Sept./Dec.)				Totals
24		Yes/Yes	Yes/No	No/Yes	No/No	
25	Yes/Yes	15.49	0.01	0.05	15.48	31.03
26 Watched	Yes/No	2.64	3.65	2.56	1.91	10.75
27 Program (Sept./Dec.)	No/Yes	0.26	2.57	4.06	0.64	7.53
28	No/No	18.12	0.15	0.23	20.91	39.42
29 Totals		36.51	6.38	6.91	38.94	88.73

From the table above, the calculated chi-square, X^2, is equal to 88.73.

6. Calculate the degrees of freedom.

D.F. $= (4 - 1)(4 - 1) = 9$.

7. At á = 0.05, test the significance of advertising on purchasing decisions.

$X^2_{0.05}$ from the chi-square table with 9 degrees of freedom is equal to 16.919.

Since 88.73 > 16.919, we reject H_0 and conclude that advertising and purchasing decisions are dependent variables.

REFERENCES

1. Aaker, Davis A., *Strategic Market Management*, 6th Edition ((New York: John Wiley & Sons, Inc., 2001), pp. 4547, 69-75,123-126.
2. *A Chronology of Computer History, http://www.cyberstreet.com/hcs/museum/chron.htm.*
3. *Acronym Alley, http://www.geocities.com/SiliconValley/Park/9104/.*
4. *Acronyms Online, http://www.acronymsonline.com/.*
5. *A History of Computers, http://www.maxmon.com/history.htm.*
6. Berenson, M.L. and Levine, D.M., *Basic Business Statistics: Concepts and Applications* (Englewood Cliffs, N.J.: Prentice-Hall, 1979).
7. Blattner, Patrick, Ulrich, Laurie, Cook, Ken, and Dyck, Timothy, *Using Microsoft Excel 2000*, (Indianapolis, Indiana: Que Corporation/A Division of Macmillan Computer Publishing, 1999).
8. Boone, Louis and Kurtz, David, *Contemporary Marketing*, 10th Edition (Fort Worth, TX: Harcourt College Publishers, 2001), pp. 501-508.
9. Brigham, Eugene F. and Houston, Joel F., *Fundamentals of Financial Management* (Fort Worth, TX: The Dryden Press: Harcourt Brace College Publishers, 1998).
10. Budnick, F.S., Mcleavey, D. and Mojena, R., *Principles of Operations Research for Management* (Homewood, Illinois: Richard D. Irwin, Inc., 1988).
11. Business Plan, *http://www.bplans.com/spv/3055/.*
12. *Canada/BC Business Service Centre, http://www.sb.gov.bc.ca/smallbus/workshop/download/samplebp.html.*
13. *Chronology of Personal Computers, http://www.islandnet.com/~kpolsson/comphist/.*
14. Churchill, Jr., Gilbert A., *Marketing Research: Methodological Foundations*, (Fort Worth, TX: The Dryden Press: Harcourt Brace College Publishers, 1999).
15. *Computer Dictionary Online, http://www.computer-dictionary-online.org/.*
16. *Computer Acronym Collection, http://www.jimspages.com/Acronyms2.html.*
17. Cosmas, Stephen C., *Market Analysis and Control: Student Workbook*, (Pomona, CA: International Business & Marketing Department, California State Polytechnic University).

18. Dibb, Sally and Siskin, Lyndon, *The Marketing Casebook: Cases and Concepts*, 2nd Edition (High Holborn, London: Thomson Learning, 2001), pp. 221-228, 230, 295.

19. *Discovering Computers*, 2004, *http://www.scsite.com/dc2004/index. cfm?action=sites&chapter=home.*

20. *Excel For Statistical Data Analysis, http://home.ubalt.edu/ntsbarsh/excel/ excel.htm.*

21. Groebner, D.F. and Shannon, P.W., *Business Statistics: A Decision-Making Approach* (Columbus, Ohio: Charles E. Merril, 2nd Edition, 1985).

22. Hart-Davis, Guy, *Microsoft® Office: Excel 2003* (Emeryville, California: McGraw-Hill/Osborne, 2003).

23. Hays, W.L. and Winkler, R.L., *Statistics: Probability, Inference, and Decision* (New York: Holt, Rinehart and Winston, 1971).

24. Hillier, F.S. and Lieberman, G.J., *Introduction to Operations Research* (San Fransisco: Holden-Day Inc., 1974).

25. *History of Computers, http://history.acusd.edu/gen/recording/computer2. html.*

26. Holt, Jack, *Cases and Applications in Lotus 123 with HAL* (New York: Richard D. Irwin, 1988).

27. Holzner, Steven, *HTML Black Book* (Scottsdale, AZ: The Coriolis Group, LLC, 2000)

28. *Introduction to Computers, http://www97.intel.com/discover/JourneyInside/ TJI_Intro/default.aspx.*

29. Kohler, Heinz, *Statistics for Business and Economics, 2nd Edition* (Glenview, Illinois: Scott, Foresman and Company, 1988).

30. Kramer, Eric, *HTML: Your Visual Blueprint for Designing Effective Web Pages* (New York: Wiley Publishing, Inc., 2000).

31. *Learn to Speak Computer, http://www.su.edu/instcomp/Virtual_HelpDesk/ glossary.htm.*

32. *Management Information Systems, http://en.wikipedia.org/wiki/Management_information_system.*

33. Marvasti, Frank, *MS/PC Disk Operating System: A resource book for the IBM PC and Compatible Machines* (1998).

34. Marvasti, Frank, *PC-STATISTICS, V 2.1 and 2.5: Statistical Software and Manual for the IBM PC and Compatibles* (Wilsonville, OR: Franklin, Beedle & Associates, 1990, 1991).

35. Marvasti, Frank, *PC-STATISTICS, V 3.5: Statistical Software and Manual for the IBM PC and Compatibles* (2001).

36. Mason, R.D., *Statistical Techniques in Business and Economics* (Homewood, Ill.: Richard D. Irwin, 1982).

37. Metz, Cade, "A History of Personal Computing," as compiled by Nancy Sirapyan, *PC Magazine* (www.pcmag.com), September 4, 2001, pp.186-191.

38. Microsoft® Corporation, *Excel Program*, any version.

39. Neter, J. and Wasserman, W., *Applied Linear Statistical Models: Regression, Analysis of Variance, and Experimental Designs* (Homewood, Ill.: Richard D. Irwin, 1974).

40. Oliver, Dick, *Sams Teach Yourself HTML 4 in 24 Hours, 4th Edition* (Indianapolis, In. Sams, A Division of Macmillan Computer Publishing, 1999).

41. Olps, Lynn A., *Business Applications for Personal Computers, Introduction to Computers, http://powayusd.sdcoe.k12.ca.us/teachers/lolps/IntrotoCptrs_04/IntroAssign.htm.*

42. *Operating System, http://www.computerhope.com/os.htm.*

43. *PC World*, "Computing Through the Ages," 2001.

44. Prosise, Jeff, "A Guide to Computer Acronyms," *PC Magazine*, January 9, 1995, pp. 259, 262, 266.

45. Prosise, Jeff, "A Guide to Computer Acronyms," Part II, *PC Magazine*, January 23, 1996, pp. 211, 212, 217.

46. Reedy, Joel, Schullo, Shauna, and Zimmerman, Kenneth, *Electronic Marketing* (Forth Worth, TX: The Dryden Press: Harcourt Brace College Publishers, 2000).

47. Ross, Kenton E., Gilbertson, Claudia B., Lehman, Mark W., and Hanson, Robert D., *Fundamentals of Accounting* (Mason, OH: Thomson/South-Western Publishing Co., 1998).

48. Stauble, Vernon, *Marketing Strategy: A Global Perspective* (Forth Worth, TX: The Dryden Press: Harcourt Brace College Publishers, 2000), pp.306-320.

49. Taylor III, B.W., *Introduction to Management Science* (Dubuque, Iowa: Wm. C. Brown Publishers, 1986).

50. *The History of Computers, http://www2.fht-esslingen.de/studentisches/Computer_Geschichte.*

51. Tom, Paul L., *Managing Information as a Corporate Resource*, 2nd Edition, (New York: Harper-Collins Publishers, 1991).

52. Turban, E. and Meredith, J.R., *Fundamentals of Management Science* (Plano, Texas: Business Publication, Inc., 1988).

53. Walkenbach, John, *Excel 2003 Bible*, (Indianapolis, IN: Wiley Publishing, Inc., 2003).
54. Walpole, R.E. and Meyers, R.H., *Probability and Statistics for Engineers and Scientists* (New York: Macmillan, 1978).
55. *Wikipedia: The Free Encyclopedia*, *http://en.wikipedia.org/wiki/Main_Page*.

INDEX

absolute addressing..............................35
Acronyms.....................................261, 262
Advanced logical statements 63
Advantages of computers........................4
Allocation..153
AMD 5
Amortization...49
Amortization table 54
Analysis of variance 170, 180
Annual data...187
ANOVA...170
Applications of computers......................3
Application software.............................11
Assets 43
Autocorrelation 180
Balance sheet..42
Bar graph 115
BCG Growth share matrix 125
BIOS..14
BIT 5
Brand loyalty......................................124
Breakeven analysis 214
Business plan.......................................218
BYT 5
Cash cows 126
CD ROM 9
Cell width and heights 32
Central processing unit...........................5
CGA 7
Character 16
Chi-square test 206
Class width..131

Classical multiplicative model 196
Coefficient of correlation.....................166
Coefficient of variation........................135
Command-line.......................................11
Competitive analysis............................221
Competitive grid statement 127
Competitive strength grid 127
Compound logical statements 38
Computer hardware 4
Constraints..153
Contingency 206, 209
Contingency table 209
Correlation...166
CPU..5
Coss-classification 206
Customer service 119
Cyclical-irregular relatives............188, 197
Cyclical analysis...................................197
Cyclical component.......................187, 196
Daisy-wheel...10
Data...16
Data base 16
Data base administer 18
Data base management system 18
Data table type I............................89, 105
Data table type II 92, 108
DBA 18
Decision support system 26
Descriptive summary measures.............133
Detail reports 17
Disk drive...8
Dispersion...134

Diversification 121
Dogs 126
DOS 12
Dot-matrix 10
Drawing tool 125
Drawing toolbar 117
DSS 26
Dual 157
DVD 9
E-mail marketing 221
EGA 7
Excels drawing toolbar 117
Exception reports 17
Exchange rate 100
Executive summary 218
Expense report 111
exponential smoothing 189
Fear 3
Fence-sitters 124
Field 16
File 16
File organizations 17
Financial statements 42
Fixed costs 214
Flash drives 10
Forecasting 83
forecasting 28, 196
Formatting 28
Formulas 33
Frequency distribution 131
George dantzig 155
Goodness-of-fit 206
Graphical presentation 95
Graphing 113
Gaphing techniques 95
Grouped data 137
Growth-share matrix 125
GUI 11
Hardware 4

Hard disks 8
Homoscedasticity 167
HTML 246
IBM 12
If-then-else 37
Income statement 42
Income tax 56
Indexed sequential file organization 17
Information 16
Information technologies 1
Input devices 2, 6
Integrated circuit 2
Intel 5
International trade 100, 101
Interquartile range 135
Irregular 187
Irregular component 188, 196
Liabilities 43
Linear programming 153
Linear regression 166
Line graph 95
Linux 12
Loan 49
Logical statements 37
Mainframe 4
Management information system 15
Management reports 17
Market analysis 117, 120
Market development 121
Market penetration 122, 123
Market segmentation 124
Matrix 126
Mean 133
Media 128
Median 133
Media schedule 128
Microcomputers 4
Microprocessor 2
Microsoft 12

MIS...15
Mixed addressing...........................35
Mode 134
Monitor 7
Motherboard.....................................5
Moving average 189
MS-DOS 12
Multi-user 12
Multiple regression analysis 177
Multiplicative model 187
Multiprocessing...............................12
Multitasking.....................................12
Multithreading................................12
Nested if statement...........................38
Notepad 246
On-demand reports............................17
Operating system 11
Output devices....................................7
PC-DOS 12
Penetration....................................120
Permanent storage 2
Pie chart..113
Positioning....................................221
Pricing strategy..............................220
Printers..10
Printing..33
Problem children...........................126
Product-market strategies 120
Productivity......................................24
Product development 120
Product positioning...........................121
Promotion/sales..............................220
Promotion strategy...........................128
Pro forma..100
Pro forma financial statement 83
Pro forma income statements 88, 104
Quadrant 120, 121
Qualitative analysis.............................21
Quarterly time-series 196

Quartiles 133
QWERTY...6
RAM..2, 6
Random (direct) file organization...........17
Random access memory 2
Range 134
Ratio-to-moving-average 197
Record..16
Regression analysis 166
Relative addressing 35
Residuals 170, 180
ROM 2, 6, 14
Scarce resources.............................153
Seasonal-irregular 197
Seasonal analysis.............................196
Seasonal component...................187, 196
Seasonal indices.............................197
Segmentation 124, 221
Sensitivity..84
Sensitivity analysis....................26, 28, 88
Sequential file organization....................17
Simplex method 155
Simplex tableau..............................156
Simple logical statement.......................37
Simple regression analysis.....................166
Skewness 136
Smoothing......................................189
Solver..163
Standard deviation 135
Stars..126
Store..2
STP...221
Sturges 132
Summary reports...............................17
SVGA 7
SWOT..127
System chassis 5
System software................................11
Tags..246

Targeting...221
Tax liability..57
Tax on base...56
Tax rate..56
Time series...................................187, 188
Time series analysis............................196
Total cost...215
Total revenue.......................................215
Transportation problem................159, 290
Trend...187
Trend component.........................188, 196
Ungrouped data....................................131
UNIX..12

USB...10
Variable costs.......................................214
Variance...135
VGA..7
Website..246
Web page...246
What if...84
Windows..12
Zip drive..9

CPSIA information can be obtained
at www.ICGtesting.com
Printed in the USA
FSHW021252250820
73285FS